DAWN
of all
THINGS
A Novel

BY

W. JASON PETRUZZI

Copyright 2019 © W. Jason Petruzzi
All Rights Reserved

No part of this publication may be reproduced, stored in a retrieval system or transmitted, in any form or by any means—electronic, mechanical, photocopying, recording, or otherwise—without prior written permission from the publisher, except for the use of brief quotations for purposes of review.

ISBN: 978-1-7338804-1-1 (paperback)
ISBN: 978-1-7338804-0-4 (eBook)

Cover Art: Altar for Strange Gods—
painted by Ruth K. Gross, 1970—Scarsdale, N.Y.

Cover & Interior Book Design by www.TeaBerryCreative.com

CONTENTS

INTRODUCTION v
PROLOGUE vii
CHAPTER 1 1
CHAPTER 2 11
CHAPTER 3 19
CHAPTER 4 35
CHAPTER 5 53
CHAPTER 6 65
CHAPTER 7 73
CHAPTER 8 91
CHAPTER 9 107
CHAPTER 10 115
CHAPTER 11 131
CHAPTER 12 137
CHAPTER 13 141
CHAPTER 14 145
CHAPTER 15 153
CHAPTER 16 183
CHAPTER 17 199
CHAPTER 18 203
CHAPTER 19 215
CHAPTER 20 223
CHAPTER 21 227
CHAPTER 22 233
CHAPTER 23 251
CHAPTER 24 263
ABOUT THE AUTHOR 265

INTRODUCTION

Dawn of All Things begins in the early 2000's with a group of sexually and ethnically diverse friends working through life's issues, including careers, goals, past and present relationships, entertainment venues, and curiosity about religion and the afterlife. Their 'playground' is Washington, D.C. and surrounding communities.

The story focuses on a young man who meets a mysterious young woman claiming to be God who is observing her world but not wanting to interrupt the balance and harmony of good and evil. The twist is they were sweethearts in high school. After seeing her preaching to several followers, he becomes consumed with her dramatic life change since he last saw her. The young man wants to know everything about his former girlfriend's evolution and enlightenment, and whether by claiming to be God, she is delusional or psychotic. The longer he searches, the more he falls in love again, uncertain of the outcome.

PROLOGUE

In dark silence, she opened her eyes, and the universe was born. She sat on the grass in the park in the full lotus, watching with peace and attention the vibrant flow of life that surrounded her. The joggers, the dog-walkers, the summer tourists, both youthful and elderly; the pleasant hushed busyness of it enveloped her. She was in West Potomac Park, which surrounded the Tidal Basin and was adjacent to the National Mall. This was where Washington's famous cherry trees stood, though by this time of year their beautiful pink flowers had already given way to a canopy of thick green leaves. Yet the air was still sweet with a clean, garden smell, and she breathed it in deeply, a tiny smile playing across her face.

After some time had passed, she got up to stretch her legs and went for a walk, across the Mall, past the Reflecting Pool and the Lincoln Memorial, past the dark stone of the Vietnam Memorial, and across Constitution Avenue, out of the park, and into the city proper, into the subdued frenzy of the capital of the free world.

Her walk was leisurely, slow and measured, and people parted around her, rushing past, like a river around a rock. She moved without being jostled, without being touched. Unreflectingly she observed everything, taking it in, the bright sunlight glinting off the windows of stone buildings, cars slowly bumping their way through the stop-and-go traffic, chic and grungy people alike chattering noisily into their cell phones without losing their step; everything filled her head with its vibrancy before floating dreamily away. She felt apart from them, above them.

Sitting on a bench, with his back to the iron fence surrounding some ancient building, his legs splayed out, was a coarse-looking man in a soiled, threadbare jacket and jeans, and a styrofoam cup in his hand which he would occasionally hold up in a silent plea for change. He saw her through the moving crowd, standing alone, watching him from across the street. His eyes followed her as she took a lackadaisical path up to the stoplight, then across the street, then down the sidewalk again, coming over to where he sat. She stopped and stood in front of him, gazing down.

Standing perfectly still, she looked down at him, saying nothing. She was young, early-to-mid-twenties, dressed in a casual way: jeans, a loose, plain white tee, and sandals; but her eyes stood out, clear and focused, as though she knew him from somewhere, and was waiting expectantly for him to remember. Her long auburn hair fluttered momentarily in the breeze.

He held his cup in the air and waved it at her a little. "Spare some change?" he grunted, his voice weak. She remained silent, and he began to dread her stare, which peered through him in some indescribable way. He was used to condescension, of course, but her stare wasn't angry or judgmental or demeaning; rather it had a soft, honest empathy about it.

She bent down to him, reached out, and gently put her hand on his cheek. He jerked away instinctively, and she let her hand drift down to rest on his shoulder. It made him nervous, suspicious, ready to jump up, and ready to fight. Nobody ever touched him. But he looked into her eyes, which reflected only kindness, and felt comforted.

"I'm sorry," she said quietly, and it sounded absolutely genuine, afflicted with some great sadness. For a moment he was afraid she had come to him purposefully, bearing bad news, news of some tragedy that would surely devastate him.

But she said nothing else, only stared.

"For what?" he asked, after a heartbeat passed.

"For everything," she said, never taking her eyes from his. "For all the misery you've lived through, for all the things that haven't been the way they should have been, for not giving you what you want, for making the world unfair."

This was too much. He chuckled dryly, and pushed her hand off his shoulder, carefully but not gently. "Making the world? What are you, God?"

Now she smiled, ever so faintly, but compared to the sorrow on her face a moment ago, it was like the clearing of gray skies. "Yes," she said, her voice almost a whisper. "But please, call me Dawn."

He was about to laugh, but didn't, because it wasn't funny. She was too unassuming for him to think she was trying to pull something. Perhaps she meant it. In all his years living on the street, he had met some pretty crazy people, some paranoid folks who believed the strangest, most incoherent things. He had a touch of it himself, voices which would come and go, guiding him, telling him where to go and what to say, pushing him away from any sense of a normal life. And though some of those people he knew would hear the voice of God, or at the very least claimed they did, he'd never met anyone who actually thought they were God. This young girl lived in a special madness of her own.

It was his turn to pity her. He knew from experience it was often more than useless to try to talk someone out of a delusion, but once in a while talking could get through to a person. So he said to her, "I don't believe you."

"I don't ask you to believe me. I don't expect you to. I only wanted to come and tell you I was sorry."

This poor girl, he thought. "If you were really God, you could do something about it, instead of just apologizing."

"Come with me," she said at once. It was not a command, or even a request. It was an offer, given in hopeful, honest solicitude.

But he wasn't going to humor her. "I'm not going to become some disciple. I don't need to be saved. Why can't you do something more practical?"

"Like what?"

He held out his cup again. It wasn't the right thing to say, to try to take advantage of someone in her condition, but he couldn't help it, he was hungry. "If you were really God, you'd give me some money."

Her smile faded away, and she looked terribly crestfallen. "Money? But I'm all powerful. I can give you anything, anything you could possibly want. Surely you can dream better?"

Poor, deluded girl. "No, a little cash would be enough."

She sighed quietly. "Well, okay, if all you want is money..." She stood up straight, suddenly thrust her hands up into the sky, and instantly it was raining money. Bills, scores of them, gently floated down like fat green leaves, turning and twisting in the air. He was shocked, then started frantically grabbing at the cash, and dropped to the ground to collect those he'd missed. He crouched there on the ground, clutching at fistfuls of bills as the rain stopped, singles and fives all, maybe forty, fifty bucks total. People around him gaped in amazement to see the floating currency, but, confused and not wanting to risk getting involved in what they didn't understand, let their wariness outweigh their own impulse to try and snatch some for themselves.

But he knew others had seen, and he would have to get out of sight quickly. He stuffed all the bills into his own pockets, and looked around, but by this time the girl had vanished. He slipped away himself, and spent the rest of the day in a bewildered stupor of shifting emotions, elated at his fortune one moment, then disturbed by his callousness the next. Part of his mind swore he saw the bills fall straight from the sky, and part swore he had seen her holding them in her hand and tossing them up in the air. He was confused, but either way he felt at a loss. He was fearful he had conned a poor innocent, and terrified he had offended the divine.

CHAPTER 1

I could smell the warm, comforting goodness of pancakes even before I opened my eyes. At first I thought they were the last vestiges of a dream, but no, they were real. My brother Paul had cooked pancakes for breakfast that morning, and their scent roused me from a smooth sleep of pleasant, disconnected visions, as refreshing as any night could be. The vibrantly bright morning sunlight seeped in beneath the shades of my window, and hit me explosively, momentarily burning my eyes and kicking me into wakefulness when I let them fly open. The sun filled my little room, enlivening it, and I felt the excited anticipation of an unstructured July weekend before me, a glorious weekend of freedom.

Those warm, fluffy, syrup-drenched dollar coins of batter were the breakfast of childhood. Our mother used to cook pancakes on Sunday mornings when we were kids; it was a delicious little ritual that I missed. Of course, she had made them from scratch, while I knew Paul was just using a box of instant mix I kept in the cupboard. Still, I wasn't going to complain. Pancakes were pancakes.

I yawned as I glanced in the mirror to pat my tousled brown hair into some semblance of order, and ambled out into our sparse living room in my undershirt and boxers. Our living room contains a bookshelf that came with the place and now holds my TV/stereo entertainment center, along with some books, a small coffee table in front of it, and a white sofa with orange stripes that also came with the place and which I'm pretty sure was manufactured back in the Seventies. Behind the sofa was a small, circular wooden table with two chairs where we'd usually have our meals, but it was empty. Paul, fit and tan, with sandy-blond hair, was sitting on the sofa eating from a plate of half-finished pancakes. I was momentarily startled to see that he wasn't alone. This bothered me but I was striving to not to let it bother me; I've been trying to get used to finding strangers in my apartment since Paul moved in. He had a lot of friends, and would bring them over all the time, usually unannounced, to study, have drinks, go jogging with, or whatever.

The guy sitting next to him, though, was different. First off, he seemed to be an Arab and so perhaps also a Muslim, a change from his usual companions. He was slight but in good shape, with short black curls and comparatively light brown skin. He was wearing short jeans, sandals, and a light gray tee shirt that read "GWU." He had a beard, but it was just a few days' worth of stubble. The shirt let me conclude he was a classmate of Paul's, which made me feel a little more at ease. Paul was a junior political sciences major at George Washington University; actually, a rising senior now, since the school year was over. This summer he had an internship at some sub-department at the State Department, called the Bureau of Economic, Energy, and Business Affairs, which was truly impressive; yet he was actually disappointed because he hadn't gotten a position on Capital Hill. He minored in economics, and sometimes talked about getting an MBA after he graduated and going into investment banking, although he was already working on his law school application. But I could see Paul as an investment banker, one of those fund-managing, entrepreneurial, greedy sons of bitches who make money by making money. He already had a small investment portfolio amounting to a few gold coins and a couple of hundred dollars in a few stocks. He did some very basic day trading, but I don't think he made a dime from any of it—I think his profits and losses evened out—but he went on and on about how important the learning experience was, et cetera. I never knew whether to be amused or jealous.

"Hey," he said to me in between bites, "glad you're up. I made some for you. Better get 'em while they're still warm." They were watching a news show; the talking heads were saying something or other about Iraq, no surprise. There was a picture of Condoleezza Rice on the screen.

I walked into the little kitchenette, where, sure enough, there was a plate of pancakes waiting for me on the counter. They were no longer piping hot, so I put them in the microwave for a dozen seconds while I poured a cup of coffee. As silly as it seemed, I felt a slight stab of disappointment, knowing Paul had gone through the trouble of making these to share with his friend, not with me. I know making pancakes hardly constitutes some significant family ritual, but all the same, I was piqued. When they were appropriately sizzling, I poured some maple syrup over them. I came around to the front of the counter and leaned on it as I began eating, so I could talk to him. "Going to introduce me?" I asked as I took a bite.

"No," said Paul, sounding mildly surprised. "You've met him. Ahmed? He was here for the party. Don't you remember?" Of course I remembered the party. He had thrown a mild get together for a dozen of his friends when he moved in back in May. Before that I'd had a different roommate, and Paul had lived in an apartment near the campus. But my roommate got another job and was leaving the area, and Paul wanted someplace new. I liked the idea of not having to worry about searching for someone unknown and enduring the time it took to build up trust, so it worked out perfectly. I was worried about his plan for a party—a bunch of drinking-age college kids in my home that I bore sole responsibility for. It was very strange, actually. The thing I most remember is spending the whole time with a paranoid fear that someone was going to break or steal something, or have a medical emergency. It made me feel so old. But it turned out to be surprisingly mild. The music was loud but not blasting, the alcohol was no more than a few six-packs. Paul's a pretty straight-laced guy, and most of his friends are equally conservative, or at least the school friends he brought with him. They aren't the only crowd he hangs out with, unfortunately. Having just turned 21 in April, he'd been taking his liberty clubbing every weekend. He never gets drunk or anything -- that's not what I was worried about.

"I don't remember; my apologies." I had a vague recollection of seeing him before—all of Paul's other friends were white, so how could I not? But I wouldn't have been able to place him without being told. I trusted Paul's judgment enough to believe Ahmed was a safe character. But still, he was probably a Muslim. There was something more going on here.

Paul looked over at Ahmed, smiled and shook his head gently. Ahmed, speaking over his head, said, "Then I'm pleased to meet you again, Court." His voice was clipped, with a light accent, and I guessed he was a genuine Arab immigrant.

"Yeah," I shrugged, taking a sip of coffee. "You a poly-sci major, too? I mean, I take it you're not in his Bible study group."

"No, no I'm not," he said, with a polite chuckle. "Not that he hasn't asked." I smiled at that, too. He paused, unsure whether to continue, and then said, "I'm actually a graduate student."

"Uh-huh. Good for you." I took another bite. "Poly-sci or economics?"

"Medicine."

I stopped chewing and blinked. Paul was looking down at his plate; he looked almost embarrassed, which was not an emotion he often showed. I had been right; there was more going on here, and I could already guess what it was.

"Paul…" I sighed.

He looked up, flashed an exasperated glance at Ahmed, and then smiled at me. "Yeah, I was getting around to telling you, eventually. Ahmed's my new boyfriend."

I sighed again, and set my cup on the counter. "Ooookay."

"What?" he said, suddenly aggrieved. He wasn't going to say anything, and now *he* was annoyed.

"He was here the whole night, in my apartment, and you didn't tell me."

"So? I need your permission, now?"

I didn't understand the now part, since this situation was obviously unique. We had never had much of a discussion about it, either. But I'd assumed some argument with his previous roommates over his homosexuality, perhaps over some incident exactly like this, was the real reason he had been so keen on staying with me. There wasn't any other reason, since I lived well outside the city; the nearest Metro stop was five miles away. I couldn't very well throw my own brother out, after all. My assumption was probably correct, considering how touchy he'd suddenly become. "I just don't feel safe with some complete stranger in my apartment."

He laughed maliciously. "Don't even dare, Court. And he's not a stranger. I told you, he was here for the party. It's not my fault if you've got a lousy memory."

"Okay, Paul. Okay." I picked up my cup again and drained it. There was no point arguing. He was right—although he hadn't introduced Ahmed as his boyfriend at the party; I would have remembered that, at least—and I could see I wasn't going to win. I just wanted to finish breakfast and get out of here.

"I don't want to create any problems here," Ahmed said directly to Paul, but loud enough so I could hear. "You said he knew."

"He does know, just not about us." He put his hand on Ahmed's shoulder. "Don't worry about it."

I finished my breakfast; on the television they were now discussing the recent Israeli actions against Hezbollah in Lebanon and flashing a picture of Prime Minister Ehud Olmert. When I went to the sink to rinse my dish, Paul came over and said he was sorry, which surprised me a little. He wasn't one to admit mistakes, and he objected when anyone, especially me, made any negative comments about his orientation. Actually, I should correct that—it only applied to me. I don't want to paint him as some kind of activist, because he wasn't. Hell, no. Far from it. Paul was never, ever, going to march in any parades or join any protests. He was a devout Christian and very conservative. He always voted Republican, too. Gay rights issues somehow weren't significant enough to swing his political opinions much. Were the issue ever on the ballot, he wouldn't vote against gay marriage himself, but he routinely voted for politicians who did. He even tried to justify the issue once, telling me marriage was a big deal and it should be advanced slowly, to give people time to adjust; pushing it would endanger society, the social fabric, "true" marriage, et cetera. No, I guess it was only me he expected better from, but I can't blame him for that.

I leaned over the counter. "Tell me Paul, an Arab? Probably Muslim?"

"What?" he said, uptight again.

"Well, since 9/11, you did say *they* were the enemy. I'm surprised you don't think he's a terrorist."

"I never said that, and I understand most Muslims aren't terrorists!" he insisted, looking genuinely hurt; but Ahmed had a faint smile, so I was sure he knew better.

I considered pressing the issue further with a few more jokes, but I really didn't feel in the mood. Truth be told, I have met very few of Paul's boyfriends before, and I felt uncomfortable with him sitting there. I wondered when they had met, since he'd been here for the party but Paul had told me when he moved in that he wasn't seeing anyone. But I thought if I questioned him about it, it would lead to another pointless argument. So instead I asked something simpler, more obvious. "Where are you from, Ahmed?"

"Egypt," he said. Yes, then, definitely an immigrant. I wanted to warn him he was friends with a guy who spoke empathetically about the need for an extensive wall along the U.S.-Mexico border, but I suspected he already knew that, too. And I was equally confident I didn't have to ask if he was familiar with Paul's opinion on the Iraq war.

"And I can trust you, right?" I asked with quiet amiability. "So when I ask you if you've ever spent the night in my apartment without my knowing, before last night, you'll tell me the truth, won't you?"

"Oh, let it go, Court," Paul protested immediately. "I said I was sorry."

"I just want to know."

"The answer is no," said Ahmed, quickly jumping in. He was lying, I was certain of it. It was a conspiracy against me.

"Okay," I shrugged, then started back to my bedroom to get dressed.

Paul watched me get halfway down the hall before calling, "Hey, Nate called earlier."

I stopped and turned back. "Oh?" Nate was my old college roommate and best friend. He and his wife Sandy lived in a townhouse in Montgomery County, Maryland, just a little outside DC.

"He wants to play Hide and Seek. He said to meet him in front of the Air & Space Museum at one."

"Okay." Now at least I had something specific to do with my Saturday. I had been planning on spending it just hanging around with my girlfriend Kim, which would probably entail going to the mall, so this was much better.

I turned back and continued down the hall, and Paul said, "We're coming, too."

Craning around, I said, "With Ahmed?"

"It sounds like fun," Ahmed replied. "I'm sure it'll make a great story to tell my parents next time I write." I shrugged and returned to my bedroom.

I called Kim and let her know about our invitation, and then went and took a shower, feeling a little frustrated and annoyed. It wasn't the homosexuality that bothered me, at least not entirely.

What I really hated was the hypocrisy. Paul wasn't exactly a card-carrying member of the Religious Right, but he was more than amenable to their moral crusading. He endorsed things like decency standards in entertainment, abstinence-only sex education, restrictions on abortion but not guns, things like that. While he told me he was primarily conservative on financial issues, which I thought was problematic in itself, he had a high tolerance for most of the Republican Party's insane policies, from supply-sided economics to aggressive interrogations. Other than the anti-homosexual hate-mongering, he was, generally speaking, on their side. He claimed it was only the professional politicians, forced to appeal to the lowest common denominator, who were stridently anti-gay; most actual Republicans believed in equality, so there was no problem. Someday, he promised me, he would run for office. No surprise; he studied political sciences for a reason. That's the name of the game for most high-flyers here in the DC area. In New York everyone wants to work for hedge funds, in LA they all want to be movie stars, and here inside the Beltway it's all politics. I don't know how far he'd ever get; there are some gay office-holders, even as Republicans, but their power is ephemeral, especially here in Virginia, which is, let's not forget, below the Mason-Dixon Line. He thought the bias would eventually dissipate, but I figured he, or someone like him, would never have a chance at being, say, governor, let alone president. But at the very least he fully planned on holding some small local office someday, maybe a seat on the county Board of Supervisors, if nothing else. He'd been involved in student government all during high school, and every fall he volunteered for some campaign or other (fortunately for him, local and state elections in Virginia are scheduled for odd years, so here the dog and pony show never ends). In this situation, at least, I felt sorry for him.

But the politics are only part of my concern. After all, he's not unique there. I think I read somewhere that the Log Cabin society, a group of gay Republicans, has 10,000 members. It's Paul's religious devotion which confuses me. On the one hand, he is an evangelical Christian who believes in the literal truth of the Bible, and on the other hand, he's an openly gay man with an active sex life. He criticizes me for not caring about faith to a rather exasperating extent. I don't know how many times he's told me I needed to find Jesus and be saved. I know he seriously thinks I'm going to hell. I used to think it was kind of sweet, that he was so earnest about my soul, but these days it's all I can do not to tell him to just shut up. I used to go to church and youth fellowship when I was in high school, but it stopped having any meaning for me long ago. He doesn't criticize me over my own sex life. His hypocrisy isn't as blatant as that, though sometimes he gives me a look which communicates clearly how much he wants to. Yet he doesn't feel the slightest bit of guilt, as far as I can tell, over his own actions. He did take seriously the proclamations of his favorite televangelists that all gays went to hell; he was familiar with all the silly scripture passages they cited, about what an abomination God considered same-sex relations to be. And yet he didn't care. I was never able to feel any *schadenfreude* over it because it didn't mean anything to him. He was cheeky about it. He had once told me that while he agreed sodomy was a grievous sin, he didn't actually think he himself was in any danger; his Personal Lord and Savior Jesus Christ would forgive him and keep him safe, no matter what he did. I didn't understand it, and I still don't. He wrapped it in solemn notes of grace, but I thought he was crazy.

Paul didn't come out until college, and then just embraced being gay. He had an active social life, going out to gay nightclubs, hanging with his numerous gay friends, dating. People knew about him, his past roommates, his friends, our parents. And he had never tried to use his faith, as sincere as he held it, to become "cured," either alone or by turning to one of those ridiculous ex-gay groups. On the other hand, he never did anything that smacked of a stereotype. He dressed well but plainly, never even sporting an earring, let alone anything pink. He had no interest in domestic things like cooking or decorating.

And now there was this Arab, his new boyfriend. A gay Muslim—was there even such a thing? I suppose it was no different than a gay Christian, but it still seemed even more ludicrous. The whole situation was so bizarre. The only thing I could think of was that Paul was interested in him because he was different. But on that basis, how long could their relationship last?

CHAPTER 2

We climbed into my car, an eight-year-old blue-green Toyota Tercel. Paul and Ahmed sat together in the back, even though it's economy-class tight; it's still better than Paul's car, which doesn't even have a backseat. Paul, believe it or not, owns a red Corvette. It's a sports coupe with a black leather interior. He loves that car, and he's very conceited about it. It's his one indulgence into flamboyancy. All his extra money, of which he does not have a whole lot, goes into paying off his car loan, yet it's completely unnecessary. There's a bus stop less than a block from our apartment which would take him to the Metro station, and would bring him directly into DC far cheaper than the fantastic sums he's pouring into his car. I can't believe he was willing to spend so much when he's still just a student, or why our parents let him. They co-signed his loan. The car is twelve years old, but it still cost at least thrice what my car cost. Needless to say, he doesn't let anyone else drive it. He wouldn't even let me take it around the block a single time.

We drove over to Kim's apartment in Annandale to pick her up. Her roommate Jenna buzzed us in, but Kim greeted us at the door with a toothy grin and an enthusiastic hello. She was just a tad overweight, but it showed clearly enough with the skimpy ensemble she was wearing today: a purple halter top, shorts, and flip-flops.

Her yellow hair was in a pixie cut, and all her nails, both finger and toe, were a bright, freshly-painted red.

We kissed briefly, then she turned to Paul and kissed him, too, on the cheek. She liked Paul; I liked to think it was in a cutesy, non-sexual way, but sometimes I felt a suspicion that she liked him in a more romantic sense, more so than she liked me. Sometimes I thought she would prefer to dump me to date him if it were an option. He introduced Ahmed to her, and she hugged him, squeezing hard.

"How are you?" he responded, maintaining his politeness despite being a bit overwhelmed.

"Joyful and rapturous!" Kim exclaimed. He seemed perplexed; she hadn't been at the party because she'd been working that night, so they'd never met. I guess we should have warned him about Kim. She was a Positive Thinker. You know, attitude is everything, see the bright side of things, every day's a new adventure, live life to the fullest, *Carpe Diem*—all that dribble from a thousand self-help books and motivational speeches and inspirational movies. She read a lot of those books, not to mention watched a lot of Oprah. But unlike most people, who close their books and then return to the daily slog through real life, she took all that stuff very seriously and actually managed through a genuine force of will to hold on to it (to actualize it, is what she would say). As a result she went around always trying to be full of life and vim and vigor, 24/7, no matter what, pretending to be happy even when she was clearly miserable. Because, you see, if you act like you're happy, you'll become happy, and you'll magically conjure up whatever you desire. Supposedly. I didn't really argue with it, mostly because arguing would be pointless with her—not to mention Negative—but because it did sort of seem to work. And I say that tentatively, because, on the one hand, her super-sunny disposition earned her some rather impressive tips from the customers at the restaurant where she waitressed. On the other hand, waitressing was the only job she had ever held, and even my administrative position was better than that. I at least didn't have to spend the day on my feet, and I had insurance benefits. On the third hand, Kim did seem to always be happy, revved up and in the mood to go somewhere and do something. It could be exhausting to keep up with her, she was so determined to have fun.

Occasionally Kim had a little too much fun. No, I don't mean drug-wise, or sex-wise, or anything like that, at least not in any serious way, at least not that I'm aware of, but she was sometimes willing to sacrifice a little self-control in the search for amusement. She has a rack of speeding tickets, for one thing. In fact, I'd actually met her at the courthouse, the Fairfax County General District Court, where I worked as a deputy clerk. Not a Clerk, you know, as in a law clerk, or a clerk for a judge, but a customer service/administrative professional. Basically I did data entry—taking data from warrants and citations and putting them into the court database, filed documents for people, and provided visitors with directions through the massive courthouse, and other mundane things. I sometimes thought, in a very vague and unfocused way, that I should try to go back and finish my bachelor's degree, or get some paralegal training, and become a Clerk, which as a managerial position pays considerably more. But frankly, the legal system isn't my passion, and I only worked there because they hired me. And yes, I know, isn't it funny, my name is Court and I work at the court, ha-ha. I have a sneaking suspicion that's the only reason I got hired in the first place. When I'm there I make sure people use the unabbreviated version of my name at all times. And no, it's not Courtney, it's Courtland, thank you very much.

Anyway, Kim was there one day for a hearing in traffic court. She'd been arrested for a DUI, after a night out barhopping with her friends. I only asked her out on a lark, because she'd flirted a little—just smiled and winked at me. It was enough. Usually people with trial dates are absorbed with their own problems and not particularly conscious of the rest of us, but Kim was different. She was trying very hard to enjoy herself. It wasn't so much that she was making light of her problem, rather she was attempting to make the most out of the unanticipated "learning experience" by putting her fairy-magic positive thinking to work.

She'd laughed at my name and was happy enough to go out with me, though I always had the feeling I wasn't exciting enough for her. She's a party girl, and almost every weekend she had free—her waitress job required her to work a lot of evenings—she dragged me to some bar or club or some such place I was always apathetic about. But she'd stuck with me for over three months now, because we got along well, we had fun, and there was possibly real potential for our relationship. That, and, having been convicted and gotten her license revoked, she needed someone to drive her around.

We stepped inside her brightly-colored apartment. Everything was in pastels. The walls were painted pastel yellow, the curtains pastel blue, the sofa pink. On one wall there was a poster of the yellow smiley-face Wal-Mart logo. The big label and tag line on top was cut off, as Kim was against retail behemoths on principle, though that didn't stop her from making the occasional shopping jaunt; but the tiny copyright name on the lower corner was untouched. On another wall was a poster of a beach, and there was a gold-hued arabesque carpet on the floor.

"This is really fantastic!" she exclaimed. "I'm glad you're being so open-minded," she said to Paul. He was mildly offended by this, as though she was implying that he was normally a racist. Ahmed, again, seemed to know well enough already, and smirked at him. She said to him, "You know, I never knew Muslims could be gay."

She realized what she'd said wasn't quite right, so she backtracked and made it worse. "I mean, isn't it against your religion?"

Ahmed, surprisingly, didn't look bothered. I guessed he'd heard this sort of comment from others before. "Yes, Kim, it is. Just as it's against his religion, too." He nodded towards Paul. "But I live with it. Does that bother you?"

"No, no. I'm sorry, I wasn't implying anything, it's just that I've never met a gay Muslim before. I didn't think there were any."

"Oh, there are," he said ruefully.

She became sympathetic. "Your family doesn't accept you, do they? You poor guy."

He was startled. "My family? My family doesn't know, and God willing, they never will." And that was all he would say about the subject.

Kim apologized again. She went on to gush over how very pleased she was to finally meet an actual boyfriend of Paul's, and declared they were a "cute couple."

We told Jenna what we were doing and offered to let her come along, but she declined. She seemed distracted, and outside Kim confided that she was having some problems at work, very serious but very vague. Or maybe it was with her boyfriend. Whatever, she'd been moody the past week. Kim spent the whole ride speculating about this, like any of the rest of us cared.

About fifteen minutes later, we arrived at the Vienna Metro Station. Paul and Ahmed both already had passes, since they used the Metro to get downtown practically every day, but I had to get a farecard. I plunked a five into the machine, and got a slip of paper with a black magnetic strip on it. I glanced at it, and it said in green letters, "Welcome to Washington, DC!" with a drawing of two pandas eating bamboo below. We took the Orange Line to the Smithsonian. It was a thirty-five minute trip into DC, and I ended up spending most of it standing holding a pole, switching between hands as I was shoved and jerked around by the train's alternate swaying and lurching. The train was pretty crowded, with hordes of people going to a Nationals game. Plus on general principle it's always kind of crowded on weekends in the summer. Damned tourists. I got squeezed in with a bunch of them, standing over Kim, trying to focus on the various intricate details of the trials and tribulations of Miss Jenna and her other assorted friends to the exclusion of the game-related musings blaring past me on all sides. Meanwhile, Paul and Ahmed had gotten seats together further back, with Paul in the aisle seat amicably chatting up total strangers. Lucky them. My head ended up hurting from all the crowd and train noise almost as much as my arms.

Finally it ended, and we took the escalator up into the bright daylight and crowded sidewalks of Jefferson Drive on the National Mall. I always felt it was a joke, the Mall. Maybe I expected something grander, but it's just a long patch of grass. I know, I know, the Mall is the space around it, the sacred monuments and buildings that define America. But whenever I go there, I tell myself, "I'm standing on the National Mall," and it's just a patch of grass. Oh, off to the west a little, there's the beautiful space between the Washington monument and the Lincoln Memorial, where the Reflecting Pool is, the space where the March on Washington was held; that's the space most people think of when they imagine the National Mall, and indeed, the grass there is much more lush and not so confined by streets and sidewalks and muddy, gravelly pathways, more in fitting with its iconic status. But it's only one section. The Mall runs down all the way to the Capitol Building, lined on either side by the various Smithsonian institutions, and most of it strikes me as a rather depressing sort of lawn. It's not even very well maintained, with numerous bald spots, and the grass left mostly to wilt in the heat of summer to a shade more pale yellow than green, almost like straw. At least people had the respect not to dump litter on it.

We walked down towards the Capitol, which towered over everything in the distance, past the street vendors hawking tee-shirts, baseball caps, pretzels and guided tours of the city; past the Freer Gallery, the cathedral-like Smithsonian Castle, the cylindrical Hirschhorn, and finally across Seventh Street to the boxy, fort-like glass and brick National Air and Space Museum, where we found Nate sitting on one of the benches with his wife, Sandy. Now, Nate and Sandy are what I'd consider a cute couple. They've been inseparable since they met in college. They're both classic computer geeks, today wearing matching Spiderman tee-shirts. Their cell phones have the *Star Wars* theme set as the ring tone, and they spend huge amounts of time playing video games together. They got up and shook hands with me, Kim, and Paul, and I introduced Ahmed.

"You're Paul's friend?" asked Nate, looking at him a bit askance, inwardly a little surprised at his nationality.

Sensing the awkwardness of Nate's comment, Sandy quickly chimed in, " Nice to meet you, Ahmed. You do understand how our game is played, right?"

"It's been explained to me," said Ahmed, and in fact, I've been to all these museums before."

"All right, that's fine," said Nate. "But, just out of curiosity, you're not, by any chance, from Iraq, are you?"

"Egypt, actually," he replied.

Sandy turned to Paul and gently asked him, "What happened to your last boyfriend? James, wasn't it?"

"Yes," said Paul, pleased she remembered and was kind enough to ask. "Nothing happened. It just didn't work out. We weren't compatible. You know how it is." I caught Ahmed rolling his eyes, which meant that he knew Paul was shorting the truth, and there was probably a long, complicated, soap-opera-like story involved, which I couldn't imagine any of us wanted to hear. But I wondered, since

I'd never even meet his last boyfriend, how did Sandy know about him? It would have had to have been a while ago; as I said, he told me he wasn't seeing anyone when he moved in, back in late May. Perhaps he came on a previous game; Paul, when he participated, usually brought several friends with him.

Changing the subject, Nate asked "So, you want to get some lunch first, or play first?"

"Let's play first," said Paul. "We're having dinner together later, aren't we?"

"Sure." Nate checked his watch. "It's now 1:10. Ten-minute head start, then you have until 4:10 to find us. Everybody understands?"

"So, wait, what, you're just automatically it?" Kim objected. She had enthused how interesting it would be to be "it" the last time we played, and had been expecting to at least be offered the opportunity this time. So she was offended that Nate was simply going to claim it for himself, ignoring her wishes so blatantly.

"Whenever possible, darling. Ciao!" It was his game, he was the master of ceremonies, so he could do as he pleased. Plus I think he liked toying with her Positive Attitude. He and Sandy turned, crossed over Jefferson Drive, and headed up the street in the direction of the Capitol, huffing as they went, until they disappeared behind some tour buses lined up in front of the museum.

"Well, isn't this fun!" Kim said with a high-pitched false cheer and a big grin, trying to get her good vibes back.

CHAPTER 3

The version of Hide and Seek we played was Nate's own creation. It had evolved from the standard adult version people play, known as geocaching, which utilizes the Global Positioning System. Geocaching works like this: People hide little boxes in various locations around the world, usually in parks, and post their longitude and latitude coordinates on the Web, then players hunt them down using their GPS units to guide them. The GPS tells you where you're located within twenty feet, and when you plug in the destination coordinates, it tells you how far and in what direction to travel to get there. Of course, the direction it points you is the fabled quickest path, a straight line from point to point, and if you can't go straight, then you have to find your own route. And since it's only accurate to within twenty feet, and these boxes can be pretty small, when you get there you still need to do a lot of rummaging, because while they're not buried, they're not out in the open, either. When you do find one, it usually has a few trinkets inside that you can take on the condition that you leave something of your own for the next player, and a little notebook, a log book to identify yourself and claim your victory. It's sort of interesting, glancing though the logs and seeing all the other people who've been there before you, and adding your own name for future players to discover in turn.

So Nate and I played this game many times during the three years we were roommates at James Madison University. He bought himself a pair of Magellan GPS 315 handsets, devices just a little larger than a cell phone, and on weekends when neither of us was too busy, we'd go out to one of several parks that were within driving distance and play, tracking down the caches we'd identified online. JMU, in rural Harrisonburg, is in between the Blue Ridge Mountains and the Appalachian mountains and surrounded by over a million acres of state and national parks.

Now I'll tell you straight out, neither of us is an outdoors person, and we did not relish trudging over miles-long hiking paths, especially through dense, insect-ladened forests. But the searching itself was exciting, filled with the rising anticipation and then the satisfying payoff of retrieving the box.

Unfortunately, this pleasure was just not enough for us. And as a video-game addict, Nate required something a little more exciting and competitive. So after the first few leisurely searches, we began splitting up and racing each other to find the cache.

Then Nate came up with the idea of dispensing with caches and bringing the game back to its childhood roots. One person would hide, then call up the other and give his GPS coordinates, then the other would seek, just as we'd sought the cache. This had the advantage of not requiring other people to plant things, so we no longer had to go out into the wilderness, which neither one of us had liked much to begin with. Now we could play on campus. And there was the fact that another person was easier to spot than some piddling box, so we could chase each other when one got close, or sneak up and scare each other. I know, I know, real mature, right? But it was fun.

The negative aspect was that there was no longer any connection to other players. It was just the three of us, including Sandy. Occasionally we got other people to play along, and one game had eight people in it, but I thought it had lost the feeling of being part of the wider world. And yes, we realized it was kind of silly, calling someone up and giving them your coordinates. Until the last component, when the seeker got close and the hider gave chase, it didn't seem much different than when we were trying to meet up on purpose—I tell them where I am, then wait around for them to find me. On that note, we experimented with letting the person who was "it" move around under various time limits. Movement without limits proved to be almost impossible for anyone to win because the "it" person had too big a lead.

Nate also tried subscribing to a car-tracking service where a unit's signals were relayed to an internet site, which you could pull up with a code number. In this game, the person who was "it" carried around the transponder, and everyone else could call into the site with their cell phones to find the coordinates at any time they wanted. This was more like a hunt than a game, and while it was definitely faster-paced, the "it" person lost the control they had, and no one needed to be clever or to think things through to play. There was no outwitting anyone here. It was just a game of chase, pure and simply, from start to finish. As a result, we, being essentially a group of computer nerds, abandoned it.

After three years, I dropped out of college, but I would still on occasion get together with Nate and some other friends to play the game with whatever new twists he'd come up with. When he graduated with a computer science degree, he got a systems programming job with some defense contractor in DC, and moved to Maryland. So now we played in the city, where the nation's capital was our game board, our little toy kingdom, with more levels and secret rooms then the vastest of digital realms.

The game we played now involved sending each other cell-phone pictures, instead of the GPS coordinates. The GPS doesn't work so well when you're indoors, not to mention underground on the Metro. Plus, Nate liked the pictures because while they're usually pretty clear in showing a location, occasionally it isn't too obvious, which added a little mystery to the proceedings, like an old-fashioned riddle game. Plus, picture phones were a bit newer, thus cooler technology than the GPS. Plus, we were in DC, traipsing over famous landmarks; the pictures themselves became souvenirs, like the trinkets we used to take from the boxes. I don't know what Nate did with his, but I kept most of mine on a devoted zip drive and made a point of going to new places on the rare instances I was "it."

Here's how the rules went: One person, or one team, as the case was this time, was "it," and went off to hide somewhere in the city, anywhere within the city limits. They selected a hiding location and went there, taking any route they chose, however direct or winding. Along the way, they took five pictures with their camera, each at a different site, and a sixth at their destination. Over the next two and a half hours, they sent those pictures to the people searching for them, the first two at fifteen minute intervals, then the rest at one every thirty minutes. After the last picture had been sent, there was a half-hour time limit for the others to find them. There was no running and catching, they just had to be found. When the half-hour was up, if they still remained hidden, they were declared the winner and the game ended.

The last time we'd played had been Kim's first game. After I explained everything to her, she wanted to know if all this adventuring implied that Nate hated his desk job, sitting in some office, staring at a computer screen all day. I told her no, Nate really was the geek he appeared to be. He would never play paintball, for instance, let alone any real sport, not even golf. What drew him to geocaching was the technology aspect of it, the idea of using the military-created GPS satellite system for his own amusement. Then when he started changing it, it became "his" game, something he'd invented, sort of, and it gave him a feeling of power. He had an ardent pride about it which compelled him to continue playing it, and roping me along for the ride, a pride that was more forceful than what was really a general dislike of the outdoors.

"So, we just stand here for ten minutes?" Ahmed asked.

"Well, we don't have to," said Paul, "But we're not going to get the first picture for fifteen minutes, and that won't even help very much. It'll take several pictures before we get some idea of where they're going. You want to get something to eat?" He motioned to the Air and Space Museum, which, in addition to a cafeteria, had an adjacent McDonald's, not to mention packets of freeze-dried ice cream in the gift shop. "We could wander around, look at the planes for a few minutes, if you'd like. Or are you not interested, since you've already seen everything?"

"Oh, no, I would love to look," said Ahmed, showing some excitement. "All the wonderful things in these museums! There's nothing anywhere else on earth like the Smithsonian. You know the Air and Space Museum has a Soviet Sputnik? You would think the Russians would want to keep it."

"I'm pretty sure there was more than one," said Paul.

"Of course there was, but still! And did you know, the National Gallery of Art," he pointed to the domed Gallery, which looked like Monticello, right across the street on the other side of the Mall, "has the only Leonardo Da Vinci painting in America, the *Ginevra de' Benci*? It was painted circa 1474/1478, and is located in the West building, Main Floor, Gallery 6.

"Gee Paul, a Muslim, an immigrant, and a nerd, all in one! You hit the jackpot," I teased.

Paul put his arm over Ahmed's shoulder and gave him a squeeze. "That's okay; opposites attract, and so forth. See you around, Court,

Kim." Ahmed waved, and they crossed the street, went up the steps and stood on the line heading into the building's glass-walled front entrance.

"So if Nate and Sandy are in the Museum, too, and they run into them, do they win automatically?" asked Kim. "Cause we have to win this one."

"No, not until the ten-minute head start is over. Besides, Nate won't be in there. If he wants to make it his destination, they'll follow some more circuitous route that takes them halfway across the city first." I stared at Paul before he vanished inside. "I'm really surprised at him."

"I know," said Kim. "It's so unfair! I wanted to be 'it' this time!" Then she realized I wasn't talking about Nate. "Oh, you mean them. What, do you not like Ahmed? I think it's great they're together, 'cause I know Paul is a teensy bit xenophobic, so maybe now he'll lighten up and reevaluate his prejudices. It's totally a good thing for him."

"I just don't get it." I shook my head.

"Well, obviously they're in love. I bet it was love at first sight, and they just can't help being drawn to each other, despite their differences. Love conquers all, you know."

"No, you don't understand." I told Kim what had happened that morning, and how it had bothered me that Ahmed had been over without my permission. Since she didn't understand my point, I explained to her how I felt Paul was belittling me, taking advantage of me.

She still didn't get it. "How is he taking advantage of you? Isn't he paying rent?"

"I just want to know who's in my apartment. It's basic security. And common courtesy."

"You just don't like that he's dating a Muslim, admit it." She waggled a finger at me. "Or are you still uncomfortable with his being gay?"

"I'm bothered that he's not bothered," I said, ignoring her last comment. "I just don't understand him. I mean, I wake up one morning, and find he's literally sleeping with the enemy, according to his previous world-view. Literally!"

"People change, Court. You can't help it. It's usually a good thing, and I would have to say definitely in this case."

My phone buzzed. My phone doesn't have a ring tone, it just rings with a simple old-fashioned *buzz* sound that a phone is supposed to have. All ring tones are annoying, and I disliked the idea of picking one favorite tune and then advertising it to the whole world. I pulled up the picture Nate had sent. He was standing some distance in front of the Capitol Building.

"Typical," I said. "Unimaginative." We could see the Capitol from were we stood, so he hadn't gone far to snap this.

"Well, he only had 15 minutes. How far did you expect him to get?"

I waved my hand around. "We're on the Mall, for christssake! God knows how many different spots you could find. Besides, look at this." I showed her the picture again. "He must be a couple hundred feet in front of it, at least. He's probably only standing on Third Street. That's what, two blocks away? It probably took him five minutes to get there. Oh, he could've done better, all right." I shook my head and put away my phone. "So what do you want to do now?"

"We should probably go back to the Metro station. He'll probably end up taking the train someplace, right? This way we'll have a head start!"

This was true. Nate was certain to take the subway; he had done so during every game we'd played here in which he'd been "it." Of course, there was also a good possibility he'd stay on the Mall, just for the sake of doing something unexpected and tripping us up. Either way, though, "It'll be at least an hour or more before we get a sense of where he's going. You really want to waste all that time sitting in some dark station, waiting?"

"Court, we are going to win this game. Think win! Win win win!" She held up her fists and shook them as she said this, a mini cheer. "Besides, what else are we going to do? Did you have anything in mind?" I shook my head. "Then what are you complaining about? Or, no, better, let's do both! We have plenty of time. Let's go somewhere. There must be something in this city we haven't seen yet. Let's go have some fun!"

I thought for a moment. "Well, I would like to see the Spy Museum. I don't know where it is, though I do remember it being on F Street."

"Okay, good!" But then she pulled out the map she'd brought with her, like a tourist, and started checking. She sort of scrunched up her mouth in a quasi-frown, and checked the index, then the map again. "Well," she said finally, delivering the bad news, her concentration still on the map, "it says it's on F Street Northwest, and F Street is divided in two by the White House, so I think it would be on the far side of it."

"That doesn't sound very far away. You were just implying I could pick anything in the city."

"I'd rather stick close to a Metro station. We should go back to Seventh Street and then north up to F Street. Then we can decide if we want to go west around the White House or just stay there, at the Museum of American Art."

"Why on earth would we want to go there?"

"Because it's right between the Gallery Place Station and Metro Center, which will give us access to all four Metro lines, so we'll be able to get to Nate anywhere."

Dear God, she'd become obsessed with winning this stupid game. She must really have wanted to be "it." All things considered, I decided it would be better to go along with her scheme. We could always come back and see the Spy Museum some other weekend, and anyway, I'd never been to the American Art Museum, so I guess it wouldn't kill me to check it out.

So we went up Seventh Street, past the National Gallery of Art, past the National Archives, crossed Pennsylvania Avenue, up to F Street and the Smithsonian American Art Museum. This particular museum was recently renovated. It used to be the Patent Office Building. It's another one of those buildings, proliferate in DC, which have that classical Greek architecture of white marble and a front façade of a row of columns. That's another thing I hate about DC—every building has to look like the damn Parthenon. Architecture in this town is so screwed up. It's a myth that there's a law stating no building can be taller than the Capitol, but there are some archaic architecture rules on the books—rules Ayn Rand would have simply hated—so that in fact there is no building taller than the Capitol. There can be no skyscrapers, which is not only why the city has such a pathetic economy, but why it has such extensive, and wealthy, suburbs and exurbs; real estate developers have to resort to building their leaning towers of capitalism in the Old Dominion.

By the time we got there, it was past time for another picture, so I called him up. "You're late," I said.

"Sorry," Nate laughed at me through static. "I'm on the Metro, so I'm waiting until we pull into the next station to send you a picture. You didn't just want to see the inside of the car, did you?"

"No, that's fine," I said, and hung up, and explained the delay to Kim.

"There you go," Kim said. "The Metro already. Now if they started from Third Street," she said, scrutinizing her map, "the closest stations are Federal Center to the south and Judiciary Square to the north."

"Don't waste your time thinking about it. He'll tell us in a minute."

So we stood there on the street corner, doing nothing but observing the traffic, as we waited for the next call. Fortunately it was only a minute before my phone buzzed again with another picture, which showed Nate sitting in the orange cushioned seat of a train car identical to the one we'd arrived in, leaning against the window. Through it we could make out faint white lettering which read, "FARRAGUT NORTH."

"On the Red Line!" said Kim. "Come on, let's go!" She grabbed my arm and we raced to the Gallery Place Station, down the escalator, and hoped aboard the next available train—another three dollars gone, but at least this one was blessedly uncrowded.

As soon as we sat down, Kim was checking the map to estimate where he'd gone. "Okay, so going east, after Farragut there's DuPont Circle, the Zoo, and, hmmm... I bet that's it, the National Zoo. He could lead us around there for hours, and go see the pandas in the bargain. I bet he'd love to see the pandas."

I sighed. "Kim, don't confuse what Nate wants with what you want. He prefers to be a little more clever. Remember our last game?" Last time we'd played, in June, Nate's final picture just showed him standing at the base of a long, narrow flight of stairs, and we didn't have the faintest idea where it was. Two of Nate's friends from work were playing along, and one of them eventually figured it out. It turned out that Nate was at the "Hitchcock Steps," on M Street in Georgetown, the 75 slate steps made famous by their appearance in the movie *The Exorcist*—the stairs the priest falls down at the end. I didn't recognize them, and I don't think Kim had even seen *The Exorcist*. Only a film buff would have even known what they were, let alone where. I told him it verged on cheating.

"Look," I said, "we should get off at DuPont Circle. There's probably more stuff there that would appeal to him. And even if that's not it, we need the next picture to know where he's going, so we can just wait out there and get some lunch, then continue on. I mean, the Zoo's the last spot I'd bet on. Neither of them is an animal lover, so let's not start speculating wildly and get ourselves off track, okay?"

"Well, I'd bet they're going to the Zoo," she said. "Going there now is taking an educated gamble. If I'm right, or even if they're going farther than the Zoo, we'll have an enormous lead over Paul and Ahmed. And if I'm wrong, we'll still have more than enough time to turn around. The best part is, no matter what, we'll have a few minutes to run in and check out the pandas! And we can get lunch there. You'd like to do that, right? Go see the pandas? Of course you would! What more could you ask for!"

Well, for starters, I recalled asking to visit the Spy Museum, but what the hell. I gave in to her demands, and we hung in until the Woodley Park-Zoo station. It was a fifteen minute trip, and fortunately for me, she'd run out of gossip on Jenna and apparently had nothing else to say about the pandas and their inherent adorableness, so she took out her iPod and spent the rest of the ride listening to music, oblivious to my existence. Which I didn't mind terribly; it gave me a chance to close my eyes and relax.

We arrived and took the escalator up to the street. I haven't been to every Metro station in DC, so I don't know how it compares to the rest, but the escalator at Woodley Park has got to be the longest escalator I have ever ridden. From the bottom you can't even see the top. It just goes up and up forever, like Mount Everest, or a literal stairway to heaven. I can't imagine how commuters survive on days when it's broken, which I understand is not that unusual an event. I gripped the handrail hard and dared not look back. After that, there's a short walkway, and then *another* escalator, albeit a much shorter one. It exits at a spot that was part of a real city, the real DC, a place with shops and restaurants and apartments and cars whizzing by and people milling about, a far cry from the over-esteemed National Mall. That's not to say I felt more comfortable there. Sitting on a bench a few feet away was a bum holding up a large piece of cardboard, a square cut in the middle for his head to appear, surrounded by the words "ME FOR PRESIDENT" and "VOTE FOR ME". I quickly averted my eyes, and noticed a second sign propped up against the bench. This one read "DAWN IS COMING". That one I stared at for a whole second and decided it was an anti-end-of-the-world sign, which was nice, I guess. We hurried along up Connecticut Avenue.

We walked past old townhouses and apartment buildings for several minutes without coming across the Zoo. Worse, the walk was all uphill, and it tired me to the point where I asked Kim if maybe we could just forget it and turn around.

"When we're so close already?" she said, pressing me onward. That's when we got Nate's third picture. Finally, I thought, salvation. But when I saw where he was, I was speechless.

It was a picture of Nate standing next to the free-standing stone word "ZOO," sitting above a bed of roses, in front of a wrought-iron fence and a cross-shaped metal pole, with two billowing green banners hanging from the arms, each featuring a panda. "Ha! I was right!" Kim said, exalting, laughing. "The Zoo, the Zoo! The pandas! We're right behind them! We are so going to win this! Win win win! Come on, they only took this a minute ago, they're still just inside. If we hurry, we can sneak up on him while he's standing around at the Panda house!"

We then had to run, and I was not in the mood for that. It still took us another five minutes to get there. Kim didn't want to let up, so I only managed to grab a breath of air when we stopped for traffic before crossing the street to the entrance, passing the very spot Nate had been standing only minutes earlier. As we darted through the sea of candy-wielding kiddies and their indulgent parents who clogged the walkways, I tried to object. "But Kim, he's only given us three pictures. There's still a long way to go. This can't be his destination. He could already be out of here." We passed a fenced-in area, and glancing over I saw a giant gray bird (identified by a sign as an emu) standing on the other side, looking back at the crowd of people snapping pictures of it, turning its head this way and that.

"Or there might be a line to see the pandas, and they'd be stuck here," said Kim. "I know it's not his destination, but it won't matter if we catch him! At this moment they can't get too far ahead of us, because we've been on their trail the entire time. We haven't wasted any time in museums or anything, remember? We took a gamble, and it's paid off. We're right on top of them! Win win win!"

After another five or so minutes of walking we arrived at the Panda Habitat. The living space of the pandas, like the space of most zoo animals, is divided into an indoors and outdoors section. To the left was a stone walkway that went past the outdoor section, right up to the fence. Beyond the fence there was a gully the animals could not cross, then the main area. For the pandas, this was a fairly spacious forest compound filled with trees, logs and other large fallen branches, grassy spaces where tufts of bamboo grew, and large flat rocks. The walkway past this had two levels, the lower one that pressed against the fence, and an elevated one allowing a wider perspective. Both happened to be packed with tourists. To the right was another pathway which led down into the indoors section of the habitat. There was no line to go inside the building, but unfortunately for us, because of the panda's popularity, the Zoo required tickets to go in, which had to be purchased in advance online, which we had not done. Nate and Sandy might have done so in the morning, knowing full well they would wind up here.

We, however, had no way inside. After a quick survey, it was clear they weren't standing outside. If they had gone inside, we had no way of knowing. Though if they had, it was unlikely they'd still be there.

We wormed our way among the crowd in the lower pathway of the outdoor section of the Panda Habitat, ducking and craning to catch a glimpse. Finally we saw it in the distance, one single Giant Panda, a tiny ball of black and white nestled in some dense grass behind a rock. It was eating bamboo, which it held between its paws, with its head moving from side to side as it tore pieces away and chewed them.

"Ooo!" squealed Kim. She whipped out her camera and started snapping pictures.

A moment later a park employee walked behind us, speaking loudly to everyone, "You can see the mother, Mei Xiang, up in the corner there. You might be able to get a better glimpse from the upper level. Tai Shan is still inside, but with his mother here, he'll likely be joining her soon."

"Okay," I said in Kim's ear. "So where now?"

"Let's stay here. I want to see the baby panda." Having come so far to see the pandas, Kim was unable to simply give up, and enjoined me to wait just a few minutes in the hope that the baby would materialize. She hopped from foot to foot, still watching the mother.

I gave it another minute, then said, "But what about Nate? We have to get going if we want to catch up with him. I thought you were desperate to win this."

She looked at her watch, trying to imagine how much longer we might have to wait to view her precious baby panda, comparing the time to our rapidly deteriorating advantage, weighing one obsession against another. True to her emotions, Kim, after having ruthlessly chased Nate and Sandy to this point, favored staying and seeing the panda herself. She was bargaining that we could still catch up to them, but I was startled to realize she was now genuinely frowning, despite her mumbling "Today is a beautiful day" under her breath. Her happy thoughts were draining away like sand in an hour glass. Oh, how Nate was going to pay for this.

CHAPTER 4

Despite all the hullabaloo made over the lack of representation in Congress and the Federal Government's tight control of the District, Washington is really just like any other city. It's just that its upper-class-*cum-glitterati* is made of mostly politicians, bureaucrats, and lobbyists, instead of actors or real estate tycoons or industrialists. Otherwise, it has what you'll find everywhere: racial division and racial politics, squabbles over neighborhood gentrification and the construction of a lofty and entirely unnecessary new baseball stadium, sub-par schools, an eccentric mayor, a functioning-but-unimpressive governing bureaucracy, the occasional scandal involving the unfortunate death of some underprivileged person that people are outraged over one week and oblivious to the next, and so on. Life as usual.

It does have some nice distinctions, though. Its baseball team, the Nationals, having only arrived in the city from Montreal the previous year, is still new enough to generate a magical, unifying pride in the city's residents. Or at least those who don't have to actually live near the stadium. The museums, of course, are among the best in the world. The Smithsonian Institute holds all kinds of cool stuff. Of course, when I say cool stuff, I mean the planes in the Air and Space Museum, but I'm sure the other ones also have interesting things in them, too. And then there's the National Zoo.

"The National Zoo," I read in a pamphlet I picked up, "is also part of the Smithsonian Institute, and is one of the few zoos in America to be home to a family of giant pandas. Its two adult pandas, Tian Tian and Mei Xiang, two of only twenty pandas living anywhere in the world outside of China, are here on a ten-year loan from the Chinese government.

"The deaths of several animals in 2003 and 2004 brought a cloud over the Zoo, calling into question its commitment to the mission of protecting the world's wildlife, but it has rebounded to new heights of popularity following the birth of a baby panda, Tai Shan, in July of 2005."

I remembered that. The papers, especially the *Washington Post*, were enthralled by his advent, and ran an excessive number of stories and updates, before, after, and ever since. "His name," it continued, "which means 'peaceful mountain,' was chosen in a contest in which more than 200,000 votes were cast." I couldn't fathom why "peaceful mountain" won out, since there are no mountains anywhere near DC, nor is there much peace. Anyway, the exhibit was always swarming with people eager for a glimpse of the black and white fuzzball.

"Okay, how about this," Kim said, breaking into a smile after pondering our position. "Why don't you go ahead and look on your own. I'm not moving until I see that panda. He's probably at the other end of the zoo by now, so why don't you head down there, and I'll catch up later."

I said nothing for a moment, concerned. "I think splitting up is cheating," I finally said.

"But we're not splitting up. We won't be looking for him separately; I'll be here the whole time. Come on, it's the only way we can keep ahead of Paul!"

"You realize he's probably still in the Space Museum. There's no need to rush around until the last two pictures, because even at this point there's still no way to narrow it down."

"Look, Nate's been following a clear pattern the whole time. He's come all the way up here, to the Zoo, and from here there's really no place else to go. He'll either stay here, or head up into Rock Creek Park, which is just beyond the north entrance of the Zoo. So whatever he's doing, that's the way he's headed."

"You don't know that."

"You're the one who said he likes obscure places. I bet he does go up into Rock Creek Park. He'll wind up at the spot where they found Chandra Levy, or something like that."

I doubted it. The dumping ground for the body of the famous missing Capitol Hill Intern seemed a little too gruesome, even for Nate. It was probably a better guess than some old Civil War fort that was also there, but really, he wasn't into that kind of thing, and even if he was, I doubted Sandy would go along with it. Honestly, I had a hard time believing my perpetually cheerful girlfriend had even thought of such a horrible thing. Besides, Levy's disappearance was back in 2001; how would he even find the place?

"I'm sure there are other things in Rock Creek Park, if that really is where he's going. But splitting up is a big gamble."

"One I'd be willing to take, considering how well my last one paid off. They were here. They probably still are, somewhere nearby. And we're still winning; we just need to press our advantage. Now, I insist you go, Court. Don't argue with me."

So I went.

I wandered down Olmstead Walk, the main thruway, a curving path made of hexagonal terra cotta tiles. I passed by a few of the buildings, and some signs pointing to various exhibits down the paths' offshoots, pausing by a cluster of vending machines to buy a bottle of water and an ice cream sandwich. I'd come all the way into DC, wasted most of my day riding the Metro, and now here I was at the National Zoo, a trip in and of itself, and except for the emu and the one panda I wasn't going to get to see any of it. It was unfair. Paul was probably savoring his time at the Air and Space Museum with his boyfriend, Nate and Sandy were presumably going somewhere they wanted, and Kim, at the very least, was going to see the fuzzball. What'd I get? Not a single thing. The whole city before me, and I couldn't enjoy any of it.

I ate my sandwich slowly as I strolled southward. I hoped we wouldn't end up having to go into Rock Creek Park, because I had no interest in that, either. It would be a long walk to get there, if easy enough. The Zoo's south entrance connected to Beach Drive, a two-lane street which runs through the park, paralleling the creek most of the way. It's closed to traffic on the weekends, so there would only be other people using it, coming and going, walking, jogging, riding bicycles. Rock Creek stretches from the Potomac River up into Maryland, as does the Park, though most of it is concentrated in upper northwest DC. All told, it's about 2000 acres in size. Supposedly there are wolves hiding somewhere in it. I don't recall even once ever having spent any time there.

As I continued on, passing a sign pointing to the Small Mammal House, I wondered what I was doing here. More specifically, I wondered if Kim was getting impatient with me, if maybe her ordering me to go on without her was a sign of an impending breakdown in our relationship. Maybe she was so determined to win this game because she already knew she wouldn't be dating me long enough to participate in the next contest. No, that was silly; she could simply play it with her own friends if she wanted. And there was nothing wrong between the two of us. I was being paranoid.

I found my ruminations repeatedly turning back to Paul and our argument this morning. I might only have been trying to justify myself after the fact, but I don't think my reaction was rooted in any prejudice. Paul was right, of course; I certainly wouldn't have required permission before he brought someone over, and hadn't with my previous roommates. But none of those people had been my own brother. I think that was my problem. I was expecting to still be the older brother, the one in charge, the one with the answers. He'd always been smarter than me, more athletic, more popular, cooler, but I'd still been older.

But I was dreaming. He hadn't been deferential to me for years. I don't think he saw me as a mature, responsible adult, and this is what bothered me. It's stupid, I know. Some people struggle with their parents' expectations of them; I struggle with my brother's.

Finally, my phone rang with Nate's next picture. Not having a map, I didn't really have any idea where I was in the Zoo in relation to the entrances, but hopefully I wouldn't have to go any further.

In the fourth photo, Nate was clearly inside a building. He was standing next to a plane of glass, hunched over so that the shot would encompass his face, the animal inside, and a sign just below it. The animal was a large snake with gray and tan stripes, curled up on some sand by a log. The sign below was hard to read, but I could make out the snake's name: "EGYPTIAN COBRA".

Oh, yes, he and Ahmed were going to be best friends, I could tell.

I called Kim and described the picture to her. She was appalled. "The Reptile House? He went to the Reptile House? He came all the way to the Zoo, and then just skipped the pandas? For some snake? How could he? How *could* he?"

"Don't like snakes?" I teased.

"Get over there!" she barked.

"Over where? The Reptile House? Come on, I don't think it takes a whole half hour to get from the entrance to there. He took a picture earlier than he needed to in order to give himself more time to get to his next destination."

"Maybe it does take a half hour. I mean, you're not there yet, are you?" She sounded both angry and disappointed in me. "You're being Negative!"

"Kim…"

"Fine, whatever. Just keep going north. I'm still betting on Rock Creek Park."

"Still no sign of the panda?" I chuckled.

"Don't you start. If I have to stand here all day to see that cute little baby, then that's what I'll do. You just get going." Then she hung up on me.

So I resumed my desolate journey, trudging onward. God, what was I doing here? I was exerting all this effort, and we were so close, yet I'd bet I was still going to lose out in the end. And then at dinner Ahmed would probably be at the center of attention, and I'd have to spend the whole evening listening to him. I wondered what he and Paul talked about. Did they argue about religion often? What kind of relationship was that?

I passed by the Great Ape House, where all of the animals must have been inside, since I could see none of them from where I was. What was up with these animals? Actually, I was starting to envy them. God, was it hot out! I was sweating terribly. I bought a second bottle of water at the next vending machine I came across. Soon enough, I came upon the Reptile House, off to my left, and continued past them. What was the point? I wasn't particularly interested in seeing the Egyptian Cobra, or any other cobra, for that matter. How did Nate know it was there? He hadn't known about Ahmed when he'd planned his trip, so he couldn't have intentionally chosen that animal. Perhaps they had just wandered around, looking for inspiration, and couldn't resist the joke when he came across it.

I walked a little further on, then plopped down on a bench for a few minutes. I'd been running, walking, and standing for nearly an hour in 90-degree weather, and was absolutely exhausted. I wished I had another ice cream sandwich, but at three dollars a pop, it was too exorbitant to justify.

For five minutes I sat there, finishing my water and resting, listening to the distant singing of the birds and the nearby chattering of children. I noticed as I looked around that behind me was a small empty space, just a little patch of grass, where a tent of blue tarp had been set up, a white plastic table beneath it. Probably a stop-off point for a tour, or some children's demonstration. But it was momentarily empty, so I went over and sat in the grass, in the blissful shade. I only stayed a minute because I kept worrying some security guard would appear and tell me to get off the grass, so I reluctantly went back to the bench. But then, fearing I might actually fall asleep, I decided to keep walking up the path. In another few minutes I came upon the Zoo's back entrance, which was just an open iron gate, devoid of the decorative flowers and signs of the front entrance.

I crossed the street into Rock Creek Park, which had no gate, and remained on the path. There was nothing I saw on the path other than some trees, and I didn't get very far before my phone mercifully rang. It was Kim, asking for an update. I told her I was in the park and hadn't seen Nate or Sandy on my way here. She told me to keep going, and she'd catch up.

She sounded chipper, like she'd gotten her happy thoughts back. "I take it you finally saw the panda," I said.

"I sure did! And he was so adorable! I could just eat him up! And he was big, too! I got a bunch of pictures I have to show you!" I though she would go on into more detail, but she'd refocused on the game and wanted to catch up as quickly as possible. She still thought Nate was in Rock Creek Park, only a little farther ahead then I was. Even so, I walked slowly, too tired to drum up much enthusiasm. Another minute went by, and then the next picture came in, and I knew I'd been right. So right I wanted to cry. All our tracking and chasing had been for naught. We had clearly lost, it was as simple as that.

The photo was of him standing outside next to a Metro sign, this one reading, "CLEVELAND PARK."

He wasn't going to Rock Creek Park at all. He'd doubled back and gotten on the train again. Maybe he'd just missed us, slipping by going out as we were coming in, or maybe he'd already left before we even got here. But he turned around and went back to the Metro, and by now he could go anywhere in the city, and we'd only know where when he sent his next and last picture. At that point we'd only have a half hour to find him, with no advantage over Paul. It looked like I might be right about the Space Museum. He would go halfway across the city, just to wind up back where he'd started.

I called Kim back. She was still in the Zoo, only having gotten as far as the Reptile House. I told her to just stay there and I would meet her, and then we could talk about what to do.

I didn't run, certainly. I took my time, but soon enough I found myself back on Olmstead Walk. I found a sign with a map posted, pointing the way to the Zoo's police station, which was fortunately also near the restrooms. I needed a bathroom break after my two bottles of water. Afterwards it was only a short walk until I found Kim sitting on a bench, eating cotton candy. I sat down next to her.

"Did you manage to get anything for lunch?" she asked after giving me a minute to catch my breath.

"Of course not. How could I, running around like this? And by the way, cotton candy doesn't qualify as lunch."

"It's just to keep up my strength. It doesn't really matter; we're having an early dinner, remember?"

"Right. No lunch, got it." I breathed deeply. "So do we go back to the Metro? I mean, the cobra makes me think his destination is the Washington Monument."

"Why would you think that?"

"Because of the cobra, the Egyptian Cobra. He obviously wants to needle Ahmed."

"Oh!" she said, understanding. "You're right!"

"The thing is, the Washington Monument just seems *too* obvious, you know? He doesn't like the obvious. I guess I really can't see him going there."

Kim thought for a minute, then shrugged. "Yeah, you're probably right. I'm getting tired of running around. Let's just stay at the Zoo until we get his next picture, then we can hail a cab." Thank God she'd finally given in to reason!

So we walked over to the nearby Great Ape House, and spent some time inside. Most of the animals there looked apathetic. The only ones that didn't were the avuncular, orange-haired orangutans, which sat near their windows watching the people watching them. One had gotten a hold of some popcorn, now spilled over the floor, and it was picking up one piece after another, grinning at us with seeming contentment. Occasionally it pressed its hand to the glass, and waited until someone mirrored the movement before resuming its eating, like it was eager to make contact, or possibly make fun of us. The gorillas, by contrast, lay curled up in the corner, staring at the wall, barely moving. It was kind of sad, actually.

After the Ape House, we walked around a circular road in the back of the zoo past the tiger enclosure. We waited there a bit, watching the animal walk around the highest level of its compound. It sauntered to one end, then turned around and began to saunter back. With its strong muscles, its graceful steps, it was magnificent. Honestly though, it looked bored. We then headed back towards the south entrance, where we'd originally come in. We stopped at the Elephant House briefly to see the elephants, and spent a couple of minutes watching the three of them lumber about and drink water from a pool.

Then break time ended as Nate's sixth and final picture came in. He was standing about fifty feet in front of what was clearly a large gothic church, with towers and arches and a larger circular stained glass window above the front doors.

"Washington National Cathedral," Kim declared instantly, holding my hand to turn the phone towards her. I sort of liked the sensation of it. It felt like things were back the way they were supposed to be. We stood like that, holding hands, our bodies touching as we sat on a bench near the Visitor Center near the entrance, listening to the squeals of several small children as they ran past, their parents calling after them.

"Are you sure? Because I know there are other big churches in this city. There's the National Shrine Basilica down by Catholic University. It's right on the Red Line, and in the last picture he'd gotten back on the Red Line. He would have had to take a cab to get to the National Cathedral."

"So, they took a cab. They probably never took the train, they just went to the station to get a cab. It can't be anything else."

"Your convictions haven't been very accurate today," I reminded her.

"Sure they have! He did go to the Zoo, just like I said. We almost had him. Now look, it's Washington National Cathedral. It's a landmark! How can you not recognize it? I mean, how long have you lived here?"

Of course she was right; I knew the difference between the Basilica and the Cathedral. I only brought it up because I didn't like the idea that Nate had only gone to the train station to take a picture. And I guess I was arguing for argument's sake; I still felt sour that I was being controlled.

But at least it wasn't the Washington Monument, thank God!

We walked back to the Zoo gate and hailed a cab, as we'd planned. There was a possibility we still had a decent chance of winning. The problem was that there weren't any cabs just sitting there, waiting. There had been when we'd arrived earlier, so we just assumed this was a regular pick-up spot. Why wouldn't it be? This was a popular tourist destination. But now there was nothing, and it cost us almost ten minutes as we stood at the curb waiting before one pulled over for us.

During the trip, Kim showed me her pictures of the panda. She oohed and aahed over images of a lot of green surrounding a tiny black and white spot. She promised me the blot was Tai Shan, but I couldn't see it. It was probably just the minuteness of the screen, and she assured me he was there—it would be clear at full size.

Washington National Cathedral, the hundred-year-old Episcopal Church, sits atop a hill 400 feet above sea level, which makes its towers the true highest point in DC. The good news was, it was unquestionably the destination spot. When we pulled up it looked exactly like it did in the photo. The bad part was we'd hit some traffic. We arrived within the deadline, but not before Paul and Ahmed. We found them standing outside, together with Nate and Sandy, off to the right of the front door, staring up at the façade.

"Well, 'bout time you got here!" cried Nate as we came up.

"You cheated!" Kim said, very sharply. "You were at the Zoo and the Metro, then suddenly you're all the way out here? That's cheating!

There's supposed to be a progression, one place leading to the next! How are we supposed to find you if you jump around randomly?"

Nate shrugged. "It's not cheating. There's no rule that says there has to be a progression. I mean usually there is, but technically I can go anywhere I want." He folded his arms. "Besides, after you guys complained about my pick last game, I figured I'd better find somewhere easy to recognize. I mean, they got here in plenty of time." He nodded to Paul.

"Yeah, we didn't even bother looking at the photos until the fifth one," Paul said.

"Were you trying to track us?" Sandy laughed.

"Of course! What's the point of having six pictures if the first five don't mean anything! Why not just do one? I mean I thought this was supposed to be a puzzle game, like *The Amazing Race*, or something!" I could see Nate knitting his brow; I knew he already shared the same concerns, and would soon come up with a brand new formulation for his game. I hope it involves a return to the GPS. The technology has advanced since we last played with it, so this time I was sure we could get it to work. Plus, using it seemed more, I don't know, adventurous.

"And another thing!" Kim continued. "How in God's name could you go all the way to the Zoo, and then not see the pandas!"

"Well, we've already seen them," said Nate. "Why? Did we mess up your plans doing that? I hope so."

"And instead you picked some stupid snake?"

"Originally we planned on the Sloth Bear, which we haven't seen. But after I met Cleopatra here," flashing him a smile, "I wanted something more appropriate. I pulled up a list of their holdings, looking for a camel, but they don't have one. The cobra was the second best choice."

"So you pre-planned your trip?" Ahmed asked. "That explains why you neglected the obelisk."

"The what?" said Nate.

"The obelisk, right on the Mall. The most overtly Egyptian site in the city. I assumed you didn't bother because it was simply *too* obvious, but I see not."

"What are you talking about?" he asked, frustrated. Everybody had little tight smiles on their faces, knowing the answer and watching him struggle.

Thankfully, and I mean that, because I was starting to worry about him, Nate realized Ahmed was referring to the Washington Monument, the towering structure that, along with the Capitol Building, dominates the skyline and everyone's image of D.C. This despite *not* looking like the damn Parthenon.

"You're right!" he said excitedly. "I can't believe we didn't even think of that! It's just so perfect! Egyptian, and a giant phallus! A perfect representation of our gay friends!"

"Hey," Paul said sharply.

Nate clapped his hands to change the subject. "Okay, enough of that. So! Dinner time! Where are we going? Hey, I know a great falafel shop in Adams Morgan. How 'bout it?"

"No thanks," said Ahmed.

"You don't like falafel?"

He shook his head. "Don't be... cute."

"Why not? I thought you liked cute guys." He laughed.

Ahmed placed his hands on his hips and asked Paul, "Are we going to have to put up with this all afternoon?"

"Jesus!" said Nate. "A little friendly teasing, and suddenly you have to 'put up' with me? Why can't any of you people just be normal?"

"I suppose," said Paul, sounding only slightly annoyed, "you put yourself in that category?"

"Damn straight!" Nate said, and winked. Then he held up his hands to wave off any impending comeback. "Hey, hey!"

"Nate, you have to understand," said Paul sharply, "Ahmed's still in the closet. You guys are among the very few straight people who know about him. He's just unsure of your intentions, that's all."

"'Are we going to have to put up with this?' doesn't sound unsure, it sounds whiny. Are you telling me he doesn't know the difference between a little joking around and getting the shit kicked out of him?"

"Sometimes one can lead to the other."

"Oh please!" Nate scoffed. "What do you know about it? When was the last time you had the shit kicked out of you, Tinkerbelle?"

"Never," Paul said coldly. "How about you?"

"Okay," said Sandy, stepping between them. "That's enough."

"Yeah, sure," Nate said, grinning again. "Sorry about that. So, okay, seriously now. You guys won, Paul, so you get to pick the restaurant. Where do you two want to eat?"

"Why don't we just stay here for a while?" said Ahmed quickly. "I'd like to look at the Cathedral first."

We all looked over at him, startled. "You would?" said Paul and Nate at almost the same time, both equally surprised.

"Oh, yes, this building is famous for its works of art. Sculptures, carvings, mosaics, and of course stained-glass windows. Did you know there's one window in particular commemorating the moon landing, with an actual piece of moon rock embedded in it?"

Paul sighed, and Kim in turn brightened up. "Looks like you guys had a lot of fun at the Space Museum," she chirped.

"Oh, yes," he said. "Lots of fun. Whole galaxies of fun." He held his hand out to emphasize the point. To Ahmed he asked, "Weren't you satisfied with the moon rock at the museum?"

"Sure. That's not the only attraction. There are a lot of famous people buried here," Ahmed offered as a hopeful enticement, seeing things were not going his way but not yet ready to give up.

But Paul shrugged and said "Okay, sure, all right. We can stay a while. The day's still young. We'd probably need tickets or something for a tour, but we can always look around by ourselves."

"You want to stay here?" I asked, surprised.

"Hey, it's a church, isn't it?"

"Ah," I nodded, understanding his meaning perfectly.

We went inside, and I was glad for that, actually. It felt nice and cool. The group wandered down the nave to the altar, and I followed for a little bit, but finally just took a seat in a nearby pew. Kim was impatient, so I told her to go on with the others; after running around all day I was tired and needed some rest. I doubt she liked that, but she followed after the others easily enough. As I watched them, Ahmed was chatting animatedly and pointing in various directions—it almost looked like he was lecturing, giving them a tour. A church and the Muslim knows more about it than any of us. What didn't he know? We'd lived here our whole lives and he was the expert on this city. I wondered why he had really wanted to stay here then, if he already knew everything. To see in life what he'd only seen in books, of course. But there was at least some preening going on, trying to show up Nate, undoubtedly. Dinner with the two of them at the same table was going to be horrible. What a lovely church it was. I stared up at the vaulted ceiling. The flags of the 50 states were hung from the pillars up and down the nave, and I spent several minutes trying to identify the state that went with each flag.

Someone said "Hey," and my head snapped up. I realized I must have briefly dozed off.

There was a girl standing around the altar where the others had been a moment before, or however long it had been. I looked around and realized that otherwise we were alone in the church. The rest of them had moved on and simply left me behind. I was sure they hadn't gone far, probably just the next room or corridor or chapel or whatever was beyond the nearest door. There were a number of doors, any of which they might have gone through, but it wouldn't be hard to find them. And if it was I could always call.

"Hey," the girl called to me, coming a few steps closer. She was small. White, with light brown hair flowing just a little past her shoulders, and looked maybe fifteen or sixteen; she was wearing a bright pink mini-skirt and matching top which was somewhat revealing, along with black pumps, a petit red leather purse, and too much make-up. Way too much. It looked inappropriate on someone as young as she was. It reminded me of one of those toddler beauty-pageant contestants. I felt uneasy and couldn't help thinking she was a child prostitute, made up like that.

"You here to see Misty?" she asked me.

"No." I didn't know anyone named Misty.

"Oh." She seemed a little disappointed. She flipped her hair back and said, "Well, God is in the garden, giving blessings. Come and get blessed if you want."

Okay, yes, we were in a church, but that was still the last thing I expected to come out of her mouth.

"I'm sorry? What did you say?"

"God is out in the garden."

"Is he now?" I asked, trying to sound cynical, but I was a little freaked out.

"She. And she's giving blessings."

I blinked. "No thanks."

The girl shrugged. "Whatever." She walked off, past the chancel and through a door on the right.

So now God was a she? These Episcopalians, getting loopier and loopier. Little pink mini-skirt was probably a bishop. Or maybe it was a setup, a trick to get me out of the dark building and into the bright sunshine where her gang could jump me and steal all $32 of my life savings. Or something.

Well, whatever was going on was simply crazy. Still, Kim would definitely be pleased to learn that God was a woman. I think Kim had referred to God as "she" on the one occasion she talked about God. To Paul, of course, not to me. He'd brought it up, but even for him, Kim's New-Age beliefs were too squishy to argue with.

She might be out there, she might not. Either way, it'd be a fun thing to talk about later, and Lord knows I needed something fun to talk about with her. So I pushed myself out of the chair and followed after the girl.

CHAPTER 5

The door she had gone through led to a corridor. I didn't see her, and there were several other doors lining the hall. I heard the click of a door closing at the far end of the hall, and when I looked I saw an exit door. I called out to her, then decided on the exit door as the best option. I hadn't actually seen anyone go out that way, but I had no idea what was in this building, and I was sure I'd get lost trying to find her wandering about. If nothing else, an exit was an exit, and she had said God was outside.

It led to a stone walkway crossing South Road and beyond that into, yes, the adjacent Bishop's Garden. It was verdant, every shrub a lush bright green, every tree thick-leaved. I followed the path, convinced she was beyond every corner or behind every tree. She wasn't, though, but I didn't have to go far to find God.

There she was, a woman with light brown hair wearing a pale yellow tee, short jeans, and sandals. Her back was to me, so I couldn't tell how old she was, but I suspected she was rather young.

She was standing amidst a small crowd of people, maybe a dozen or so, going from one to the other, putting her hand on each person's forehead. They were clumped together closely, so I kept my distance from the scene to simply watch. They were all young; several were teenagers. Some of the people wore light casual clothes, tee shirts and jeans, and some had slacks, and a few wore torn, dirty jeans and coats far too cumbersome for such stifling weather. God-lady said something to each person as she touched them, but she spoke in a low, whispering voice that I was too far away to hear. The whole thing didn't last long, maybe a minute or two; I don't know if that was it, or if whatever she was doing was intended to go on longer, but she was interrupted when the girl in pink suddenly reappeared. She came from further down the path and resolutely walked right up to God-lady, and whispered something to her, and she whispered back.

God-lady held her hands out and said something which I still couldn't hear, though it must have been goodbye, and headed off the way the girl in pink had come.

Just before she disappeared too far down the path, she glanced back at the group, and I saw her face.

And the world went all fuzzy.

It was Dawn.

I recognized her immediately, and I couldn't believe it.

My old high school sweetheart, Dawn Gardner. The girl I'd dated my senior year, the girl I'd been madly in love with. The girl I'd lost my virginity to. And I hadn't seen her in, what, six years? Not since we separated before going off to different colleges. My memories of her came flooding into my mind as I stared. Her face, so thoughtful, so kind. Her smile, so generous it caused her to squint. Her voice, quiet, breathy like a whisper, even when she was shouting. No wonder I couldn't hear what she was saying. Her voice didn't project even with a microphone. I could see her as she was, sitting across from me at my kitchen table as we studied calculus together one day, wearing a sweater, holding her pen so the cap lightly touched her lips, concentrating on the problem on the page as I watched her from the corner of my eye.

In a flash I had recollections, the time I first saw her, at school in the auditorium for some assembly, and then to the moment when I told her apprehensively that I loved her, and the flipping of my heart when she said she loved me. And the last time I saw her, the August after we graduated, the day before she left for college. We were in her front yard, and I hugged her as tight as I could as though my desperation could hold her there another day longer.

How many times had I cursed myself for letting her go? It'd been my idea to separate, but even then I'd known it was a mistake. Since then I'd always quietly cherished this secret, deeply hidden hope that I could get her back again someday, maybe when I saw her again at our class reunion, or something. I'd googled her multiple times and knew what she had been up to, or at least I thought I did. I thought she had a perfectly nice, if unusual, job, but I had never dared to approach her. But now, magically, here she was.

After she left, the group scattered, going in different directions, some going past me back to the church, some wandering off the path directly into the grass of the garden. A few did go after Dawn, but slowly, studiously avoiding the appearance of following her, at least so I thought. The girl in pink, though, sat down on a nearby metal bench and leaned forward. I could see she was out of breath. In a moment we were the only two left in that small area. I stepped over to the bench, and said, "Hey, what the hell's going on here?"

She looked up at me without lifting her head. "Did you get a blessing?"

"No!"

"Why not?"

I pointed down the path where Dawn had traveled and waved my finger. "Did you mean she's supposed to be God?"

"She sure is," she said with a smile.

"Maybe you're just misinterpreting," I suggested, getting a little desperate. "Maybe she's just a minister." I waved my hand, gesturing aimlessly. "I mean, I know who she is; she's Dawn Gardner. I thought she was a DJ." I've searched for her many times on the internet, but, of course, "Dawn Gardner" is hardly a unique name, and a search generally had five hundred or so hits; there was a bit actress with the same name, a musician named Dawn Gardner, at least one local lawyer, and a host of others. But I'd plugged through a number of them, and one name linked to a nightclub which listed her as their "guest" DJ and included her picture. That was how I knew it was her, how I knew Dawn, my quiet, thoughtful Dawn, had somehow wound up becoming a disk jockey. Now this did at the time seem a bit unusual to me; when we were dating back in high school Dawn had no significant interest in music. She listened to the radio and bought the occasional CD, of course, same as everyone, but music didn't captivate her. She didn't have any favorite groups and we never went to any concerts. To the extent she had any hobbies at all it was drawing. She would occasionally sketch things in a pad she had; I still have, stuck in the back of my old yearbook, a sketch she drew of me sitting by the window. But even with drawing she was never fanatic. She didn't carry this book around with her or anything. I don't recall her even doodling in class. So it was a little strange, but not of any concern. It had been a number of years since we parted, and people change all the time. It was just one of those things, where changes sneak up on you, what a person took years evolving through, you see all at once, and it's like, wow, what is this? And maybe for that reason, as much as I wanted to see her again, I had never gone to any of the clubs she played to try to bump into her.

I decided there needn't be a contradiction. She could be both a minister and a DJ, the DJ gig a part time job paying her way through college, and then graduate school, or seminary, or whatever it was you had to do to become a minister these days. Becoming a servant of the Lord actually seemed a little less odd pursuit than the music business. She hadn't been particularly religious, either, but she did have a bit of a philosophical, spiritual bent. No views any more sophisticated than what you'd expect from any average adolescent, but it was there, and I could see how it could have developed into more. Though, really, she hadn't been devout at all, certainly not when compared to someone like Paul. I couldn't see him becoming a minister either, but for entirely different reasons.

But God?

"No," she said, finally raising her head and looking right at me, and she certainly seemed serious. "Misty really is God. You know, God who made the world, lives in heaven, all that. She's a DJ, too, but she's also God."

Well, sure, I thought, that cleared things right up. Of course she's both God and a DJ. Why not? I mean, Jesus had a day job working as a carpenter, right? Gods've gotta eat, too, right?

Who was this girl, anyway? Was it Dawn who was insane, or her? Or maybe it was a practical joke, and she would jump out of the bushes any moment and yell "Gotcha!"

"Why do you keep calling her Misty?" I asked, because I couldn't think of anything else to say. "Her name is Dawn."

She was now leaning back in her seat, slouching, but still watching me. "Sure. That was what I said. Miss Dawn."

She'd been saying Miss D., not Misty.

"Right." I decided my conversation had gone as far was it was going to, and I should really go and find Dawn. I walked away slowly. "I think I'll be going now."

She had this look in her eyes as she watched me edge away, displeased that I wasn't taking her seriously.

I gave her a final "Thanks anyway," and turned to hurry off. Instead I almost ran into a boy coming back down the path. He was a Hispanic teenager from the crowd of people Dawn had been "blessing," one of the ones who were overdressed for the weather. He was wearing clothes which were wrinkled and stained, over which he wore an olive-green colored army-surplus jacket, and even his face was grimy. I said sorry as he passed but he ignored me. He acknowledged the girl, calling her "Mol," and bent down briefly to quietly say something to her before resuming his way. She took a deep breath, got up, and followed after him without glancing back at me.

I continued on, but not for long. I didn't see Dawn or anyone else from the little group, after going maybe a hundred yards or so. I slowed down and decided I didn't need to find Dawn now; I could simply check online and find her tonight, and if not tonight some other night. But would I, though? I could have done that at anytime before, after all, and inertia had kept me away. Although things might have been different if I had heard she was God, or at least that someone regarded her as a god. Not just a music god type of thing, but a real genuine supernatural being. I had this conviction this was just the girl's delusion, that Dawn herself was perfectly normal, even though she had been doing something which looked like a blessing. Maybe I was misinterpreting, too, and she would find it bizarre when I told her, or maybe she was already aware she had a disturbed fan, but that was surely all it was. A disturbed fan. Though there had been a small crowd, she had been interacting with them. I still didn't know what to make of that, but was confident there was a reasonable explanation.

But after walking a little further, I did find Dawn.

She was standing on the grass in a small area empty of other shrubbery, talking to two people. They were different than the other people I'd seen her with earlier, all of whom had disappeared. One of the others was a young black man sitting in a wheelchair, and a young woman standing behind him.

"Yes," I heard Dawn say when I got close enough, in her quiet, confident voice. I had to sneak in pretty close, and I felt like an intruder. "I am eternal," she continued, in a pleasant but impassive tone, as if she were commenting on the sunny weather. I stood there shocked, listening. It was true. She really did think she was God. "I have neither beginning nor end. I created the universe billions of years ago, and have existed long before that, since forever. And in that time I planned for my universe, the worlds I would create, the lives of all those who would live in them. I planned every detail. Everything is the way it's supposed to be and nothing is left to chance. Everything happens for a reason, Yvette."

"Dumb bitch," the man muttered. I could see the woman, Yvette, looked pretty upset.

"Miss D.," she said quietly, "You can do anything. I believe in you. You can heal him."

"Just shut up," the man said to her.

I stood still, feeling utterly flummoxed, wanting to scream. She was eternal? She could heal? In just a few steps I'd entered into another world, one that was very disturbing. If it had been anyone else standing there, it wouldn't have meant a thing. I would have left and gone on my way without a second thought, except maybe to joke about it later. But Dawn—I knew her. I cared about her. It hurt to watch this.

Dawn looked unperturbed by Yvette's request. I didn't for one second believe this guy was going to get up and walk. I was feeling so incredulous at that moment that even if I'd seen it, I wouldn't have believed it. I knew about faith healing, and I expected Dawn to at least try something of the sort, but I was mistaken.

Dawn calmly said, "I take it you don't believe in me, do you Tyrone?"

"Right," Tyrone drawled, wryly smirking in a way which clearly billboarded his opinion that all this was a bunch of bullshit. He was probably only here to humor the woman behind him, probably his wife or sister or something. "But I will if you heal me."

"Do you believe in Jesus?"

He stopped smiling. "Yeah."

"Why? He hasn't healed you."

I thought she was going to get smacked. Yvette's face grew wan, and Tyrone grimaced in momentary anger. "I think that's enough, bitch," he said, and started to push away.

"Tyrone," Dawn said, and he stopped. She knelt down in the grass, right in front of him, so that she was now looking up at him. Then she reached out and put her hand on his cheek. He jerked, but only a little.

"I can't heal you," she said sorrowfully. "I'm sorry. Please forgive me."

Tyrone stared at her for a moment, nonplussed. I couldn't believe her either; how could she be God and then ask for forgiveness? Certainly that wasn't very godlike.

Tyrone cracked a smile and said, "Sure I forgive you. I didn't expect nothing from you anyway."

She shook her head. "No, I don't mean forgive the silly little girl in front of you. I mean forgive God, whatever God you believe in. God has let you down, and I know you feel angry at Him, even if you don't want to admit it. You blame Him for everything, and you're right to, because everything is His responsibility. But you can't fight against God. The only thing you can do is forgive Him, and make peace with life."

There was stillness in the air as I waited to hear Tyrone's response, and I sensed this might be just the sort of thing that had gotten her some actual followers. It sounded completely wrong, yet oddly intriguing and made a certain sense.

Finally, Tyrone said simply, "You're insane."

Dawn stood up. "You can have peace."

"Peace, shit."

Dawn frowned slightly, concerned, perhaps, that her voodoo wasn't working. "All right, look," she said, and the tone of her voice dipped subtly, signaling weariness, if not surrender. "Come here and I'll tell you a secret." She waved for him to follow, then began walking away. After a few steps she turned and beckoned him again.

After taking a moment to consider whether he wanted to risk going any further down the rabbit hole, Tyron began to follow her, leaving his sister or whatever she was behind. He wheeled over to her, at a point some twenty feet away, still close but far enough to be out of earshot. For two minutes Dawn spoke with him, quietly but earnestly, sometimes making wide gestures with her hands, as if in explanation. I imagined her describing the history of the universe, while pantomiming the sweep of stars and planets. I watched quietly; it was eerily close to an atmosphere of silent reverence.

I simply had to talk to her. What was I going to say? I had no clear idea, just a vague foreboding, but I had to say something. I did want to try to help her in some way, and not just because I was eager to be the hero, to somehow rescue her and return her to the world of sanity. I wanted to help her so badly. It grieved me to watch her.

I admit in those minutes I did imagine a best-case scenario, in which I could be with her instead of Kim. Was that really the best thing? Did I really want to drop Kim to hook up with someone I haven't seen in six years? Obviously she wasn't the same person she was in high school. I was chasing a memory. I think it was nostalgia, a yearning for my lost adolescence. Dear God, I felt old. If it was like this now, when I was only 24, what would it be like when I was middle-aged? How did old people live with themselves?

Still, there was more here than just wanting to possess Dawn again. The fact that I could even dream of such things, when she'd clearly lost her mind, showed what struck me as a true depth of feeling. And I did want to help her, because what she was doing was wrong, and it had to stop.

Dawn and Tyrone finally finished speaking, and he came back over to Yvette. Dawn stayed where she was.

"What'd she say?" asked Yvette.

"That bitch," Tyron muttered back with a shake of his head, "is insane." He did not look at all angry. Bemused, but not angry. He kept going, rolling past me, onto the walk and back towards the church. Yvette followed. I watched for a moment, trying to decide if I should go after them and learn more, or just stay and try to speak to Dawn. But when I turned back, she was gone.

I walked a little further to try and spot her, and I didn't. With that, I abandoned my search and headed back the way I came. There was no point in finding her, when I knew where she'd be tonight and could speak with her then. Besides, I was too disconcerted by what I had witnessed and wanted some time to process it. I also wondered if I should tell Paul. He was more interested in theology and might know something useful to say to her, but on the other hand he had never liked her and would probably do nothing more than laugh.

Traveling along the path in reverse, I passed the bench where the girl had been sitting without seeing anyone. But when I followed it back to the side door of the church where I had come out of, I was surprised to find Dawn standing there, waiting for me.

She smiled brightly in greeting when she saw me, scrunching up the corners of her eyes. It was the same enthusiastic smile I remembered and loved. She stood there in her yellow tee, her eyes directly on me. Finally I could see her close up, in the real, close enough to touch, and I longed to stretch out my hand and touch her. She looked thin, which she had always been, but otherwise healthy, physically. She looked no different from the way I had remembered her. Well, actually, there was one difference—her eyes. They were focused and keen and lively, the eyes of someone deeply enjoying a game. Dawn had always been a dreamer, someone who could be quite content sitting alone and staring off into space, but now she seemed to be more invested in the world, and her eyes sang its colors. I thought haltingly she might be doing the same Positive-Thinking stuff that Kim was into, but Kim's cheerfulness was superficial, and this wasn't the same type of silliness. Dawn's emotions weren't as intense and unveiled, but they had a deeper range. When she smiled her happiness was unforced.

I stood there without being able to say anything, and we watched each other for a brief moment.

"You thought I didn't notice you standing there, did you?" she finally said cheerfully. She opened her arms wide and we embraced in a hug. I breathed her in and felt her body against mine, just as I had wanted; yet it was strangely awkward for me, because as much as I desired to touch her, to kiss her, there was this fear of her, because I knew something was wrong with her. I know how absurd that is, that even if she was insane, mental illness wasn't infectious, but all the same I felt uneasy holding her. We stepped apart. She was still smiling, pleased to see me, though I wasn't smiling and I'm sure she could read the worry on my face.

CHAPTER 6

"Court, it's been so long," she said merrily. "How many years has it been? Six? You haven't changed a bit. How are you doing?"

"Dawn," I began but didn't know what else to say. "I'm fine."

"And how's your brother?"

"Fine. Dawn, what's going on here? What happened to you?"

It might only have been my imagination, but I thought she looked a little nervous. She pressed her lips together and wrinkled her forehead a bit, trying to look thoughtful, deciding whether to lie or just tell me the truth. I was about to repeat my question when she sighed gently and said, simply, "Apotheosis."

"What? You've been elevated to God status?"

She shrugged. "Look, Court, I've been here all afternoon, taking about religion to one person after another, and I don't want to repeat all that with you. Let's put it all aside, forget all the theology and philosophy and psychology, and just talk, like any two people. We have a lot to catch up on, Court. It's been six years. Let's go and get something to eat and sit and just catch up. What'd do you say?" She smiled again, invitingly.

I pointed in the direction of the garden, my finger trembling slightly with an anger or maybe just sadness I could feel welling up. "You can't expect me to just forget what I saw."

"And what did you see?" she said with a slightly petulant tone. "Nothing. You saw nothing because I did nothing. Now if I'd actually healed the guy, that I wouldn't expect you to forget. But nothing happened, so it should be easy to forget."

"But those things you said, about being eternal and creating the universe…"

"Just words."

"Just words?" Was she now denying it all? And was it a good thing or bad thing, that she could so casually drop the whole affair? Was it a sign of imbalance and insanity, or some kind of strategy? I didn't know what to think anymore.

After a few moments had passed in silence, she decided my inability to respond signaled acquiescence, and asked me again, "Court, let's just talk. Tell me what you've been up to."

"Hold on." I couldn't let it go. "What was the secret you told that guy in the wheelchair?"

"Oh, that." She became somber, and looked away again, back into the garden, and said, quietly but unmistakably, "The meaning of life."

"Okay…" I took a deep breath and resisted the urge to snap at her. "Fine, I'll bite. What's the meaning of life?"

She turned back to me, but still didn't look me in the eye. "I don't think I can tell you that, sorry,"

"Why not?"

Suddenly she looked up at me and smiled again, and my anger eased. "You know, you should ask your brother. I bet he'll tell you the meaning of life."

"You can't be serious," I said. Ask Paul? Yeah, and I'd bet he'd tell me, too. I could already hear the lecture on obeying Jesus I'd get if I asked him something like that. But did Dawn know that?

He was pretty religious when we were in high school, but did she remember? "Dawn, do you even remember his name?"

"Of course I do. His name is Paul. And his boyfriend's name is Ahmed."

"Oh, very cute. Trying to prove your omniscience? And I bet you didn't happen to run into them in the church while I wasn't looking, huh?" Though as soon as I said this, I realized it wasn't the case, because had they met her, they would have called me on my cell, and she wouldn't have bothered with such an obvious ruse. It was so discouraging that I was playing this game.

"Oh, they're here with you? No, actually, I've seen them in a couple of clubs."

"Really? What, do you play everywhere? Paul's never mentioned seeing you."

"I didn't say that I spoke with him. I've only seen him. The two of them."

"Then how did you know Ahmed's name if you've never spoken to him?"

"I asked around. He's actually fairly well known. He's hardly the only gay Arab in DC, but it's a small community."

"Right. Plus he's a genius and all that shit."

"What? You don't like him?"

"No, not really," I shrugged. I thought about adding more but I didn't.

She must have guessed what else I wanted to say because she gave me a plaintive look that told me I should know better, and then changed the subject. "I do play just about everywhere, that's true. I work freelance. At all these clubs I stand in a little booth, or on a platform, above the crowd, and I watch them mingle as I play my music. I've played a lot of the clubs in this city, and I've seen so many people, so many fascinating, wonderful people. It's how I meet most of my friends."

By friends I guessed she meant her followers, which made sense. Where else would she meet someone like the girl in pink? On the other hand, a few of those people who'd been hanging around her, and certainly that kid who'd spoken to the girl, looked like they were homeless, or at least not doing too well financially, and surely it would be better if she could say she met them volunteering at soup kitchens or something.

"So that's where God hangs out these days? Nightclubs? The leper colonies of the modern era?"

She laughed, a sweet liquid chime that pained my heart. "That's very good, Court."

"Yes, well…"

"I do hang out there. And now you know the answer to the question everybody always asks."

"What question?"

"You know. Whenever anything awful happens, tsunamis, hurricanes, terrorism, whatever, people always ask, 'Where was God when this happened?' Well, now you know."

"Dawn!" I cried, shocked. "That's horrible! That's not funny at all!"

She gave a little shake of her head. "Of course it's funny. It's infinitely funny, it's just that your finite mind is too small to grasp it."

"Dawn…"

"Actually, I don't think I'd compare nightclubs *per se* to leper colonies, but certainly a lot of my friends are outcasts, and they need me."

I sighed. "I don't think I can listen to much more of this, but tell me what it is you do for these 'friends' of yours."

"I do what God should do for them. I love them unconditionally. I'm there for them, without judgment, without criticism. I accept their anger and pain and heal them with empathy and compassion."

"Ah. Of course. And this 'healing' is all emotional, right? You're not making the blind see or the lame walk or anything like that, right?"

"Not usually, but occasionally I perform a miracle."

"Right. Sure you do. But I'm positive the guy in the wheelchair was much happier with your forgiveness than with some old miracle."

"Court, didn't you hear anything I said? I offer no one forgiveness, because there's nothing they need to be forgiven for if God is responsible for fate. I created everything, I ordained the world to be the way it is, so it's my fault if people get hurt, or live in misery. It's not their fault. They've done nothing and have no need for forgiveness. I'm the one who should feel sorry. Court, lots of people in the world today are angry, and they don't even know why. They have an intense inner rage and frustration that nothing will assuage. People realize in a personal way that life truly isn't fair, and deep down they think God's responsible. They're angry at God for it, but they can't admit it, since they think being angry at God is blasphemy. But this feeling is always there, and it won't go away until it's dealt with. And when you're angry with people, the only way to deal with it is to forgive them. It's not that I forgive them, but I give them permission to forgive me, to forgive God, because for many it's the only way they'll find peace. You can't struggle against the world, you have to accept the hardships in life, make peace with its imperfections. Forgiveness is the most direct way to do that. Forgiving God... well, God personifies life."

"Okay!" I had no idea what she had just said. "Well, no wonder you've spent all day in church arguing with people."

"Maybe we should just stop."

"Hold on. What about that girl, the one in the pink skirt? She looks like, well, she looks like a whore."

"You mean Molly? She is. She's also a drug dealer, and occasionally a thief."

I shook my head, disgusted. "And you just give her love and acceptance?"

"That's what she needs."

"Uh-huh. And does giving her love and acceptance make her stop whoring and dealing drugs?"

"No."

"Than what good is it? What have you actually done for that girl?"

"I'm her friend, Court."

"Her friend? That's it? Dawn, she's what? Fifteen? Sixteen? She shouldn't be on the streets, selling her body and God knows what else. She should have a home and a family and go to school. Why don't you do something decent and use your omnipotent power to give her a normal life?"

She was annoyed. "What are you trying to do, Court? Impress me? Prove what a good person you are? Such a first-rate person that you think you're better than me? That I'm just not good enough to be God? I hear it all the time from people—they know how to run the world better than I do. Do you think that? You think I haven't been doing everything I can for Molly?"

"Well, obviously you haven't."

"Look, Court, let me tell you about Molly. She doesn't want to be helped, trust me. She's had a very hard life. People have abused her, raped her, all sorts of thing you can't begin to imagine. Her own father raped her. I've encouraged her to go to Family Services, but she refuses. She's terrified of them. She's been in and out of foster homes for years, and it always goes wrong for her. Nothing but abuse, again and again. I know, I've seen the old scars and burns on her body. I know it's terrible, but she's actually happier with things the way they are. You know what she told me once? She doesn't mind selling her body because at least that means it's hers to sell. You should ask her yourself, she'll tell you everything, and you'll understand. I can't in good conscience force her into a 'normal life' that has hurt her so much."

"Dawn—I can understand that, Dawn, but you're supposed to be God. Nothing's impossible for you, right? Yet all you have are excuses and sob stories and theories about how people think. It's all talk and no action. Like a lot of religion—God's always promising and never delivering. He loves everybody but can't lift a finger to help them out when they really need it. If you were really God, Dawn, you could do better."

She leaned forward, like she was telling me a secret. "I really shouldn't say this, but inevitability is approaching for Molly. Her problems will be over sooner rather later."

"What does that even mean?"

She shrugged. "It means there's nothing more to do than wait."

"Okay Dawn, whatever you say. Tell you what, you fix Molly and I'll believe you're God."

"Fix her?" She arched an eyebrow.

"Yeah, you know, put things right."

She leaned forward again, much closer this time. I thought she was going to kiss me, but instead she whispered in my ear, "Court, I really am God."

"You're not God, Dawn. You're not perfect. I've had sex with you."

She laughed sharply. "Is that some sort of commentary on my performance?"

"No. I'm just saying I know you better than a lot of these disciples you've fooled. I know about your mental health issues."

"Mental health issues? That's rich, coming from you." She waved her finger, scolding me. "You were there, too, let's not forget. And anyway we both know those issues didn't include schizophrenia."

"This is ridiculous, Dawn. You're insane."

"Court, have I been acting erratically? Or speaking incoherently or babbling? Do you really think I'm insane?"

"Obviously you are."

"All right, Court. We'll have that chat some other time; I really should be going." She then reached out and placed her hand on my forehead and said, "Bless you." I didn't move. Her palm was warm to the touch. She started to walk away. "I'll see you around."

"How about tonight? Tell me where you're playing and I'll be there."

She turned back momentarily, looking surprised that I had asked. "Oh—it's this place in Alexandria, the Ashland Street Club. But don't go, Court. You wouldn't like it. It's a gay bar."

CHAPTER 7

Forty minutes later we were in a little Italian place called Lucia's. It was very quaint, a petite place with a dim, candle-lit interior and red and white checkered tablecloths. We had walked from the Cathedral, straight up Wisconsin Avenue, until Paul had picked some place at random. Nate was annoyed, insisting Paul pick out something better, fancier, more expensive, or at the very least, not Italian.

"We're in DC, for God's sake!"

"So? Does DC have some kind of unique cooking style?"

"I don't know! You're the one who used to live here!"

Paul sighed. "Look, I like Italian, okay? And we're already here."

Nate glowered for a full two seconds, then gave in. "Oh, well, if we must. I guess I'll just have to order the most expensive thing on the menu."

"So, wait, does that mean no pizza?" I asked.

"Hell no. You're not getting off that easy." It was customary between us for the loser to pay for dinner. "Come on, Court," he added when I tried to protest. "This is the third game you've lost in a row. It's not my fault you stink at it."

"Let someone else be 'it' next time," said Kim, cheerfully. "Then we'll see how good you are."

We were given a rectangular table in the back, near a fresco of Venice painted on the wall. Sandy, Paul, and Ahmed sat on one side, against the wall, and Nate, Kim, and I sat on the other side. It was early in the evening, just pushing five-thirty, and for the moment the place was deserted except for an elderly couple seated in a booth on the other side, and three teenagers sharing a pizza a few booths down.

The waiter was a young Hispanic named Carlos. When he asked for our drink order, Paul beamed up at him, introduced himself, and ordered for everybody. He wasn't flirting; this was his typical behavior.

He got coffee for himself, Ahmed, and Kim, and beer for the rest of us. Kim interrupted and asked for a glass of white wine, instead. Paul grinned at her and said, "Suit yourself." Now, as a loyal, hardworking court employee, I feel duty-bound to point out that Kim, as a condition of her probation, was to abstain from any and all alcoholic beverages, so drinking wine here was a violation of her probation. If she was caught, she could, in theory, wind up in jail. Not that I was going to report her, or anything—in fact, I knew she'd pretty much have to run over somebody before she hazarded any jail time. Still, she was technically doing something illegal. I had foolishly pointed out this same mistake on our first date, and she thought I was joking and laughed. It got awkward. In the end I was thankfully granted a second date, but that's all I wound up with that evening.

"You don't drink, do you, Ahmed?" she asked, after Carlos had left.

"No, of course not."

"Well, why the heck not?" asked Nate with amusement.

"My faith prohibits it. Surely you know that?"

"Yeah, it's great," said Paul. "He's always the designated driver."

"You mean you let him drive your car?" I asked, discomfited.

"That's kind of how it works."

"What I mean is," said Nate, interrupting. "Why do you care what your faith prohibits?" He shook his head, grinning. "I mean, you're going to hell anyway, what difference is one more sin going to make?"

Paul laughed quietly to himself. Ahmed glared at him, and he quickly shifted his gaze back to his menu. Then he turned back to Nate. "I am not going to hell," he said crossly.

"Sure you are," Nate insisted. "For sodomy, right? That is against your religion, too, isn't it?"

"Yes, of course it is."

"Well, then…"

Before he could answer, Paul interrupted and, without taking his eyes from the menu, said, "Islam is a salvation-by-works religion. He believes he can still get into Paradise if he does enough good deeds to make up for it. That's why he wants to be a doctor." He glanced up at Ahmed, who eyed him tiredly. "Right?" He grinned with a smile that looked slightly sheepish, which for him was exceedingly unusual.

"Oh, you're in trouble now, Paulie," Kim laughed.

We all waited expectantly to hear Ahmed's rebuttal. But he didn't even raise his eyebrows; he just smiled. "Didn't I tell you to study up if you wanted to argue religion with me?" he said.

"I have been studying," Paul protested. He didn't seem aware of how considerate Ahmed was being. It made me wonder what they'd talked about the whole time they had been wandering around the Cathedral, since it apparently hadn't been religion. Probably architecture.

"No, clearly you haven't."

"Okay, fine. Then enlighten me."

Carlos came back at that moment with the drinks and a breadbasket, and offered to take our order. He asked this directly to Paul, but he demurred, so Carlos skipped him and went around the table.

We went with the classics, chicken Parmesan, lasagna, spaghetti and meatballs, even. Nate was the only one who ordered an appetizer, fried calamari. He also ordered the roast pork, just to annoy Ahmed, who himself ordered fettuccini.

When Carlos left, we waited for Ahmed to speak, but he took his time, putting sugar and cream in his coffee, stirring it and taking a few sips while we all watched.

"Oh, come on," said Kim. "You can tell us. What are your thoughts on that?"

"Well, I'll tell you this," he said, speaking to everybody, "Do all of you know what the essence of Islam is? The word *islam* itself means—"

"Peace!" she said proudly.

He snickered a bit. "No, not even close. Although it's nice to see the PR campaign is working. No, *islam* means 'surrender.' We surrender to God's will. Now, of course, this will is revealed through the prophets, through the Holy *Qur'an* and the *sunnah*, and yes, these forbid homosexuality. But I am the way I was born, and so I am the way God made me. Therefore, I believe that in accepting my orientation, I am in fact surrendering to the will of God."

"What crap," said Paul quietly, to himself.

"So you don't feel guilty? It really doesn't bother you?" asked Kim.

"No, it really doesn't."

"Do you think the mullahs would agree with you on that one?" asked Nate.

Ahmed shot him a scowl. "No, of course not. I have no scholarly justification, I know. But that is the way I feel. I simply don't believe I am committing a sin in this regard. I believe I am honoring God by accepting His will."

"That is just such garbage," said Paul, empathetically. "Once you say that, where does it end? It's a slippery slope. If you start deciding what is and is not a sin based on how you feel about it, then you end up with no sins at all. Kleptomaniacs can say, 'I have an inherent desire to steal, so it's not a sin.' Serial killers can say, 'I like killing, so it's not a sin.' You end up with total moral chaos. You can't go around picking and choosing. If God says it's a sin, then it is, plain and simple."

"I think there's a slight difference," said Ahmed politely.

"But I thought you believed the same thing, Paul?" said Kim.

"No, I most certainly do not. I believe what the Bible says, and it makes it very clear that sodomy is a sin."

"So, what, you're going to hell, and that's just fine with you?" asked Kim.

"No," he sighed. He'd suffered through this argument many times before. "I'm not going to hell. It's a sin, but a minor one. It isn't the end all and be all. What matters is your relationship to Jesus Christ. I have been forgiven by Jesus, whose death on the cross atoned for my sins, just as it does for anyone's sins. Really, Kim, everybody's sinned, and all sins are crimes against God. My sin is no worse than anyone else's, and Jesus will forgive me just as he will forgive all who believe."

Nate laughed at him, and Kim rolled her eyes and smiled. "Trying to convert me?"

"I'm just explaining what I believe."

"And aren't you supposed to stop sinning to get forgiven?" asked Nate, derisively. All of us, with the possible exception of Ahmed, had at one point or another already heard Paul's sermonizing. And it got to be pretty amusing, especially because he was so sincere about it.

"No. Jesus forgives us all our sins, past, present, and future. We will always have at least some sins while we are alive because the flesh has a sinful nature. Only when we die will we be made perfect. In this life it doesn't matter. It's not how good you are that gets you into heaven. You can be very good and it still won't mean anything. Salvation comes by grace alone. Only by accepting God's grace through faith will we be saved. If we are repentant and believe in Christ, he will forgive us all our sins."

"Yeah, but the point is, you're not very penitent, are you?"

"Sure I am."

"It's true," Ahmed interrupted. He'd gone quietly back to sipping his coffee, and was at that moment holding it to his lips. "He always gets on his knees and asks God to please forgive him for the sin he is about to commit." Everyone except Paul laughed.

"That's not what I meant. Besides, you do the same thing," he retorted.

"No, I don't."

"You do too. It's just that you don't let me know because your prayers are in Arabic." I didn't like where this conversation was going.

"I could teach you Arabic," said Ahmed, and at once I felt better that the subject had changed, and deftly, too.

"I told you, I don't want to learn Arabic."

"But it will help with your career later on."

Paul took it up and argued further about what would be good for his future *vis-à-vis* what would be good for the future of American business as a whole. He thought Chinese—language and investments—or even Indian, was a much surer thing than anything Middle Eastern. Unless, of course, you happened to be in a defense contracting business, as Nate was.

Carlos brought us the calamari appetizer, and we all took a piece as the conversation switched from a religious argument between Paul and Ahmed to an economics discussion between Paul and Nate. I thought, with some relief, that was how the evening would while away, but no, Paul apparently wanted to keep Ahmed talking. I don't know why, whether he liked the sound of his voice, or wanted him to show off, to impress us. Or perhaps Paul was the one who wanted to show off by scoring debate points against the med student.

Somehow over five minutes or so the conversation drifted to talk about interest rates. I'm certain Paul had done this on purpose, because he said at one point, "That's a huge problem with the Middle East economy, you know—interest. The Koran or whatever commands the faithful not to loan or borrow money at interest, and everybody takes this real seriously, so there's no interest charged, which impedes banking and investment, which prevents there from being any progress or growth. I mean, the Bible says the same thing, and people used to do that, but they gave up on it because money-lending is the only way to create anything new. New technologies, new businesses. The whole middle class is built on loans. Otherwise, a person would have to work their whole life to save enough money to buy a house, and what would the point of that be? By being able to borrow the money to buy first, then pay it back over time, they can own their own properties and businesses and accumulate real wealth. That's how you have a middle class. That doesn't exist elsewhere. All those Third World countries have a wealthy elite, and everyone else lives in poverty. I'm telling you, their religious beliefs are causing their misery."

He turned to Ahmed, expecting what would surely be an understandably sharp retort. Ahmed, though, was not interested in playing. He was slowly and deliberately buttering a piece of bread, and looked as though he hadn't heard a thing. I couldn't imagine what was wrong with Paul, why he wanted to rile him up, but it was clear that his statement, like his earlier remarks, were not a faux pas, or instances of ignorance, but intentional remarks designed to provoke Ahmed. It made sense; he was always such a glib talker, it was hard to believe him capable of saying such stupid things. The only question worth considering was why. Nate's insensitivity was simply him making fun, belittling another to raise his own self-worth. It was a perfectly ordinary activity. But why would Paul do it, especially to someone he wanted to win over? I doubted it was for the same reason as Nate, because Paul never had self-esteem problems. He had a very high opinion of himself. Nor did I think he was doing it because the rest of us were there. Ahmed's patient delays and casual answers suggested a pattern, an established dynamic between them, meaning their relationship had been going on for longer than I had been led to believe. I didn't want to inquire too deeply. I doubted anyone else did, either. We all waited to hear Ahmed's response.

"Well?" said Paul, prodding him.

"Paul, there are banks in the Middle East; most of them are secular and abide by standard Western business practices, and those that don't, the Islamic banks, still lend money and collect fees for it. It's not specifically called interest, but it works in a similar manner. Besides, if that's the cause of poverty in the Muslim world, how do you explain the poverty in Catholic South America?" He said this with mild, unhurried curiosity, like a store patron asking the price of an item he has no intention of buying. He put the bread into his mouth and tore off a chunk.

"Oh, well, those countries were set up that way. The Spanish conquistadors set themselves up as the governing oligarchy over the indigenous people, and nothing's really changed since."

Ahmed sighed, but tenderly, a little smile across his lips. I thought then that maybe they weren't involved in a pattern but were playing a game of some sort. He said, "There was colonialism in Arabia, too, and the nations are still ruled by monarchs and tyrants. I can't believe you're trying to reduce a highly complex set of geopolitical problems to something so idiotically simple as interest rates.

"Besides, you just said yourself it was a command of God that you ignored, and what has it gotten you? You Westerners spend far more than you can afford, and then notwithstanding all these fancy things, don't try to save or earn more because you can already buy whatever you want on credit. That's why real wages for your exalted middle class have been stagnant for the past decade or so, while you drown yourselves in debt. It's a wonder your whole economy doesn't collapse. And if foreigners stopped investing in your country, it would, unquestionably. Just wait, eventually you're going to run out of money."

"Wages have nothing to do with easy credit."

"Of course they do."

Sandy leaned in and said, directly to Ahmed, "You should blame everything on Bush's tax cuts for the rich. That drives Paul nuts."

"No," Ahmed replied. "What really drives him nuts is criticizing his reckless spending on that vehicle of his."

"Hey," said Paul testily. "Leave the Corvette out of this."

"You see?"

"Oh, hey, speaking of the car," chimed Nate. "Now we can finally get an answer. Tell us," he motioned to Ahmed. "Is he compensating for something?"

Everyone ignored him.

Paul said to Ahmed, "But look, what I said earlier, about you having to do good works to make up for your sins, that is right, isn't it?"

"You're losing an argument in your area of expertise, so you want to change the subject." Ahmed said, making not a question but a statement, though a lighthearted one.

"I'm not losing. I really want to know."

"You just don't want to have to defend Bush's tax cuts," said Sandy.

Paul ignored her. "Come on, Ahmed."

"The ancient Egyptians did believe in a system like that, where your soul was weighed on a balance after you died. Today we are not so picky about it. Certainly it is possible, and ideal, that your good outweighs your evil, because Muslims do not believe, as Christians do, that man's nature is inherently one of depravity. But it is beside the point. We believe, as you do, that God is merciful, and will forgive our sins. The difference is, we don't believe God needs any complicated sleight-of-hand to do so."

"Sleight-of-hand?"

"Yes, this silly theology you have, that the Prophet Jesus, peace be upon him, died for your sins, as a sacrifice in your place. If God wants to forgive us, he can simply do it. Nobody has to be sacrificed for anything."

"But then God isn't just."

"You make it sound as though there is some spirit of justice more powerful than God, who can require a penalty be paid. But there is nothing greater than God. God has decreed the laws, and the punishment for their violation, and God can enforce them or set them aside in mercy, as He wills."

"You mean Allah," said Kim.

"*Allah* is simply the Arabic word for God. I generally don't use it when speaking in English."

"It's an old philosophical problem," said Paul. "Are things good or evil because there's an intrinsic standard of good and evil, or simply because God says that's what they are? If you say it's just God picking things, and then just ignoring His own standards at His pleasure, then you've made God into a hypocrite."

"That's a bit much, don't you think? God decides everything. Nothing is beyond His control. It's called *al-Qadar*, divine predestination."

"No, my point is, how can you judge God? We all say God is good, and righteous, and holy, but what standards are we basing that on? If holiness is just whatever God says it is, then what does it mean to say God is holy?"

Ahmed shook his head. "Paul, you're trying too hard. You Westerners debate these things far too much, and work yourselves up into migraines over nothing. God is infinite, that is all. God is infinite, therefore He is perfect."

"You won't even consider it?" Paul had been speaking for this whole time in a conversational tone, so I was sure there was more here than just an effort at proselytizing. It was like they had a little routine they were acting out for us.

"Consider what? Your whole religion is absurd, as far as I'm concerned. How can you believe a man, any man, even a great and powerful prophet, could be God? How could the infinite, limitless power of God be contained in the finite form of a man?"

"God can do that if He wants. He's omnipotent; He can do anything."

Ahmed frowned briefly in annoyance. He said sourly, "Honestly, Paul. If someone walked up to you and said, 'I'm God,' would you even give him a moment's consideration?" I had an unsettling feeling, as I reflected on my afternoon with Dawn, and how I said pretty much that very thing to her. I hadn't mentioned this meeting yet, and I was planning on putting it off as long as I could. Any mention of her was not going to go over well with either Kim or Paul. But I intended on being at her club tonight; I just had to figure out a way to get there.

Paul said, "But Jesus proved himself by doing great miracles."

"So what? All prophets perform miracles. But no miracle, no matter how great, is enough to prove that a mere man is the infinite God who created the universe."

"But you're missing the whole point. The glory of Christianity is the idea that God loves us so much he became one of us, living and dying as a human being. It gives glory to humanity because God chose to manifest Himself as one of us. You lose out on so much by not seeing that, by not seeing the sanctity God gives every life."

"Please, let's not forget, Christians have a pretty long history of killing in the name of God, too, sanctity notwithstanding."

Paul sighed, "Okay, I'm probably going to regret this, but if you want to say that no miracle is good enough, then what did Mohammed do to make you believe in him?"

"The Blessed Prophet is the prophet of God. He never claimed to *be* God. What he taught—the root of Islam—is simply that there is no God but God, that is, there is only one God."

"And that," said Kim, suddenly jumping in, "is something we can all agree on, so let's leave it at that!"

"Well, yes," said Ahmed, taken aback. "That was where I was going."

"Tired of the subject?" asked Paul, giving her a smile.

"Christ!" she sighed. "Do you guys argue about this stuff all the time?"

"Actually, no," said Ahmed. "We hardly ever do. It's pointless, as you can see. Really, we should make an agreement not to discuss religion anymore at all."

Paul simply laughed. He said, "So, Kim, you and Court actually tried to catch Nate before he even got to the Cathedral?" And just like that, we were on a different subject. Religion was spent, and we were on to recounting our day's journey. We told it straight, including how we split up, which Nate agreed was not cheating, just pointless, as we'd only have won if we found him together. Then Paul talked about how he and Ahmed devoted their afternoon to touring the Air and Space Museum, and how Ahmed had gushed over every little thing, with a school boy's combination of wonder and exhaustively memorized trivia.

"Could have gone into engineering, you know," he said.

"No," shrugged Ahmed. "My parents wanted me to be a doctor, so that's that."

"So what, you just did it, just like that?" asked Kim.

"Well, I suppose I could have done anything. I am exceptionally intelligent. But I like medicine. I like the power it has to help people so directly and dramatically."

"He has a full scholarship, you know," Paul said to Nate, beaming proudly, like a parent.

"What, to med school?" he said, surprised. Nate cherished his intellectual ability, so pointing out Ahmed was smarter was an intentional insult. Recompense for his earlier jabs.

"Yes, and college before that," said Ahmed. "Which is very good, because my parents are poor shopkeepers; I'd never have gotten here without it. The school pays my tuition in full, all my books and lab fees, my relocation expenses for when I moved here from Egypt, and a stipend for living expenses. The only thing they don't pay for is my daily commute."

"Damn. And all that because…"

Ahmed shrugged. "My academic record is perfect. I have never received anything less than the highest marks in all classes, papers, and exams. I have been in accelerated learning courses since elementary school, when my IQ was tested at 174."

"Hoo-hoo!" said Kim.

"And this was in Egypt?" asked Nate.

"Yes. When I was six I memorized the entire *Qur'an*, and my parents—"

"Really?"

"Yes. It's not as unusual as it sounds. Many devout people memorize the *Qur'an*. It's only the length of a regular book, about as long as the New Testament, and it's written in poetry form, so it's not that hard. You recite it in a cadence, so it's more like memorizing song lyrics than dry prose. It's so common, that in many places memorization is considered a rite of passage, called *ameen*, which may be undertaken by children as young as ten. What I did was remarkable only because I was merely six, and did it without being required to." He smiled. "I was bored. Now, other parents might have taken this to be a blessing from God, and put me on the path of an 'alim, an Islamic scholar. But my parents, fortunately, were more secular in their outlook, so they bought me science books to read and took me to Cairo University to be tested by a psychologist. And it went on from there. Now I am fluent in four languages, I have a Bachelor of Science degree with a double major in biology and chemistry, and am in my third year of medical school at the age of twenty-three."

"Jesus H. Christ.," said Nate, shaking his head. "It's so not fair."

"And you only want to be a doctor?" said Sandy. "You could do a lot better, sounds like."

"Oh, I am. I'm in a research program. I'm actually in the process of writing a paper with my advisor."

"Oh really? In what?"

"My field is molecular genetics," he said.

"Good God," said Nate.

"Ahmed," Kim said suddenly, "you're an optimist, right?"

"Kim," I groaned.

"In some things," said Ahmed. "But in others I'm not. It depends on circumstances. The world is very complicated."

"Thank you," I said emphatically.

"But Ahmed, you have to be an optimist! All geniuses are optimists! Mozart was an optimist!" Kim was certain of this, because she had read it in one of her self-help books; it was one of the many pieces of evidence proving the value of Positive Thinking she had bombarded me with.

"All geniuses aren't optimists," he replied. "Many are quite neurotic. And I don't think anyone is ever entirely one thing or the other. So many things happen to us, and we're subjected to so many different emotions throughout our lives. I suppose I am optimistic about my own future, but I feel very pessimistic in regards to the advancement of humanity and the progress of human rights."

"But Ahmed," she pleaded, sounding less than positive herself. She wanted him to validate her life's devotion, and he just wasn't going to give her satisfaction.

"And by human rights you mean gay rights?" asked Nate.

"No, I mean all rights, for all people. But yes, I do have a special concern for the rights of sexual minorities."

"So do you think there's a gay gene?" said Nate. Paul shook his head, warning him.

"Actually, I'm sure there is something like that," said Ahmed, turning morose. "And it's inevitable it will be discovered. And when it is, that will be the end of us."

"You mean there'll be a cure?" asked Sandy.

"No, he thinks people will test their fetuses and abort their gay children," said Paul, reflectively gloomy. "That's what he's so pessimistic about. I've told him it's absurd considering the abortion controversy, at least in this country. It might happen occasionally, but not in significantly large numbers, but he doesn't believe me."

That brought the conversation to a halt. Fortunately the pause didn't last long enough to become awkward, as Carlos arrived with our food. So far the conversation was going exactly as I'd expected it would, with Ahmed at the center of attention. I glanced around and noticed the restaurant had filled somewhat, though it was still nowhere near capacity.

Without anyone having to say anything, we all folded our hands and closed our eyes, even Ahmed. We knew Paul wanted to say grace, as he did before every meal, and we went along with it because it was easier to just do it than to argue about it. He recited a short prayer thanking God for our meal and our friendship, and I wondered whether Muslims did the same thing.

Afterwards, we ate in silence for a few minutes, but Nate must have been using his time to contemplate a way to regain the upper hand, because he said, out of the blue, "So, Ahmed, speaking of gay rights, it must have been pretty hard being a queer in Egypt. Don't they, like, cut your head off if they catch you?"

Ahmed sighed and put down his fork "In some countries it is a capital offense, yes. Saudi Arabia and Iran, specifically. But Egypt is an officially secular nation. Believe it or not, they used to be quite proud of the fact that, unlike even in some Western countries, homosexuality is not prohibited by law." He nudged Paul.

"The Supreme Court overturned that," Paul mumbled. "*Lawrence v. Texas.*"

"And when was that? 2003?"

"So it's okay there?" asked Kim.

"Oh, no, certainly not. It is not acceptable at all. The police still arrest plenty of people for it. I remember a huge raid on a disco on the Nile called Queen Boat not too long before I left. The state newspapers depicted them as devil-worshipers. I heard a number of people simply disappeared. Normally though, when they arrest people, the charge is not homosexuality but being a male prostitute."

"And what does that get you?"

"Up to five years," he said, eliciting astonishment from us. "It's not as bad as decapitation, of course, but on the other hand, because the punishment is less severe and therefore less noticed by international rights groups, far more people are arrested. But most people aren't sent to prison. They're just beaten, often severely, and released when they or their families pay a bribe."

"And that never happened to you?"

"Of course not. Otherwise I doubt I would be here now. But I did meet some people who had suffered such a fate. One poor fellow had his leg shattered, and will probably walk with a limp for the remainder of his life. Another had most of his teeth knocked out. Still, it wasn't so bad. I met a lot of nice people in Cairo's gay bars. Yes, there are gay bars in Cairo, just like here, except of course there they don't advertise. They are all underground, and you usually have to know someone to get in. That was just in Cairo, though. Cairo has fourteen million people living in it, so it's a pretty cosmopolitan city, and you can find just about anything you want. The rest of the country is much more conservative, and much more limited. Very Third-World."

"So did you date guys while you were there?"

"A few, sure. But most of my relationships were very brief. Only one was ever serious, a very special young man named Kamal; but because of his extremely strict family situation (with his father being a police officer), he was always afraid of his true nature being discovered. So we couldn't be together, and not long after I last saw him, I found out he had hung himself."

This was so completely unexpected that we were all shocked into silence for several moments. "I'm so sorry," said Kim finally, deeply moved.

"Yes, I know," said Ahmed, with a melancholy sigh. "I miss him."

There was silence all around for a few moments. Everyone there pretty much knew Paul's personal history, but Sandy turned to him with a question. "Does Ahmed know how well you did in school? Class president, track team star, and those religious study groups—and no one knew your orientation then, at all."

"Well", Paul said, "I was never outed at school, but I don't think it would have mattered anyway. I was basically a very popular guy, and even dated some girls!"

Nobody at our family church ever found out either, even today, and Paul still goes there. He continued his story, saying "I never dated any guys until I got to college. And there I found Ahmed... he's the best part of my life now!"

So that was how dinner went.

CHAPTER 8

After we finished with dinner, we took a Metrobus to the Cleveland Park station, and took the subway to Metro Center, where the four of us said adieu to Nate and Sandy. Nate promised we'd play again in a few weeks, and next time would be even better. They continued on the Red Line into Maryland, and we got on the Orange Line heading back to the Vienna station. The train was less crowded and we were able to sit together.

"So what are you guys doing tonight?" Kim asked.

Paul shrugged. "We'll go club hopping, same as always. Swimming with the guppies," he said, meaning gay urban professionals. He went clubbing almost every weekend. The fact that Paul used such a '90s term like *guppies* showed how dismissive he was with me. He knew I didn't want to hear about the subject, and didn't want to discuss it in front of me. "How about you? You have to work tonight?"

Kim, as I said, worked a lot of evenings. She honestly enjoyed her waitress job, it suited her personality perfectly; her cheery disposition pulled in huge tips. I have no idea what her long term plans were, or where she wanted to go from there, but it wasn't a pressing issue for her. Her job, unlike mine, was more than just a way for her to earn money; she took it fairly seriously. But it did keep her busy, even on weekends. She worked every Friday evening, but had every other Saturday off. Not completely off; she was usually on "on call" status, meaning they could require her to come in if someone else was out unexpectedly, or if there was a particularly heavy crowd. This month, though, the holiday had thrown off her schedule and she'd gotten both last Saturday and this Saturday off.

"No, I'm free. We'll probably go to a movie," said Kim, already sounding bored just from the thought of it. I could bet she wanted to go dancing, too, but we didn't as often as she preferred, because I'm not a good dancer. It's not something which appeals to me. But here I saw my moment, a golden opportunity to get what I wanted and make everyone else happy, too.

"Hey, Paul," I said suddenly. "Let me ask you something. Have you ever heard of a club called Ashland Street?" He shook his head. "It's in Alexandria," I said.

He shrugged and glanced at Ahmed, who lived in Alexandria (because it's also a city in Egypt? I wondered absently). He also shook his head.

"It's a gay bar."

His eyes lit up, and he laughed. "Somebody at work make a recommendation?"

"Something like that. Listen, why don't we all go out together?"

"Go out... to this club?" He asked slowly, uncertain of my meaning. "You want to go to a gay nightclub?" he said, amazed when I nodded.

Kim was instantly enamored. I knew she would like it; she had suggested in the past that we take Paul out and find him a date, and I had received this idea quite coldly. "What a wonderful idea!" she said. "Let's do it!"

"That's nice of you, Court," he said. "Sure we can do that. But you know, while I'm always fond of discovering a new hangout, this place sounds kind of sketchy. It can't be all that great if neither of us have heard of it before. Why don't we go somewhere else? I know a lot of really excellent clubs in DuPont Circle. They're all popular, lively, and safe. And I'm sure, this being your first time, so to speak, you'd want nothing less."

"Did you know," Ahmed interjected, "that a number of gay nightclubs in the area advertise themselves as being 'straight-friendly'? I always found it to be rather amusing."

"No, it's this or we don't bother. I don't want to go to DuPont Circle, or anywhere else; I've had enough of DC for one day."

Paul grinned at me. "Okay, sure, if that's what you want, we'll be happy to go."

"Does this amuse you? Are you surprised? I know Kim would love a double date, so why not? I'm not homophobic, you know. I don't lie awake at night terrified that a man will make a pass at me. I'm hurt you have such a poor opinion of me."

He chuckled. "That's good, Court. Real fine. I never thought otherwise of you.

After we arrived back at the Metro station, I offered to take Ahmed home first, but he declined, so we drove Kim to her place, then returned to my apartment. Paul left with Ahmed to drive him home himself.

I checked the mail and then turned on my computer to search for the club, found its website, and printed out a page with directions. Ashland Street Club was, of course, on Ashland Street. Then I tried searching for Dawn again. I added such words as "god," "enlightened," and even "Washington DC" to her name in the search criteria, but none of the results stood out, and a few of the things I clicked on clearly didn't relate to her, at least that I could tell. Apparently there's a Dawn Gardner who actually is a minister, but she lives in Spokane. Without any more information, I was at a loss. Hopefully I would learn something more tonight. Maybe tomorrow I could try going over to the house she'd lived in when we were in high school, and see if her father still lived there, or if I could find him. He might be able to tell me something, and if he couldn't, it would mean he was completely ignorant of everything that was going on in his daughter's life, and I would be doing him a favor by telling him.

When I was finished searching, I went out to the kitchenette and left the page with the directions on the counter, then I sat on the sofa in the living room just as Paul returned. He was in an upbeat mood and plopped down right next to me. "So," he said, by way of a greeting, "did Kim put you up to this?"

"No. I mean, she's suggested it before, but this was my own initiative."

"Really. You know, I'm actually rather pleased."

"What the heck for?"

He shrugged. "Well, just so you're aware, there's really no difference between a gay and a straight bar, except there's fewer women. And guys kissing."

"I wouldn't expect otherwise."

"Just want to be sure you know what you're getting yourself into."

I sighed. I had thought it was clever, getting everyone to go with me, but Paul thought I was doing this for him; he would be furious when he found out I was only chasing some girl.

"So tell me", Paul asked, "what did you think of Ahmed?"

"He's alright, I guess." Despite my earlier feelings, I decided I didn't really dislike Ahmed. I didn't quite like him, either. I guess I really didn't have much of an opinion one way or the other, or maybe I held both opinions at the same time. I was uncomfortable around him because I'd just met him, but at the same time I was able to dismiss it because it wasn't his fault. And, I admitted to myself, I held a bias against him; but again, I thought I could ignore it and form an honest opinion.

"He's gorgeous, isn't he?"

I choked. "Gorgeous?"

"Okay, okay, I take it that's not a word you'd use to describe another guy, huh? Ok, how about handsome? You'd agree with that, right? He's quite handsome. And he's so smart, and so self-possessed. He's really wonderful, isn't he?"

I stared at him, but he was in earnest. He watched me, his eyes shining, hanging on my response. "I'm sorry," I said. "You actually care what I think?"

"Well, I just want you to get along with him. He might be here a lot."

Dear God, that didn't sound good at all. I turned to face him square, and held up my hands. "Okay, what's really going on here?"

"Nothing," he said, grinning with embarrassment. "I'm in love."

"Really? In love with him? Are you serious?"

"I sure am. Isn't it amazing? I've never been in love before. I mean, I've had crushes before, but nothing like this. This is real. My head is swimming and I think about him all the time." His voice had momentarily taken on a childish lilt.

"But, Paul, he's an Arab! A Muslim!"

"So?" he said, hurt. "Those are just surface differences. Really, our outlook on the world is actually very similar."

"Yeah, you both think it's a sin to be gay but you're not going to hell. That's a great thing to build a relationship on. And since when did your Personal Lord and Savior Jesus Christ become a surface difference?"

"Stop it. You know what I mean. I actually like arguing with him. He's always so careful and reasoned. It's not like arguing with other people I know. You know, everyone these days is so partisan, and they do nothing but repeat the same sound-bites over and over again. And so many Muslims out there are pretty racist themselves.

But Ahmed makes me feel better about the world, showing there's some hope for things. He has a totally unique perspective on everything. And not just because he's so smart. He's like those racially mixed people who have such expanded viewpoints because they live in two different worlds, only he lives in four. Four! He's the most amazing person I've ever met. He *understands* me, Court. Like at the restaurant, when everybody was after me, *again*, about why I'm not afraid God's going to come after me. How many times have I tried to explain it? Every single person I know has asked me that same stupid question. Everybody wants me to give up on God or deny who I am, except Ahmed. He *gets* it, Court. He knows exactly what I mean. We have a real connection. Frankly, I think he's the only person I've ever really felt was my equal in every way."

I had to laugh at his display of ego. "Mr. Genius Doctor, and he's only your equal?"

He waved the comment aside. "Oh, well, you know what I mean. I'm just saying I feel I can really talk to Ahmed. We have very meaningful discussions."

"Is that why you were being so insulting to his culture earlier?"

"I wasn't doing anything of the sort. We were playing, that's all. I told you, he understands, trust me."

Well of course it was a game. "And how long have you been, uh, dating him? Be honest with me."

"Since the end of June."

"Don't lie to me, Paul. This is not the behavior of people who've only been dating a few weeks."

"And what, you're a behavior expert now? I swear, end of June. Really. I was completely truthful when I told you I wasn't seeing anybody, back in May."

It seemed hard to believe, but I kept my doubts to myself. In the meantime I changed the subject. "Is he really a genius?"

"Well, I didn't test his IQ, but I got him to let me read his paper. I made it through the whole first paragraph before I gave up. I understood it was about mutations, because it had the word 'mutation' in it, but that's all I got out of it; everything else was technical jargon. He had to tell me it was only about one specific mutation to one piece of one gene on one chromosome."

"He studies this stuff even though he thinks it'll bring doom to your... group."

"He only started thinking that way *because* he was studying it. But yeah, it's pretty tough for him, which is why I keep telling him to go into something else. He knows everything."

"He's a real nerd, huh?"

He chuckled. "Don't I know it. All afternoon, he went on and on about the magnificence of the universe and the space program and whatnot. He could actually tell the difference between all those damn satellites. He could name the moons of Saturn, right off the top of his head. He knew the name of the third guy on Apollo 11."

"Third guy?"

"Yeah, you know, Neil Armstrong, Buzz Aldrin, and the third guy nobody remembers because he stayed aboard the rocket and never walked on the moon."

"Who was it?'

"Michael Collins. The point is, he knows all sorts of trivia, especially the science stuff. He was birthday-boy excited by this thing called *Spaceship One*, even though it looks like a giant preschool toy. Personally, I preferred seeing the Wright Flyer. He could probably do the same know-it-all routine at the other museums, even though I have to confess thinking about how it's a little frightening. I asked him what else was in the National Gallery besides the Da Vinci, and he rattled off the names of a bunch of Van Gogh's, and then I asked what *else* was in there, and he named some statues by Degas, and then I asked him what *else* there was and he finally got annoyed and wanted to know if I'd like him to list their entire collection. I don't know if he was just bluffing or if he could really do it, but I would bet he could. Sometimes my buddies and I play trivia games with Ahmed, just to see if there's anything he doesn't know, and pretty much sports stuff is the only time he draws a blank. Unless it's soccer, which he knows all about. So yeah, he's a nerd, but it's fine. I still think he's gorgeous."

I didn't want to hear anymore, yet I wanted to question him anyway, to be certain he was serious. But I'm sure he was; I realized this was the reason Ahmed stayed for breakfast. Paul had never introduced any of his previous boyfriends to me. I'd seen him occasionally over the years with people whom I figured he was involved with but he never said and I never asked. There was one person he brought to our family's Thanksgiving dinner two years ago who he said was his boyfriend, although it was just that one time; I never saw him again. I wasn't sure if this was because Paul was discrete by nature or because he thought I would be hostile.

I thought about Paul in love, and I thought about how tightly I held on to Dawn that day in the park. Was it really the same thing? I wanted to ask him about this, and about his claim he'd never been in love before. I recalled that he had made a high school virginity pledge, and while he had seemed serious enough at the time, I'd never thought he'd stick to it. I can't imagine anybody did. It became doubly true when he came out in college, so I wasn't surprised to learn about his relationships there. But I had assumed that while his pledge was always a white lie, since gays couldn't get married back then, he had at least been honest in his intentions; he had abandoned it only because he'd fallen in love with someone and realized how silly it was.

I had had enough of that line of thought for now, so I said I had some errands to run and would be back later, and left.

I had no idea what I was going to do as I walked down to my car, but then I recalled my desire to find Dawn's father and see if he knew what was going on. What I was hoping for was some way to restore her sanity, make her see she wasn't God, and bring back the old Dawn I knew and loved and would be happy to know and love again. I dimly thought maybe she and her father had been apart, and if I could reconcile them somehow, I'd fix whatever was wrong with her. Or maybe I would discover some terrible dark secret, something that drove her over the edge into a displaced personality. I saw it all the time in the movies and on TV. Some devastating tragedy had broken her mind, but it could be made right again with some appropriately poignant words and swelling background music.

I'd planned on going tomorrow, but I could always go now; it was only late afternoon and I had plenty of time. Unfortunately I no longer remembered the address. I remembered approximately where it was, since I had driven there often enough back in high school, and I thought I might still be able to find my way there by instinct, but I preferred the certainty of having the address. I knew where I had written it down, too. It was on the inside of the back flap of the notebook I had been using that year. I didn't know if it was still around, but if it was it would be with my other school things at my parent's house. So I drove there.

My parents lived in a standard, yellow and beige- colored split-level house that looked exactly like every other house in our Fairfax neighborhood, about eight miles away.

I pulled up to the curb in front of the house fifteen minutes later. I could hear the faint sounds of the lawn mower in the back, so I walked around before heading in. I could see my father off in the back end of the yard pushing the mower. He waved, and I waved back. My mother was sitting in their little garden. It's very little, only about three feet wide and twenty feet long, on the far right edge of the property, right up against the chain-link fence. It's not a flower patch but a real garden where they grow, or try to grow, their own little vegetables, mostly tomatoes. The vines wrapped up around wooden stakes piled in every few inches, swaying in the wind like mini skyscrapers.

Mom sat on a ragged throw pillow in the dirt, digging at something. I walked up to her, and she looked up. She was almost sixty, but her face was still tight, and her hair was cut short and curved around her face, and included bangs, which made her look school-girlish.

"Hi, Mom," I said, without bending down.

"Hi, Court," she said, pleased, squinting up at me through her sunglasses. "How are you?"

"Oh, I'm fine. Same as always. I just stopped by to get something."

"All right. Back door's unlocked. So everything's still working out well, with you and Paul sharing an apartment?"

"Yes, it's fine. I'm glad I get to spend a little more time with him, but sometimes, you know…"

"No, what?" she said, innocently.

I leaned in a little closer, as though I were going to tell her a secret. "You know, he's got a new boyfriend."

"You mean Ahmed? Sure, I know; he already told me."

I stood up straight again, shocked and somewhat offended. "He did? When?"

"When he called last week."

I extended my hands, palms up, in exasperation. The nerve of him. "So he tells you before he tells me? They're sleeping together in my apartment, and I have to be the last to know?"

She gave me her own look of exasperation, and turned back to her spading, or whatever she was doing.

"And you're perfectly okay with all this?"

"Okay with what?" she said, amused, tuning back to me.

I shrugged. "Nothing. Anyway, I'll talk to you later. See you, Mom."

"'Bye, Court."

I went into the house and poured myself a glass of soda, then went upstairs to my old bedroom. I liked being here. It was strange; when I'd lived here, I couldn't wait to be free, and now that I had my own place, I routinely felt drawn back to the comforting embraces of home.

My room was stripped of furniture, except for the desk and a half-filled bookcase, and was otherwise filled with boxes of various junk they were now storing, sorting through old stuff from around the house to see what could be thrown away. Someday, I'm sure, they would move into a smaller place, somewhere a little more rural, where the property taxes weren't so brutal.

I looked through the few pieces of mail my mom had left sitting on my desk. Just a bunch of useless credit card offers. I tossed them in the corner trash can.

Then I rummaged around the bookcase, and pulled out all my old stuff from high school: a couple of notebooks, a photo album, my senior yearbook. I was sure I had her number and probably her address written down somewhere.

As I sipped my soda, I took some time to flip through the Fairfax High yearbook, letting the nostalgia for those glorious days gone by briefly sweep through me. The school, the teachers, the friends I'd half forgotten, or completely forgotten.

There were two pictures of me in there—not counting the Senior Class group photo of everyone standing outside on the bleachers—the individual photo and one with the Latin Club, the only club I'd ever joined, which I did because I had no choice. I needed some extra-curricular activity for my college application, and the teacher was a neighbor of ours. There were also two pictures of Dawn; in the individual photo she wore a black dress, and had her hair coiffed in some unnaturally elaborate fashion. Her smile was off as well, because she was deliberately trying to keep her eyes open. Really, it wasn't her best picture.

In the second picture, she stood with a group of other kids, standing around an upside-down car. They were all unsmiling, dressed in black, and had their faces painted white. This was the club she had joined, the SADD club—Students Against Drunk Driving. One day a year, in the spring, they had their Day of Silence, in which they would dress all in black, paint their faces white, and go to their usual classes without saying a single word all day. They were supposed to be dead, representatives of the legions of teenagers who'd died in alcohol-related car accidents. The smashed car was provided by MADD around the same time of year, and would sit for a week or two on some grassy spot as a visual reminder of what can happen in a car accident. I remember thinking how horribly morbid it all was. Yes, it was an important message, but still… Dawn had actually tried to talk me into joining but there was no way I would do something like that. I even tried to talk her out of it, because her interest scared me, but she thought she doing something noble. I still can't understand why no one was concerned by her participation (except Paul; he, naturally, thought she was crazy). After all, Dawn had never known anyone who was killed by drunk driving; I made it a point to ask.

So why had she done it? I thought I knew, but now I wasn't so sure. She had told me she was being idealistic and trying to "make a difference." I hadn't believed her, but maybe it really was true.

Stuck in the back of the book was an envelope with some individual shots of her, and of the two of us together, some extra pictures I'd never gotten around to putting in the album: us leaning against a car at school, Dawn sitting in my kitchen, Dawn and some friend of hers whose name I couldn't recall, us next to a snow man, Dawn in some dress she was trying on at the mall. I peered at them intently, and it was incredible how little difference there was between then and now. She even had her long, straight hair exactly the same. It didn't seem to have grown a millimeter in six years. Though I must admit, I was pleased to have remembered her well enough to have noticed this.

There was also a folded up piece of paper in the envelope, which turned out to be a pencil sketch of me. I remembered sitting on my bed, trying not to move, watching her drawing in broad strokes, sometimes sticking out her tongue and licking her lips unconsciously as she concentrated especially hard. It was actually pretty good, certainly a hell of a lot better than what I could do. Dawn never quite fancied herself a budding artist; I think she only drew this because she was in an art class that year. I encouraged her to pursue it, because drawing was the sort of "quiet," introspective activity she liked.

I remembered that very well, how Dawn would stare out at things off in the distance, absentmindedly, sizing them up in her head, collecting "inspiration," as she claimed. She was the dreamer, visionary type, but sometimes I had the sense that she didn't just slip into daydreams and stare off into space, but was looking intently at something real, something right there, something she could see and I couldn't. Often we would just sit around, at a table, in peace and quiet, just watching the world. I remembered that Dawn was the only person with whom I could be comfortable with, without talking. Silence was not just an awkward pause in the conversation, as it is with Kim, but it was an essential element of the conversation, and what wasn't said was every bit as important as what was said.

I slipped the picture of the two of us leaning against a car into my pocket, and kept searching. I think I spent a full half-hour searching through the yearbook, the album, and all the notebooks, yet managed to come up empty. Wherever it was that I'd written down her phone number and address, it wasn't here. As I put everything away, I wracked my brain trying to remember either of them, and couldn't.

I was left with three alternatives. One, I could run through the phone book, except I didn't know what Dawn's father's first name was. The right address might jump out at me, but only if he still lived there. Two, I could ask Mom. She might have written it down somewhere. Did she ever actually go there? I couldn't remember. In any case, I'd have to explain why I was looking for Dawn's address, which I had not the slightest interest in doing.

The third choice was just to get in my car and drive around in the general area where she lived, and try to feel my way there, maybe get lucky. I'd never been good with directions, but I thought I could remember enough landmarks to make it work. It could take a while, but I still had more than enough time.

I remember Dawn used to live in a good-sized Colonial over in Oakton, only a few miles away. No cookie-cutter homes over there. The houses were built to spec, in widely spaced lots brimming with trees. They had the feel of real homes, avoiding the oppressive sameness of the over-developed tract house suburbia. The road was heavily trafficked, but was winding and hilly and only two lanes, giving it an almost rural feel. No, more than just rural. Some spots here had so many trees, filtering the sunlight into a handful of isolated rays, that it looked the way I imagined a rustic cabin, hidden in the woods, looked. I had loved going there; I felt like I was really out in nature.

So that's what I did, I drove around and let my instincts point me down one road, then another, until lo and behold I found myself standing at her door. And it had only taken a half hour to find it, but I felt so satisfied I wouldn't have cared had it taken all night.

Even better, it turned out her father, whose first name I was starting to think was John, did still live there. He opened the door after I buzzed, but it took a few minutes, and I'm certain I caught him peeking out the curtains of a side window. He was heavyset and had a noticeably tired look on his face, enough so that I hoped I hadn't woken him from a nap.

"May I help you?"

"Mr. Gardner, hi, um, I'm Courtland Richards, you may not remember me, um, but I used to be friends with your daughter."

He half-smiled. "Right, Court, sure I remember you. How've you been?"

I was so pleased he recognized me; I was always pleased when people remembered me. "Oh, fine. I ran into Dawn not too long ago, and she was acting kind of funny. I was wondering if you knew what was going on…"

"Funny?" His eyebrows knit together in concern. "In what way?"

"She was saying strange things."

"What things?"

I hadn't wanted to be so specific, at least not right up front, but it looked like he was going to force me. "About God. She told me and several other people that she *was* God."

He was silent for a moment, then waved me inside. Closing the door, he led me into the living room just off the hall. The room had a fireplace at one end, and there was a small picture of Dawn on the mantle, the same one as in the yearbook, as well as a photo of her mother. She was pretty, too, but there wasn't much resemblance that I could see. There was a black leather sofa against the wall across from a big-screen television, and I noticed above it there was a framed photo of the Manhattan skyline against the setting sun. It didn't say when the photo was taken, but the Twin Towers were prominently featured, brightly lit against a wash of purple and red twilight.

I gave him a brief synopsis of my encounter with Dawn at the church. He listened impassively.

"I haven't noticed anything unusual with Dawn, other than she's still deejaying instead of looking for a real job. Did she mention that? But a few weeks ago, there was this guy who showed up asking about her. Braxton. Black fellow, mid-thirties. Said he's a Professor—at Howard University, mind you—and he's doing some kind of research project, and Dawn was involved. At first I was curious, but his questions seemed awfully personal—about her medical history, her mother. Without a signed release form, I should add. Rather galling. But he said Dawn had joined some kind of cult. So naturally I called her and asked her about it. She said she was doing some volunteer work at a youth shelter, and she had talked to the kids about God, and, well, actually I'm not sure what the connection was or how this Professor got involved, but she assured me it was just a misunderstanding. So I left it at that. But you think maybe he was right?"

"Well, I don't know anything about a cult," I said carefully. "But it was strange, and I was worried about her."

He mused a moment. "You know, he gave me his card but I threw it out. I guess I will have talk to her again."

He showed me out, and I left both disappointed not to have learned more and disappointed he wasn't more deeply concerned. He was going to call her? That was it? Who knows, maybe something had happened between them.

But at least I had a next step in mind—to find this Professor Braxton and see what he knew.

CHAPTER 9

I went to a drive-thru and got a couple of burgers on my way home. Paul was sitting on the sofa watching the news when I arrived. Without saying anything I handed him his burger and then retreated to my room. Searching Howard University's website, I found a listing for Scott Braxton, PhD, Professor of Theology at the School of Divinity, and sent him a quick email expressing my interest in his project and mentioning I knew Dawn back in high school. I figured I wouldn't get a response until Monday, at the earliest. There was also the possibility that, this being summer, he was off for the semester and was not reading his university email at all. I decided that if I hadn't heard from him in a week, I would go in person to the school's offices with a handwritten letter and see if they would forward it to his home.

Then I reconsidered. They surely weren't open on Saturdays; was I willing to take a day off from work just to mail a letter? But fortunately I didn't have to worry about that. After I finished my sandwich and got dressed for the evening—a pair of slacks, a dark gray shirt, and loafers—and sat back down at my desk, I had a response waiting for me. He said he'd be happy to talk to me, gave me his address, and asked me to drop by anytime tomorrow afternoon.

Professor Braxton's response was much better than I had expected. Another step in the investigation; I was moving right along. I felt like a detective. Plus now I had something to do tomorrow. The best part was that the Professor lived in Chantilly, despite teaching in DC. I didn't know the reason and I didn't care. It wasn't too far away, and thank God I wouldn't have to go back into DC.

As I waited for the minutes to tick away, I sat idly web surfing and wondering just what I was going to say to Dawn this evening. What could I add to our conversation from this afternoon that would make any difference? I also realized I hadn't considered what I was going to say to the others, which was the problem I most dreaded. Kim would not like that I was showing any interest, no matter how kind-heartedly, towards an ex-girlfriend, and Paul, well… he had always thought Dawn was more or less crazy. How would he react when he learned he'd been right? Would he laugh at her? Would he get angry at her? Angry at me? Maybe I didn't want them together after all. I suppose he would try to argue with her, although I doubted that would do much good, not if his conversation with Ahmed at dinner was an indication.

Paul knocked on my door at nine and told me it was time to leave. He was wearing a sports coat and still smirking. We got in the car and left. We took my car, since it had more room, but I let Paul drive, because he had a better sense of direction than I did. And because he always drives.

As we went along, he said to me, out of the blue, "You know what he's thinking of doing?"

"Who?"

"Ahmed. He tells me that after he gets his degree, he wants to go back to Egypt. Can you believe it? Why on earth would he want to go back there? I mean, to visit, sure, but who would want to live in place like that? I keep telling him to stay here, apply for citizenship. He'd make a lot more money, certainly. He might not even be able to get a job there. What kind of molecular genetics research does he think he's going to be doing in the Middle East? Is there any place for that at all over there? And of course the worst part is he'd have to get married. His family would insist on it. He'd have to get married, and make both of them miserable, and then he'd either have to give up having any gay relationships, or else go sneaking around behind everybody's back, risking disgrace and arrest and the ruination of whatever career he has. Here there wouldn't be any of that; he could live with whomever he wants to. Spend his life with someone he really cares about. But no, he wants to go help the underprivileged Third-World kids, or whatever. He thinks with his credentials he'll be able to get some kind of government job in the Health Ministry and maybe effect some change. Plus he says, 'There're too many doctors in America already.' Can you believe that? Come on, how the heck can you have too many doctors? I mean, what does that even mean? Personally, I think Ahmed's mostly interested in the political situation over there. He wants to be on the inside, working on changing the government behind the scenes and helping to set up a democratic system when Mubarak is no longer in control, and all that sort of thing. Which is fine, except that it runs its own risks. He could still do a lot of good from here, maybe get involved in an international organization or something. Do you understand what I'm saying?"

"Yeah."

"Course, even if he stays here, he's very insistent on remaining in good standing with the Muslim community, so he still thinks he should get married. To a girl, I mean. How could he want to do that? I mean, I know gays have been hiding for centuries, trying to pass for straight, but I just can't see it. It's so much better to be open. Why pretend if you don't have to? And what kind of girl would go along with it? What, is he going to lead a double life, here? I mean, he's trying to do that already, but I doubt his roommates approve of his disappearing overnight, even if they think he's just with a woman. Those people are very strict. He was speculating on trying to arrange a 'marriage of convenience.' You know, a gay marring a lesbian, and they're married for appearances' sake, but they never sleep together and have their own separate lives and other relationships. Like being roommates, basically."

"People do that?"

"Oh, yeah, I'm sure plenty of people do, though not as many as you might think. I read about it somewhere, how difficult they are to arrange. Especially nowadays, when plenty of people remain unmarried because there's no longer any stigma against it. And you'd still have to find someone you like and would be willing to spend years living with, and who knows, maybe even adopt a child together or something. I know there are guys who are interested in such a situation, but not too many lesbians. Being a lesbian just isn't as contemptible as being gay."

We picked up Kim from her apartment, and she and I sat in the back while Paul drove to Ahmed's place, because I had no idea where it was. On the way over he repeated to Kim what he'd been telling me, and she agreed wholeheartedly that it was just crazy for Ahmed to want to live in Egypt. Paul didn't mention that he had decided he was in love.

Ahmed was waiting for us, and walked over to the car as soon as we pulled into a space. He was wearing a sleeveless black tee shirt tucked into his black jeans, and he had on a beaded necklace. I couldn't believe he would let people, particularly his conservative roommates, see him dressed like that, but I elected not to make any comments. He opened the front door and leaned in and grinned at us.

"Hi," said Paul. "Get in."

He took his seat but left the door open. "*Is salaam 'alaykum,*" he said to Paul.

"What?"

"Your response is '*wa 'alaykum is salaam.*' It's a formal greeting. I say 'Peace be upon you,' '*Is salaam 'alaykum,*' and you reply, 'And upon you be peace,' '*wa 'alaykum is salaam.*'" He smiled at Paul with real expectation that he would follow along with this.

When Paul just stared he went on, "If you prefer, we could use the colloquial hello, '*ahlan,*' since we're all good friends."

"Ahmed, I told you, I'm not learning Arabic. Now shut the door."

"I can't. First I would like to borrow Kim," he said, leaning in to the back seat. He gave her a diffident smile. "I hate to do this. I know I just met you today, Kim, but would you help me? Would you come upstairs and let me introduce you to my roommates as my girlfriend?"

"I'd love to!" she said.

"You see? What I'd tell you?" Paul said to us. "Can I come too?" he asked Ahmed. "I'd like to see your place."

"That would defeat the point," he said, as politely as he could.

We circled around until Paul found a place to park the car, then we sat there for ten minutes and waited. Paul didn't say much, he just fiddled with the radio. I figured he was dejected, though what could he have expected?

When they came back Ahmed looked relieved. Kim began describing his apartment, which was in poor condition and very cluttered. His roommates—only two of the three were there—didn't speak to her. They were both older and taller than he was. Apparently he'd given her a brief tour, because she saw his bedroom, which was crammed with two beds and two desks. Ahmed's desk was the only spot it the entire place that looked neat and organized.

"It went better than I expected," said Ahmed.

"What were you expecting?"

"I don't know. An argument, maybe a quiz."

"They don't want you sleeping with an infidel girl, huh?" teased Kim.

"Actually, no, it's far preferable to sleeping with a Muslim girl. Then I'd be defiling her purity and dishonoring her family, and it would be entirely unacceptable. But you, well, many Muslims consider Western women in general to be whores, so it's less of an issue."

"Well, gee, thanks," Kim pouted.

"And sleeping with whores is okay?" asked Paul.

"No; of course I shouldn't be sleeping with anyone. But we have a different way of looking at things. We all agree it's immoral to be lustful, but you Christians blame the person who has those thoughts, as though you could turn your mind on and off. We, on the other hand, recognize how human nature works, how our emotions are excited by outside stimuli. This is why our culture encourages moderate dress for women. That way there'll be less temptations, and less lust, and hence fewer immoral acts."

"Oh, right, blame the woman!" said Kim.

"No, it's not blame, it just a pragmatic understanding of how our emotions work. Your culture is awash in sexual images, which is one of the reasons it is so vilified. It's as though you're going out of your way to force people to sin and degrade themselves. On an individual level it's naturally very difficult to resist. So my roommates don't hold it against me that I often sleep with my American girlfriend, as they imagine. It just means I lack self-control. Moderately shameful, certainly, but not the crime you assume. When I get married to a good Muslim woman, God willing, it will all be forgotten."

The trip to the club only took ten minutes, which Paul spent arguing with Ahmed about this theory of morality, and whether it justified the gross oppression of woman prevalent in the Muslin world. Kim backed him up, while Ahmed was forced to explain how innocuous headscarves and veils were, and how they prevented woman from being objectified, which was really just a different form of oppression. Kim dared him to defend the burkas, and he allowed it might go a little too far without actually saying there was anything wrong with it. I spent the time observing the skyline out the window.

CHAPTER 10

The bar was housed in an squat, inconspicuous brick building, with only a small neon sign and the faint thumping of a heavy bass to inform us we'd found it. It looked to me like the kind of place you go to buy drugs from dealers. There was a $2 cover charge. Inside, the place seemed crowded, if small. I quickly scanned the dim room, and it was what I'd expected: a whole lot of men, of all ages and races, and very few women. I looked for Dawn, and didn't notice her. What I did notice was that, across the modest dance floor, there was a stage, where some poor waif was screeching along to a recording of Bobby Darin's "Mack the Knife."

"What the hell is this?" I asked Paul, loudly.

"It's called karaoke," he said, grinning from ear to ear. "Ever heard of it? Don't worry, you're going to love it. Karaoke in a gay bar means only one thing: drag queens! You two are in for a treat!"

"There's no DJ?" I asked, bewildered.

"Nope," he said, then looked at me seriously for a moment. "You didn't know?" he said finally, already laughing. "You printed out the page from their website. Didn't you read it? It said it right there."

Sure I had read it. I had searched the entire site diligently for any mention of Dawn, and I just assumed her absence and the mention of karaoke meant the site hadn't been updated recently. Never did I consider the possibility she had lied to me. Why would she? I mean, she's God, and gods don't lie, right?

She did specifically tell me not to come, though.

And now I was stuck. I'd dragged them all here; I couldn't very well turn around and leave.

Paul patted me on the shoulder and said, "Go find a table, and I'll get some drinks." As we stood searching, he strode over to the bar, to our left, and leaned in between people sitting on the stools and talked to the bartender, a long-haired man in his thirties with a white shirt and bow tie. He was drinking from a glass of his own, I noticed.

We managed to find a booth in the back of the club, and sat down.

"This is really great!" said Kim. We had to talk a bit louder than normal because of the volume in the room, but it wasn't as bad as most clubs I've been to, and the booth added some extra isolation. We weren't required to shout. "We'll all have to sing something."

"Hell no," I said.

"Especially you. It was your idea."

"There's no freaking way I'm singing. Certainly not here, for God's sake. I didn't know it was karaoke." The room was filled entirely with men. I kept my eyes down.

Paul took an awfully long time, but eventually he arrived holding four glasses: three with a dark brown liquid that turned out to be scotch, on the rocks, and one with Coke.

"Scotch?" said Kim, surprised.

"Jesus, Paul," I said.

"Why not? A little something special. I've never had one before. Surely you didn't just want another beer?" Since he turned 21 Paul's not only been going clubbing, he's been experimenting with various types of alcohol. Well, taste-tasting, mostly. I don't think he's ever actually been drunk, or at least not that I've seen. He took a sip, and his eyes widened as he inhaled sharply. "Good stuff," he said breathlessly. "Anyway, the bartender said Gladys will be doing a show around midnight."

"Gladys?"

He pointed to the corner, where Gladys the drag queen sat, wearing heavy mascara and a gown of sparkling green sequins. She, or he, had long black hair that was very rigid. In the same booth were two other similarly attired drag queens—backup singers, perhaps?—and two regular men sitting with her. Or him.

I sighed. "Well, at least there's only those three."

"Are you disappointed? Don't worry; there'll be more later, once the evening gets going. She'll sing Madonna songs."

"Madonna?"

"You bet. All us queers love Madonna." He winked.

"Really? Not Cher?"

He laughed. "You watch too much TV."

"So this is the kind of place you spend your evenings at."

"Uh, no, not really. Usually the places I go to are way trendier than this—I mean, let's be honest here, this is pretty lame. It's basically dead. The crowd here is about half the size of the ones at say, JR's. And it seems a little seedy, too. I mean, I'll give it the benefit of the doubt and assume we're simply here way too early. But yeah, it's your typical gay nightclub. It's not so terrible, now is it? I love gay nightclubs. It's so great being in a place where everybody's just like me." He let his eyes wander for a moment, then grinned at me. "How does it feel, Court? To be the one person in the room who's completely different from everyone else?"

A muscular, well-built man with short, spiky, blond hair wearing a thin tee shirt walked by our booth just then, and Kim, Paul, and Ahmed all turned their heads and leaned over to follow him. When he was out of sight, Paul turned back to me and smiled, slightly embarrassed. Kim, I noticed, wasn't embarrassed at all.

She finished her drink and asked for another one. "In fact, why don't you just get us a pitcher of beer."

"Be happy to. Don't go anywhere." Paul got up and glided through the crowd on his way back to the bar.

"Now why did you do that, Kim?" asked Ahmed. "He'll be gone forever again."

"You worried he's going flirting?" she laughed.

I looked around, still nursing my scotch. All the guys there, most of them young, a lot wearing tight-fitting clothes. At one table I saw one man lean over and kiss another on the mouth. It was brief but intense. To me, it was curious, but no more. I was surprised it didn't mean anything. All I could think of was that I'd never seen Paul kiss a guy before. I've seen him looking at guys with, shall we say, interest, and I've seen him touch people in tender, suggestive manners, but never kiss. I mean, until he moved in with me we hardly ever spent all that much time together, but I couldn't help imagining he was doing it on purpose, to try and shield me, as though he didn't want to upset me because I was too sensitive. It was insulting.

I hated how this, coming here, was being made into such a big deal for me, but it was what he did every weekend. I regretted coming, and I felt angry at Dawn for having tricked me like this. God, if only I could talk to her again, make her come to her senses. It relieved me a little, to concentrate on her.

Paul came back with a pitcher of beer, and poured some out for Kim.

"Good," she said. "Now who's going to sing?"

"Not me," I said quickly.

"We should all go up and sing that song—by the Bangles, wasn't it?—'Walk Like an Egyptian,'" said Paul.

"Please don't," said Ahmed, looking annoyed.

"Oh, come on. It'll be fun. It's not even about Egypt."

"I know what it's about."

"Well then, what's the big deal? It's all in fun."

Ahmed looked to us plaintively. "Change the subject, Kim."

"Okay," she said. "Speaking of Egypt, why on earth do you want to go back there?"

"Oh, he told you about that, did he?" He glanced at Paul. "But is it so hard to accept? I am homesick. I want to see my family. I want to return to the places where I grew up. I want to live in a Muslim society again. I love my country, Kim, as flawed as it may be. Don't you love your country?"

"Mine? Hell no," she said, laughing. "America is the Great Satan, as everyone knows. We're responsible for all the world's problems. If only there were no America, there would be peace and harmony and equality everywhere on earth."

Ahmed rolled his eyes.

"So how is it there are too many doctors in America?"

Ahmed sighed. "That's not what I meant. We were discussing the rising cost of medical care here, with the great gap between the insured and uninsured, and I was saying that the situation could not last forever, that there would inevitably be some sort of dramatic shift. Possibly the whole system will collapse, or at least become entirely regulated by the government. There's going to be a lot of very restrictive legislation. Plus, with the advent of Web-based reference guides and the proliferation of over-the-counter medicines and so-called natural remedies, a lot more people are going to be to self-medicating. And then there's insurance. Malpractice insurance is already sky-rocketing, and filling out all the necessary paperwork to collect any money consumes more and more of every physician's time and resources. I'm just speculating here, but I think it's going to be very hard to be a doctor in America in the coming decades."

"Well it sounds pretty bleak. I guess I was wrong about you being an optimist. But at least there'll be lower costs for us poor working folk!"

"No, I'm afraid not. It will probably mean the opposite," he said.

"It's all the fault of illegal immigrants," said Paul. "They come here and take and take and take without paying for anything. They flood the emergency rooms for every minor ache because they can't afford regular office visits. Now don't say it's not their fault, because it is. If they just played by the rules like everybody else they could get decent wages, but they come here and get exploited into accepting below minimum wages, which screws everyone else over coming and going. They take jobs away from real Americans, send half what they make back home, leeching us dry, then because they can't pay for anything, they abuse public services and take money right out of the pockets of hardworking taxpayers like us. Really, getting rid of them would be for their own good."

"Okay!" Kim held up her hand and smiled broadly. "New subject! Tell me, Ahmed, are you a Sunni or Shitte?" He looked up at her in surprise.

"Well now, that's an interesting jump. But, Kim, if I told you, would you have any idea what it meant? Do you even know what the difference is between the two?"

"Nope! Just making conversation. What is the difference?"

He smiled. "Well, the difference between them is actually very similar to the difference between the Catholic and Protestant branches of Christianity. Catholics believe the authority of their religious leaders derives from an institution which descends directly from the apostles. Similarly, the authority of Shiite religious leaders derives from their direct descent from Ali, the Blessed Prophet's son-in-law and heir. And I mean that. Their imams are literally direct biological descendents. The Sunnis, like the Protestants, drawn their religious leaders from the common men of the local community and derive their authority entirely from religious orthodoxy."

"Wow," said Kim, impressed. "That makes things so simple. So which are you?"

"Like the majority of Egyptians, and indeed the majority of Muslims the world over, I am Sunni."

"That's not how you explained it to me when I asked," said Paul, frowning.

"Yes, well, that's because you said the only thing you know about Sunnis is that they're the terrorists in Iraq."

"Paul, you didn't!" squealed Kim, sounding awfully delighted about it.

"You see, and this is the guy who wants me to sleep with him, not to mention convert to his religion. He exasperates me with his ignorance. I, for one, having lived here for five years, have learned much of your nation's history and culture, and have studied your religion earnestly. I know what Christianity teaches, and I know what the difference is between the Protestant, Catholic, and Orthodox branches, both historically and theologically. Yet Paul thinks he can convert me without learning the first thing about Islam. I don't know why I put up with him."

"Well," said Kim, "why do you put up with him?"

"Oh, well," he chuckled. "He's very cute." Paul blushed instantly. "And he can be very amusing as well!"

Ahmed turned back to Kim. "But seriously, let me tell you what I like about Paul. When I first met him, I was very hesitant to become involved with him, because of his strong religious views. It wasn't just his carelessness about my own, or his crude efforts to convert me, it was a worry that he was, beneath his cheerful countenance, an extreme example of the many guilt-ridden religious homosexuals I've met. Many gay men have so absorbed the censure of society that no matter what they claim, deep down they are convinced God hates them. Many of them even defended themselves with clever theological arguments, like Paul, yet still believe they're going to *jahannam*, to hell. But not Paul. He isn't ashamed; he doesn't suffer from self-loathing. He's happy with himself, and he trusts his God. Our outlook on life is very similar. We understand each other."

Damn. Paul had said something similar earlier. This *was* serious.

"Well, that's very nice of you," Paul said to him. "But I think you're wrong, or at least exaggerating. I know God loves me. The problem with these other people is they don't understand their faith. They have too little religion, not too much. And I don't know anybody racked with self-hatred. You just think that because of Kamal. So now because of him you're paranoid and can't get too close to anybody."

"That's not true at all. I've been close to people, and I'm just saying I find you to be different from every one of them. You're completely at ease with your sexuality, and you've been able to reconcile your faith with your orientation, the way I have. I'm saying this is a unique connection we have. Other people simply aren't as well-adjusted as you are."

Paul chuckled. "You hear that, Court? I'm well-adjusted. What are we, in third grade here?"

I wondered if what Ahmed was saying was right. I'd occasionally wondered whether or not Paul had a guilt complex, or serious doubts. His religious views, after all, simply weren't overly nuanced. I could never fathom how he could be gay and yet devoted to a religion teaching that gays were evil and hell-bound, but at the same time I had difficulty imagining Paul being, even deep down, eaten up with anxiety. He just never struck me as a deep thinker. He must have had struggles, he must have; but he failed to express them, or show that he was ever bothered by them, even a little. Maybe he was compartmentalizing, or maybe he simply never thought about it, but I doubted Paul had some secret understanding of Christian theology everyone else had missed. His attitude surely wasn't as exceptional as Ahmed made it out to be.

"Paul has a deeper understanding of the will of God than most," Ahmed continued. "He's very self-confident, and I find that appealing."

"And yet you want to run back to Egypt and hide in a marriage and throw away your own freedom," Paul said, suddenly angry.

Ahmed shook his head sadly. "No, Paul. Ultimately, I'm afraid I don't have any freedom, no matter where in the world I go."

"Sure you do. You're free here."

"No, I'm not. And neither are you, your emotions aside. You may think you are, but you aren't. We don't have freedom in this world."

"Of course we do."

He shook his head; he must have still been thinking about the future disaster we'd discussed earlier. "Don't fool yourself, Paul. You think this is freedom?" He motioned to the dance floor, where people were jumping up and down and shouting. But the gesture was also in my direction, and I had the impression that he included me, and by inference the heterosexual society at large. No matter how unconcerned he was regarding others, Paul kept his behavior in check around me, but I'm sure it was just out of a general low opinion he had of me, that he needed to protect me. But otherwise the point was clear. If, for whatever reason, he felt he needed to do things to shield me, his own brother, and if I, in turn, could not be comfortable with him, then what chance did they have against the wider world?

Whatever larger implications he meant, Paul certainly didn't see it, or at least chose not to. He said, "Nobody's hiding here, Ahmed.

We're not underground anymore. There are even places where gays can get married. I don't know what you're talking about."

Distressed, Kim said, "Ahmed! That sounds pessimistic! Stop it!"

Before Ahmed could respond, Molly appeared at our booth.

I hadn't seen her approach, so I couldn't say where she came from. Suddenly she was just there, leaning over and grinning, a bit out of breath. She was wearing the same pink outfit from this afternoon.

"Hi guys!" she said cheerfully. "Hi, Mr. Paul! Hi Mr. Court! Hi, You!" This last greeting was directed to Ahmed.

I was shocked. How did she know them? Hell, how did she know my name? This superseded the fear that she was about to mention Dawn and expose the real reason I'd brought them all here. Though maybe, possibly, if she was here it meant Dawn was also here, though I couldn't see how. Much more likely she had brought a message.

The others glanced at me and then back at Molly. "Hi," said Paul. "What are you doing here? Where's your God?"

"Oh, she's not *here*," said Molly definitively. For some reason her emphasis on the "here" made the others laugh.

"Well of course God's not here," said Kim. "What god would come to this filthy den of sin and iniquity?"

They kept laughing, and Molly continued smiling but also looked a little bewildered. "No," she said slowly. "She's been here before. She's just not here now."

"Really?" said Paul, amused. "God comes here to rescue poor sinners?"

"Yeah!" exclaimed Molly, brightening up again.

"Okay, you know what, I think we've heard enough from you today. Go bother somebody else," said Paul, becoming serious again. He made a motion with his hands to shoo her off, and she left, reluctantly and clearly disappointed. I was wholeheartedly relieved; I desperately wanted to know what her message was, but not delivered in front of everyone.

"What the hell was that?" I asked after she was far enough away.

"What do you mean what was that?" said Paul. "You talked to her, right?"

Well, she knew my name so I couldn't very well deny it. "Yes. And she talked to you, too?" And then added, suddenly understanding, "At the Cathedral?"

"Sure. We ran into her. She and a few other people were talking about God, which you'd expect at a church, but then she tells us that God was in the garden and we should go out and see her and get a blessing—apparently she worships a female deity. At first I assumed it was some sort of metaphor, but she doesn't look like the kind of person who knows much about metaphors, so I had to ask. Seems Molly actually believed God was literally right outside, just waiting for us to drop by. Yet when I asked her about Jesus she didn't appear to understand. It was very bizarre."

"You didn't go out and see, did you?"

"No, of course not. Did you?"

I shook my head. "It was too hot out."

Kim snorted. "Yeah, right."

"I don't get it," I said to her. "I thought you'd like hearing that God was a woman."

"Well, yeah, that's great and all. I thought about going, but it wasn't enough to get me to follow that girl."

"No?"

Ahmed smiled at me. "Court, did you notice anything particularly unusual about her?"

"What do you mean? No, I didn't notice anything. Well, other than that she's obviously too young to be in here. How do you think she got in?"

He shrugged. "A bribe, probably. I think they let her sneak by because she brings in more customers, too."

"How? I mean, I kind of assume she's a prostitute, but this is a gay nightclub. Can't be too many interested people here, right?"

He and Paul exchanged smiles, amused by my ignorance. "No, quite the opposite. You see, our little evangelist is actually a boy."

"What?" I quickly glanced out at the crowd to pick out Molly. "That's ridiculous," I said, turning back when I couldn't immediately find her. "I mean she clearly has breasts."

He nodded. "Sure she does. She's a transsexual."

I grinned stupidly, hoping he was making a joke. "Wait, you mean a person with both, um, both parts?"

"No, that's a hermaphrodite. A transsexual is a person who is born one sex but identifies as the opposite sex, and may try to change their sex through surgery. Our friend is a boy but identifies as a girl. I'm pretty sure she's pre-op, though, meaning she hasn't had sex reassignment surgery yet, but she's on hormone therapy. That's why she's grown breasts, and why her voice is so high-pitched. I think she may have been taking estrogen for a long time, since before puberty, even, because her growth seems stunted."

"But how can you be sure?"

"Cause he's a doctor, you idiot," Kim said.

"Did you notice her Adam's apple?" asked Ahmed, pointing to the lump on his own throat. "Only males have those."

I was still confused. "But what about the dressing up, the drag queens?"

"No, those are transvestites. Completely different. They just dress up for fun, just to pretend. And they can be straight. This girl's serious."

"Boy, we're learning all kinds of fun things today, aren't we?" said Kim, pouring herself another beer.

All I could do was shake my head. It was horrifying, that someone would want to do that to themselves. And I had been fooled—by a kid. Not that it really mattered, couldn't matter, but it was still unsettling. But wasn't there a connection with the rest of Molly's history? Or was that just another lie Dawn had told me?

Kim drank most of her beer, then said, "Okay, come on, that's enough, time for singing. Ahmed's gotta sing 'Walk Like an Egyptian.'"

"What?" he cried. "Now you expect *me* to sing it?"

"Yeah, go sing it," commanded Paul.

"Never."

"Well, you could sing 'Rock the Kasbah' instead, if you'd like," suggested Kim.

"Come on." Paul leaned in and put his hand on Ahmed's chest. "Sing it for me and I'll do anything you want."

"Well...," Ahmed wavered. "All right, but you have to sing something too."

"For you, anything. What'd you have in mind?"

"Oh!" said Kim. "I know the perfect song! Paul should sing that one by Vanilla Ice."

"Okay," Paul said, nonchalant.

"*Ice Ice Baby*," Ahmed said with a grin.

"You are Mr. Cool," I added.

"Fine, I'll do it. What are we going to make Court sing?"

"I'll think of something, don't worry. You guys go first." She stood up and then held out her hand to me. "Come on, let's dance."

"No way. There is no way in hell I'm dancing in this place."

"I thought you weren't scared of the queer people."

I leaned back in my seat. "I'm just going to stay right here."

"Chicken. Well fortunately there are plenty of other men here."

"No there aren't."

Paul held out his hand. "I'll dance with you, Kim."

Ahmed jumped up and took her hand as she held it out. "No, I'll dance with her. You sing first."

"Bye Court," she said. "If anyone else asks you to dance, tell them you already have a boyfriend." The three of them moved out onto the dance floor as music started and another singer began butchering a classic 80's pop song. Paul looked back at me and wiggled his eyebrows as they went.

I sat there fuming. I should have just gone and done it. Kim was mad at me now, and she'd probably pick some horribly embarrassing song for me to sing as revenge. I could always refuse, but if I didn't play along I'd be sleeping alone tonight. And worse, how could I sleep in my own bed, knowing those two were right next door?

Reluctantly I stood up and glanced around for her. I couldn't find her, but I did see Paul standing in a short line of people behind the stage, wait their turns to make fools of themselves. I also noticed Molly, standing at the edge of the bar, talking to someone.

Now was probably the best, if not the only, chance I would get to find out Dawn's message, while everyone else was busy. So I walked over to her. She was talking to a black woman, young but probably old enough to get in here legally, or at least have a credible fake ID; she was dressed very casually, in short jeans and a dark blue tee shirt, and I thought I recognized her from the Cathedral garden this afternoon, among the people Dawn had blessed with her touch. They stopped talking when I approached, and Molly again grinned.

"Hi, Mr. Court!"

"So, did Dawn give you a message for me?"

"You want us to tell you where she really is tonight?" asked the woman.

I shook my head. "Thanks, but there's no point. I came with some other people, so I can't just leave. But she gave you a message for me, right? That's why you're here, right?"

"Yeah, come on, let's go to the back where it's quieter," she said, motioning to a little hallway further down. She grabbed her purse off the table and turned and started for the hall immediately, not giving me a chance to respond. The woman smirked at me, and I followed Molly.

CHAPTER 11

Down the hall there were several doors. Two were bathrooms, one men's and one women's. Why, I wondered, did a gay bar have a separate woman's bathroom? Why not just a unisex restroom, and use the other for storage or something? Did enough women come here to justify the expense?

"Look," I began to say as I caught up to her, but Molly shook her head.

"No, no, let's go outside." She led me all the way to the end of the hall, where there was a door with an exit sign above it, and pushed it open. I understood at once what Molly thought was going on, and I was disgusted and about to refuse, but honestly, it really was much quieter outside, so I grudgingly followed. The door opened out to an alley at the back of the club, and we stepped into the night air, which had cooled down considerably but was still hot and humid. There was trash littering the street, surrounding a garbage bin at one end. Otherwise it was deserted. Molly used her foot to shove a beer can into the door to prop it open. Then we went a little further down the alley, and she suddenly stepped up close to me, her chest forward, actually brushing up against me. Even in her heels, she was several inches below my height. Now that I saw her close up, I saw clearly the angular, masculine face hiding beneath the make-up, and couldn't believe I had been so deceived. I hated that she'd made an idiot out of me. I hated that she thought I might want her. . . in that way.

She said, giggling as she did, "I know what you want. Normally it's two hundred bucks, three hundred if you don't have a condom, but I'll only charge you for half because Miss D. said you're her friend. And besides, I like you, you're kinda cute." She put her hands on my belt suggestively. I pushed her away forcefully; she almost tripped stepping back. "Get off me, you little freak," I said, rather loudly.

Apparently she really did like me, because she looked shocked, hurt. But, ever streetwise, she bounced back and sneered at me, putting her hands on her hips. "Like I haven't heard that before. If you're going to insult me, you could at least say something new."

"I am not interested," I said, trying to be my sternest.

"Sure you are," she said smiling. It was the weirdest feeling. I felt nauseous, so disgusted I was on the verge of heaving. "Don't touch me." I held my hand up to ward her off, and as I did, a whole new, and far more disturbing idea came to me. "I thought Dawn gave you a message for me. What is this? Did Dawn send you here you to have sex with me? What is she now, a pimp?"

"No," she snickered. "She didn't tell me to have sex with you. She just said you were interested in me."

I gaped at her a moment, sure there was no way Dawn would ever have said anything like that, when I realized with a shock what she was talking about. "No, God no, not in that way," I said quickly. "Jesus Christ. I was interested in your personal life. Dawn was telling me about all the horrible stuff you've been through and how you're a happy hooker now. That's all I meant; that's the only thing I expressed interest in. You—God, I can't believe I felt sorry for you."

"Hey, I don't need your pity."

"You know, Dawn told me this whole story about how you'd had this horrendous life, how you'd been abused and raped and sent from foster home to foster home. Maybe you even dressed up in your mother's clothes, or your sister's, or whatever, and you'd get beaten for it, right? You finally had to run away just so you could wear a dress and pretend to be a girl." I understood it all clearly now. I'd asked Dawn to help this person, and Dawn had told me she couldn't be helped because of the pain she'd suffered in her past. But I guess I hadn't taken her seriously enough, so she sent the girl here, specifically to talk to me. Molly wasn't here to deliver any message, she was here so I could understand who she really was and maybe hear her sob story first hand, and even be more gracious when Dawn failed to pull off the miracle I asked for. In a way, knowing the truth did let me accept the impossibility of the task, because I could see I'd been wrong. The unfortunate circumstances here were her miserable foster homes and her gender unhappiness, but she didn't have to be on the streets as a prostitute. That was her choice. No amount of magic was going to set this sad, desperate person right.

"I am a girl," she pouted.

"Do you like living like this? Do you like dealing with drunken strangers, or risking your life selling sex and drugs to crackheads and junkies? You're going to end up in jail or dead."

She shrugged, like it was no big deal. "No, I don't like it, but I need money for my surgery."

"Right, so some doctor can mutilate you...God, how could you honestly want that?" She folded her arms and glowered. "Look, are you just going to stand there and lecture me? 'Cause I don't need it, okay. We might as well go back inside so I can start making some money."

She started for the door, and I grabbed her arm. "Hey!"

"Wait a minute; I'm not done with you yet." I still wanted to ask her about Dawn. Hopefully she could help me figure out what Dawn was doing.

But it was a mistake to touch her. Her demeanor turned very aggressive; she looked back up at me again, furious, and simultaneously reached into a pocket with her free hand and flicked open a knife. "Let go!" she yelled, pointing it at my face.

I dropped her arm and put my hands up. "Molly…"

She waved the knife in the air. "I don't need you insulting me and lecturing me! Maybe I ought to cut off something important to you, and see how you'd like it!"

"Molly, put down the knife…"

"Miss Dawn loves me! You're not her friend! You're not my friend either!"

Given how tiny Molly was, and how loosely she was swinging the knife, I wagered I could take it from her before she did anything destructive with it. So that's what I did, or tried to do, anyway. I grabbed her hand with my own, and tried to pull the knife out of her grip, but she held it fast.

"Let go!" she yelled as we struggled. And I decided a better tactic was just to run back inside, so I let go.

Her arm jerked back and the knife slashed across her midriff. A bright red line appeared on her stomach. She looked down at it and started screaming. And then, before I could say anything, she fainted.

She fell to the ground, dropping the knife. I stood still for a moment. "Molly?" I tentatively asked.

Her eyes were open and she was breathing hard, very hard. She didn't say anything but her look conveyed both fear and pain. I didn't know what had happened, but was terrified. I crouched down.

"Stay right there, Molly. I'll be right back with a doctor."

I found Ahmed standing on the same line Paul had been in when I left. I guess I had missed Paul's singing. Now Molly didn't appear to be breathing, so Ahmed started CPR until the paramedics arrived and zapped her with their paddles. I hated how they stared at me as they put Molly on a stretcher and into their van, like I was the lowest scum on the earth. I said I was just talking to Molly, and she got angry when I told her she was mistaken about my intentions. And that she then pulled out her knife and waved it at me, but only ended up scratching herself and unexpectedly collapsing. I assured them I wasn't going to press any charges against her for threatening me, so they never called the police. They believed me that I hadn't caused the knife wound on her belly, which was no more than a scratch. I'd had paper cuts worse than that. It could even have been made worse by her fall, as there were a lot of sharp rocks, tin cans and other trash in the alley. Still, from their looks to the shocked faces of my brother and girlfriend, I felt more shame than I had ever felt in my entire life, and I hadn't even done anything. Information about Dawn was all I had wanted from Molly.

CHAPTER 12

Kim was humming a little ditty. Over and over again, very loudly. It was the most upset I had ever seen her. She had lost all her happy thoughts, had nothing positive to say, and were she to open her mouth only curses would come out, so the humming was the only thing she could do to keep up her good vibes. She'd been humming since we left the club. I figured our night was ruined and was just going to drop her off at her building, but when she got out she just stood there, waiting for me. So I got out and followed her in. I couldn't believe it when she let me into her apartment. It was dark and looked empty, but Jenna's door was closed so I couldn't be sure. Her tabby cat, Spanish, appeared and rubbed against her legs, meowing. I asked her the first time I came here why she had given him such a ridiculous name, but she had a reasonable story—something to do with a poodle from her childhood named Frenchie. She bent down and patted him on the head but still kept humming. She just dropped her purse on the kitchenette counter and turned around to stare at me.

"Tell me again what the hell you were doing with that girl?" she asked, coldly. I repeated my explanation, which I already given several times that night, about how I had only wanted to talk to her, and how Molly had made a mistaken assumption about my intentions and led me outside. What we had talked about I left vague, because

I still couldn't mention Dawn, and I couldn't let on that I knew as much about Molly's history as I did.

"I just felt sorry for her and I wanted to know how she wound up like that," I said. "She's obviously very young to be in a bar like that…"

"Uh-huh. You sure you didn't want to see for yourself what she was?"

I stood there for a moment, not answering her. "You don't believe me?"

"And then she just suddenly collapsed? Just like that? Without you even touching her?"

"I told you what happened when she pulled out her knife…and accidently cut herself and then…"

"She just what—had a heart attack? At sixteen?"

"Yeah," I shrugged. I had no idea what had happened to her. Ahmed hadn't known either.

Kim sighed. "Well, okay, I know you didn't have sex with her. I made sure to ask Ahmed. I just don't know why you refused to dance with me but you went to hide outside with that strange little girl. Boy. Whatever."

I felt slightly relieved. "Is that it? You feel jealous?"

"I'm not jealous," she snapped. "I just find this whole thing pretty damn creepy."

She didn't say this loudly, but it was the angriest she'd ever been with me, and it was kind of shocking. "So then why did you let me in here?

"If you must know, she said, no less chilly, "You can stay here tonight but you will sleep on the couch."

"Really, you want me to sleep on the couch?"

"Yes, because I don't want you to go back to your own place. I want Paul and Ahmed to have the place to themselves, to be free to do whatever they want without worrying about you interfering."

"Paul and Ahmed?"

"Ahmed deserves a reward for saving Molly's life. Paul does, too. I guess you missed his singing. He was awesome. People were cheering, singing along. The two of them deserve to be free for the night, alone, together."

"So you only want me here to keep me away from my own apartment?"

"Basically, yeah; you owe them that much."

I went over to the couch. "Great."

CHAPTER 13

I woke the next morning when I heard Kim getting out of bed to open the shades and let the sun flood the room. She raised her arms up, over her head, all the way into the air, and cheerfully called out to the sunlight, "Good morning, morning!"

I'd heard Kim's morning ritual many times before, and more often than not it made me smile, sometimes with reflected contentment, sometimes with derision. A few times, with her encouragement, I'd even managed to get up and do it with her. Today, though, I closed my eyes again and fell back asleep.

Later I woke up again, to the aroma of strong coffee and a mild headache from the night before. I was hopeful that today I could get things smoothed over with Kim.

I had not really undressed last night, as I just slept on the couch. I got up and walked over to Kim, who was sitting at the kitchenette counter eating a bowl of her favorite cereal, Lucky Charms, while talking to Jenna. Jenna looked up at me as I came over to them.

"Morning, Court," she said, unemotionally. Kim turned her head to glance at me.

"Good morning," I said, trying to sound cheerful. "And how're you doing, Kim?"

"Upright and breathing!" she said with a grin. So she was still mad at me. She said stuff like that when she was down, mantras which inspired Positivity by reminding her that no matter how bad things were, at least she was still alive.

"Kim was telling me all about your lovely adventure," Jenna said.

I went to the cupboard and took down a mug. "No, no adventure," I said, pouring a cup of coffee. "A girl fainted, although apparently with some sort of heart complications, and was taken away in an ambulance."

"No, I mean before that part."

I stirred in the sugar and milk. "What'd she tell you?" I didn't really want to have to explain everything again, but I guess there wouldn't be much choice. Jenna didn't say anything, though; she just shrugged and looked back to Kim.

"We were just talking," I said.

"Court, why don't you just get showered," Kim said pleasantly.

"Sure. What are we doing today?" I gulped down my coffee, and Kim went back to eating her cereal.

"I haven't decided. We'll think of something."

"Sounds good to me," I said, trying to stay as equally pleasant. Whatever she wanted to do, I would do it, to make up for last night. Any thoughts I had of trying to sneak in my visit to Professor Braxton were abandoned. I would just have to email him an apology and try to see him some other day. Kim would be working next weekend, so I could meet him then. Or I could go over to his house any day of the week in the evening, after work. He didn't live too far away, and I'm sure he had a light teaching schedule for the summer.

I finished my coffee and then took a shower. I shaved afterwards with a razor of mine that I kept there, and changed into a green tee shirt and short jeans that were among the few pairs of clothes that I also kept there. I didn't have an extra pair of shoes, though, so I had to continue wearing my loafers. Hopefully we could stop off at my place before we went wherever we were going so I could get my sneakers.

When I was done I went back out the living area. Jenna was sill sitting at the counter, leafing through a magazine, while Kim had moved to the sofa. She sat in front of the television, but it wasn't on. I took a bowl from the cupboard and was about to fill it with cereal when she called me over, patting the seat next to her. So I went and sat down.

"So what are we doing today?"

She looked me in the eyes. "Court, I just want you to know that I think you're a decent guy, and I don't want you to be angry, but I've been thinking about this for a while and…"

"Wait—you're not breaking up with me, are you?"

She nodded. "This relationship just isn't working out, Court."

The thing was, I knew that. I had been thinking the same thing myself, but I still couldn't believe this was happening. "I thought we were having fun."

"Not really, Court. I hate to say this, but you're a Negative person. And you're boring."

"Boring?" I said, surprised. I knew I wasn't as energetic as she was, but boring? "How am I a Negative person? What about yesterday? We had a lot of fun, right?"

"Sure, I had plenty of fun yesterday. But it wasn't because of you; it was in spite of you." She ticked off yesterday's failures on her fingers. "You didn't care about winning the game, you didn't care that Nate was cheating, you blew me off in the Cathedral, I don't think you said a single word during dinner except to mock me, and then, when you actually came up with a great idea for the evening, you decided just showing up was enough. You weren't going to participate, and then you snuck off with some whore—"

"Hold on—"

"And I don't even know what happened after that, but it was pretty bad."

"I didn't do anything!"

"You're just sending out Negative vibes, Court, and I have to cut you loose before you pull me down, too."

"Okay..." I slumped down in my seat.

"Anyway, you're a not a bad person, and I hope you can see this is really for the best, for the both of us. You have to think positively!"

I wasn't going to stubbornly refuse or try to plead for forgiveness when I knew she was right about us. I had certainly always thought it was a fun relationship, but that was all it was. I never really thought Kim was someone I could spend my whole life with, and I don't think I would have wanted to. So I went and gathered up all my things and said my goodbyes to Kim, Jenna, and Spanish. And Kim said she'd still be willing to join in next time I played Hide and Seek with Nate, if I wanted to give her a call.

CHAPTER 14

I was surprised by how late I had slept in. By the time I got home, it was almost noon. I put my things away and changed my shoes. I considered wearing my nicer clothes again for my interview with Professor Braxton, which was now apparently the only thing I was going to be doing today, but decided against it. It was still too hot for anything but shorts.

I fixed myself a sandwich and ate it while I watched the news. I finished and washed the plate and clicked off the TV. I made sure I had the picture of me and Dawn that I had taken with me yesterday, and then decided I was ready to leave. I sat down on the couch and waited, though. It didn't matter that I would be gone most of the afternoon, I'm sure, but I felt the urge to tell Paul that Kim had dumped me. I wanted to complain about her characterization of me, at least a little. Well, maybe I didn't; I wasn't sure Paul would entirely disagree. But surely he would find it amusing that Kim wanted me to stay at her place just to give him and Ahmed some privacy.

When Paul arrived, though, he down looked at me, frowned, and said, "You're in big trouble, Courtland." He was dressed in a shirt and tie for church.

"Um, hi," I said. "Where's Ahmed?"

"I dropped him off at home."

"He didn't go to church with you?"

"Of course not. I tried to get him to come, but he won't unless I go to mosque with him."

"So maybe you should go."

"Hey, don't change the subject," he said crossly. "You're in big trouble."

I sighed. "Okay, what now?"

He leaned against the kitchenette counter. "Last night, Ahmed insisted we go to the hospital. He wanted to find out what happened to that trans-girl. I told him they weren't going to tell him anything—HIPPA and all that. He should know that himself, but he thought they might because he'd saved her life, or because he was in the guild, or whatever. And of course I was right. But he decided to hang around and try his luck with someone else, and we both ended up falling asleep in the waiting room. And you'll never guess who shook me awake at three-thirty in the morning."

He paused, waiting me for to guess. It was obvious what had happened, and why I was in trouble. "Sorry, no clue…"

He sighed. "I was shocked to discover Dawn Gardner was *that* Dawn Gardner. I thought she moved to California. But, no, there she was, back again. She even remembered my name."

"What do you mean? Is there some other Dawn Gardner?"

"Heck, I thought there was. A DJ goes mad and tells everyone she's God, and you don't think people aren't going to notice that? People talk. You and Kim go to a lot of clubs; haven't you heard? The mad DJ, the divine Miss Dawn? Ahmed even met her once; he mentioned it to me a few weeks ago, and I thought, hey, a crazy girl with the same name as that other crazy girl, won't Court be amused. How long have you known?"

"Only since yesterday."

"That was the first time you've seen her, at the Cathedral? So you did go out to see the god in the garden, huh?" he said, nodding. "And you didn't even know. Jeeze. But you didn't think to say anything to the rest of us, did you? And of course you had to tell her I was gay."

"I didn't tell her, Paul. She already knew."

"How could she know that?"

"She said she's seen you around, in some of the clubs she's played."

He shrugged. "Fine. But now I know why you were so dismayed by the karaoke last night. I can't believe you suckered us into going there. Kim's going to be furious when I tell her."

"Right, went to a gay bar to meet a girl. How ironic. Don't waste any effort on Kim, by the way. We already broke up."

"Oh, you did, huh?" He smiled at me.

"You don't have to look so pleased. She said I was too Negative for her; interfering with her Positive mojo. And boring. She said I was boring."

"Yeah, well," he said, still smiling. "That sounds about right."

"Hey! Come on, now."

He shrugged again. "What do you want me to say?"

I shook my head. "Well, I hope you're happy, at least. Kim insisted I stay there last night, but the only reason was so that I would stay away from here so you and Ahmed could have some privacy."

"Well," Paul said, "we were hardly home at all. I told you, we fell asleep in the hospital waiting room, and then we were talking with Dawn, so it was almost four thirty, a quarter to five, before we got home. Ahmed slept on the couch. I told him to sleep in your bed, since you weren't here and it was your fault anyway, but he was too polite to do that."

"So he slept on the couch?" I asked. "And you couldn't have, maybe, I don't know, just skipped church for once?" I felt a little odd, encouraging him.

"It's wasn't only that. We had this fight."

I perked up. "What about?"

"Some stupid joke. I don't know why he was so worked up about it."

"Finally crossed a boundary insulting Islam?"

"It wasn't about that at all! It was something Dawn said."

"What?"

"You know, we had a pretty strange conversation with her. I don't think I've ever talked to someone who was genuinely insane. Although I have to admit, she didn't look bad. And she seemed pretty focused, too, which was a little surprising. But you remember what I said about her before? I always said she was crazy. I told you she'd come to a bad end, and now look at her. I guess it's not her fault. I don't know what you were trying to do, Court, but you should forget her."

"Come on, Paul, she was no crazier than I was."

"That's not true and you know it. You got over it; she didn't. And now she's slid way past the edge and into a total abyss."

"I want to help her."

"Forget it; there's nothing you can do for her. She needs professional help and some powerful anti-psychotics. Maybe even a stint in a mental ward."

"Right, so they can make her normal with shock therapy, just like they did to gays in the Fifties."

I immediately regretted saying that. I thought he was going to become angry, maybe say something about what else shock therapy could cure, but he just shifted his stance. "Don't defend her, Court. You know, she told me that same joke last night. I warned her she was going to go to hell for blasphemy if she didn't repent, and her response was to tell me that Dante's *Inferno* puts blasphemers and sodomites together in the same circle of hell."

I smiled, but only briefly. "So what was the problem with that?"

"That's not what we were arguing over. What happened was Dawn thanked Ahmed for saving Molly, and then offered to repay him with a miracle."

"Really? She refused when I saw her yesterday."

"Well, don't tell Ahmed you asked her, apparently that's a no-no. That just plays into her delusion."

"But if she promises a miracle and then can't deliver, isn't that a convincing demonstration she's not all powerful?"

"Well, that's what I thought, but apparently that's incorrect. Ahmed's not a psychologist, but he was pretty insistent that asking her for anything, or talking theology, or doing anything she might interpret as treating her seriously only ingrains her delusion even further into her mind. The inconsistencies, the failures, those don't prove anything. She just explains them away, or ignores them, or forgets them entirely."

I gave it a moment's curious pause, then continued, "So I take it he didn't ask her for anything?"

He cleared his throat, suddenly embarrassed. "No, he didn't. I did."

"Ah, well I guess I can see what happened. What did you ask for?"

"We were in a hospital, right? So I figured this would be obvious. Healing the sick, raising the dead, that sort of thing. But she tells me not to play any games with her, to be real. What would I ask if she were actually God?"

"Which would mean taking her seriously, which feeds her delusion. Ahmed must have been upset."

"Yeah, well, he just told me not to do it; he didn't explain all the reasons until after I'd already gone and done it. So I thought to myself, if Jesus appeared and offered me anything, what would I want? And you know, my life's pretty good. There was only one thing I could think of that I would actually ask for."

"And what would that be?"

I waited while he walked into the kitchenette and got a glass from the cupboard. "Maybe I shouldn't tell you," he said as he pulled a soda bottle from the refrigerator. "You'll only laugh."

"No I won't."

"Of course you will." He filled the glass, returned the bottle, then came back around to the front and resumed leaning against the counter. He sighed, but went ahead and said it. "I told her to make me straight."

He was right; I did laugh. It was the last thing I had expected. He took a long gulp from his glass to mask his annoyance.

Watching him, seeing him in a new light, I asked, "I thought you liked being gay?"

"I do!" he said. "But what else would I ask God?" It was a curiously honest answer. Asking if he liked being gay was another one of those topics I wasn't supposed to broach. He would feel obligated to insist he had no say in the matter; that it was simply something he was—yet he wasn't broken up about it and clearly enjoyed his sexuality. But I can see how he'd feel a need to deny it if he ever did have a choice. "Now Ahmed's disappointed with me, because he said all that stuff about how well-adjusted I am."

"Paul, you said this to a crazy girl. Ahmed's got a point. Whatever your religious convictions, whatever you *would* say to God, why on earth would you treat Dawn so seriously?"

He shrugged, helplessly. "This will probably sound stupid, but I wanted to hear what Dawn's response would be. If she's so concerned with that transgender prostitute, it's obvious what her cosmology is. If she's a god, then she's obviously one of those liberal, morally relative, new-age gods. She was almost as horrified as Ahmed that I had even asked that. She was all, 'Oh, no, I made you just the way you are, you have nothing to feel guilty about, blah, blah, blah.' What rot."

Considering what she had said to me yesterday, I could only agree with Paul's assessment of her theology. "Okay, then what?"

He scowled. "She put her hand on my forehead and said, 'Now you're straight,' just like that. And then the most ridiculous part of all; she said 'Don't come complaining to me if you don't like it.' I swear." He shook his head, then took his drink and wandered back to his bedroom, shaking his head again as he did. I figured we were done, but then I remembered something.

"Hey, Paul?" I called to him.

"Yeah?" he turned back.

"What's the meaning of life?"

He stared at me. "What?"

"Sorry. When I spoke to Dawn yesterday, I asked her what the meaning of life was. She said you knew."

He came back into the living room. "She said I knew?"

I nodded. "I can imagine your answer pretty well, but I can't figure what she's getting at, since her outlook is a little different from yours."

"Yeah, well." He thought for a moment. "The meaning of life is to obey God and do His will. To know and obey God through a relationship with His Son, Jesus Christ, who is God Incarnate, God made man."

I sighed, "Yeah, I figured that's what you'd say." Of course, Dawn also thought she was God incarnate, but I didn't see how that had anything to do with the meaning of life. At least now I could leave. I told Paul I was going out for the afternoon.

CHAPTER 15

Professor Braxton lived in Chantilly, almost thirty minutes away, straight up Route 50.

I was anxious to see what he was up to, because I was terribly curious about why he was studying Dawn and what he might be able to tell me about her. It was a good thing I had my whole afternoon free, because he could very well have a whole cornucopia of information. How much of it he'd consent to reveal to me, though, I didn't know, but the information I had about Dawn, what her father never would have told him even if he'd been in a speaking mood, would make his day.

I knew Dawn and I shared a special bond, and felt I'd be able to reach her in a way no one else could, not even her father, once I knew the whole story. I could find a way to get her to agree to obtain the treatment she needed.

Though, suppose I did help her, and then I got involved with her again? Suppose things worked out exactly the way I hoped, would I really want to spend my life caring for someone so impaired? I mean, when you stripped away the crazy God-stuff, what was left anymore? The girl I had loved might no longer exist. Would I want some shell of her, some unadorned semblance?

But I was getting ahead of myself again. It would all work out, I assured myself.

Braxton lived in some pleasant new development, in one of a row of townhouses, each identical to the others, the same peach roofs and white siding. I parked in an empty space not too far away, which was probably reserved for some other homeowner, and composed myself before buzzing.

After another minute or two, a man answered the door. He was a tall, wiry, black man, young-looking for a college professor, maybe in his early thirties at the most. He was dressed in khakis and a short sleeve shirt, and looked down at me with puzzlement, trying to place me. "Can I help you?"

"Professor Braxton?"

"Yes?" Fortunately for me, since I hadn't confirmed an appointment time, he was polite enough, without any gruff annoyance because of the intrusion. However, he did have a blank look on his face. For some reason I'd been expecting him to recognize me, not just because I had a standing appointment, but because I'd assumed he would have seen the yearbook photos, or heard something about me. Though I don't know why Dawn or anyone she might know would mention me, after six years. It presumed she hadn't dated since then, which, as nice as that was to imagine, was unrealistic.

"Hi, I'm Court Richards. You sent me an email that I should drop by."

He nodded. "Right, you said you went to high school with Dawn Gardner."

"That's right." I pulled out the photo of us, feeling very glad to have brought it with me, and held it up for him to see. He took it out of my hand and peered at it closely.

"Interesting," he said, handing it back. "Come on in."

I stepped into the blessed air-conditioning. "I spoke with her father; he told me a little about what you're doing."

His face relaxed, and he said, "Oh really? I doubt he said anything good about me. Come on, Court, my office is on the third floor. And is it Courtland? Like Courtland Milloy? *Washington Post* columnist. Ever read him?"

"No," I said. "And I just go by Court."

"Right, Court for short," he said, amused, as he shut the door. I knew he had made that whole comment just for that last joke; other people had done it before. I recalled a nick-name I was teased with in elementary school, "Shortland," which had been particularly grating when used by sixth-grade bullies playing keep-away with my backpack. On the plus side, at least he hadn't asked if my name was "Courtney."

He led me up the stairs to the third floor, where he and his wife kept their respective offices. His wife's name, he told me, was Sherri, and she was out on some work-related assignment, so it was just the two of us. I peeked into her office, which had a neat desk and chairs and bookcase, and a poster of a wide-eyed child.

A little further down the hall was Braxton's office. It was a nice room, with oak paneling, an easy chair, and a spacious desk, but it was filled with stuff: books and papers and folders and knick-knacks—which included mugs, vacation souvenir palm trees, and little statuettes of the Virgin Mary. Not quite bad enough to be called a mess—there was an overall arrangement to everything, it seemed—but it was hard to see where you'd put anything else. A small camcorder sitting on a folded-up tripod was leaning against a bookshelf that covered the entire back wall, and was crammed with books. Books and sacks of paper sat in piles on the floor, as well. There was no cork board on the wall, but papers were taped up all around. One posted prominently was a large-sized cartoon. It was a single panel, and at the top it read, "An Intelligent Design Theorist Plays Poker." In it, two men are sitting across a table with a pile of chips in the center, with their cards showing. A bushy-bearded man on the right has four aces. The man on the left, angry and pointing at the other, has an assortment of random cards. In the caption the man was saying, "Win? Hardly! The odds of getting four aces is 311,875,200 to 1. It is far too unlikely to have happened by mere chance! Clearly there has been some intelligent intervention—namely you, cheating! So I win! Ha-ha!"

I didn't get it.

Also, I was shocked, though I don't know why, to see there were several pictures of Dawn taped up. Most pictures weren't very clear for one reason or another, but I definitely knew it was her, and I felt a little thrill to see them. All of them were dark indoor pictures, probably from inside clubs, which struck me as odd in spite of her occupation. I'd found her preaching out in the open, like you'd expect a self-declared deity to be doing, and assumed that was her standard *modus operandi*.

He motioned to the easy chair, and he pulled out his desk chair to face me. "So you knew her in high school?"

"We dated, actually, yes." He raised his eyebrows. "Look, let me just get one thing straight here, Professor Braxton."

"Please, Scott."

"Okay, Scott. I came here to talk to you because I want to know what happened to Dawn that led her to such a state. I don't know how much you already know about her, but I'm offering to tell you what I know in exchange."

"Uh-huh. An exchange," he said, leaning back and putting his hand on his chin. "And what makes you think anything happened to her?"

"I ran into her yesterday, at the National Cathedral, and she told me she was God. Now, that's not normal behavior, is it?"

"No, it's not," he said with a smile.

"So then I went to Mr. Gardner's house to see if he could tell me what was up, and he said you were studying Dawn because she joined some cult."

He leaned forward again. "Yes, well," he said.

"He was offended by your research."

"Well, he's not the only one. None of Dawn's roommates from college, at least those that I could find, were willing to talk to me once they found out the reason. But you are?"

"I want to help her. I just need more information."

"You want to help her. Very noble. Though I doubt you'll have much luck." Braxton turned around partly and took a folder off his desk, and placed it in his lap. He opened it, and reached back to grab a pen, and scribbled something on the top page before returning it.

He looked back up at me. "Look, let me just tell you, right up front, there's nothing racial about this project. I know what you're thinking—professor from Howard—but there's nothing here that corresponds to any construct of black theology. After all, Dawn is white and her followers are multi-racial. I thought there might be some aspects of social justice to it, given the penury of her cohorts, but she doesn't focus her concerns on economic equality, and even if she did, they're too immature to care. Of course, her claiming to be a divine incarnation does engender discussions of God's imminence, but since she's not really God that relates more to her personal psychopathology than to any theological imperative."

I held up my hand. "Wait, there's a black theology?"

Braxton raised his head in peals of laughter while I looked on in bewilderment. Finally he turned back to me, still grinning. "Okay, 101 for you. I'll keep it traditional. Anyway, I'm not teaching any classes over the summer semester, and I'd planned to use the time to make some headway on my new book; but then I got involved in trying to help this girl, and it became a distraction from my work, facilitating a natural tendency to procrastinate, until I found myself rather consumed by it. Eventually I figured, I may not be able to help her, but if I get enough information, at least I can turn it into an article or something to justify the time spent."

"What kind of article?" I said. I liked that he wasn't just using her to advance his career but was interested in helping her, too; but if he'd already written her off, what more could I do?

"About cults, of course. But I never said she'd joined a cult, more like she's trying to start one. The Cult of Dawn."

"The Cult of Dawn," I repeated slowly, filled with sorrow at the depths to which she had fallen. But of course; hadn't Molly been recruiting?

Braxton continued: "Now, she's not very serious about it. Or organized. No compound or henchman or anything, or even a membership list, just a bunch of people hanging out, teens mostly. None of her putative followers have been brainwashed, as far as I can tell. No glazed-over expressions here. She works at it so little it's amazing she has as many devotees as she does. Though on the other hand it's not really surprising; there are always some people who will gladly follow any spiritual nonsense. Look, it's a hot topic in the field, you know, emerging religions. What she preaches here is just the usual New Age crap you can find anywhere, but she's got a bunch of actual people listening to her. And not just the homeless ones either; I've seen college kids, even some government interns, sitting around, awe-struck, soaking up her gibberish. I know, it's not all gibberish. Some of what I've heard from her is pretty slick, I'll tell you. Nevertheless."

"Do you think she's schizophrenic? Can't someone help her?"

The Professor shrugged. "Schizophrenia? Sure, there are treatments, medications to control it. But there's no way to get her committed or force her into therapy. Involuntary commitment is only if you're a danger to yourself or others, not for simple delusions. This doesn't qualify. Besides, I'm not entirely sure she is schizophrenic. She probably is. You don't just claim to be God without being seriously delusional. But it's not the standard form of schizophrenia I'm sure you're familiar with. She doesn't have hallucinations or hear voices, at least according to her. I rather foolishly forgot myself once and asked if she heard the voice of God, and she smugly replied, 'Every time I speak.' But look, I talked to her, my wife talked to her, and I showed a video I made to one of my colleagues in the Psych Department, to try to get a diagnosis. He said her behavior, her speech, her emotions, are all rational and controlled, not like you'd find in classical schizophrenia. She doesn't have any negative symptoms at all, and her only positive symptom is her delusion that she's God. That's her only symptom, period, though it's a pretty major one. She doesn't suffer from paranoia, or extreme anxiety, or social detachment, or any other intense negative emotions. Yet her delusion is too far-ranging to be just an initial symptom of a late-emerging illness. It doesn't just develop in the late teens, you know; it can appear later in life. So we're all perplexed. He thought it might be something closer to a pure psychological breakdown than the more biological schizophrenia."

"So she had a breakdown?" I was getting more and more confused.

Braxton then said: "God only knows. I'm just saying nobody really knows what's wrong with her. She's obviously insane, but my shrink friend says he needs to interview her personally before he could make a confident diagnosis. I plan on trying to arrange it at some point.

"But look, let me tell you how I got involved with Dawn in the first place. First you should know that my wife Sherri is a social worker. She works for the Department of Child Welfare in the District, and deals with a lot of runaways, and abused kids. She goes around to the Youth Shelters in the city to talk to them, try to keep tabs on them. Sherri first saw Dawn in one shelter, down in Anacostia, I think it was. Dawn wasn't staying there, that was clear enough. She's too old. But she wasn't an employee, either, or even a volunteer. She just showed up to hang around for a while, then disappeared again. The fellow who runs the place, Ortega, I think, thought she was harmless, so he paid her no mind. She wasn't selling them drugs, or anything, which was probably his only concern. But one day Sherri was talking to one girl, and this girl mentioned Dawn had taken away her 'bad feelings,' as she put it. She was instantly suspicious, as you can imagine, and asked her how Dawn had done this, and the girl said Dawn had put her hands on her head. She started questioning the others kids and finally someone admitted to her that Dawn had told them she was God."

"Doing miracles for them?"

"It seemed like it. So the next time she saw Dawn she asked her about this, and Dawn admitted it, very casually. She wouldn't do a miracle for her, of course, at least not just then, but she said she would be at this nightclub later that night, and she could come by and talk at length if she wanted to. So she went, and obviously brought me along, because I'm an expert in the field of theology. This was back in May, and I've been tracking her and debating her ever since. Usually I find her at the various clubs and bars she plays at—do you know she is a DJ? Unbelievable, huh? What kind of job is that for a god?—and we have little impromptu debates. As for the rest of her life, you have no idea how much detective work I've put in trying to piece together her life, and I still have no idea where she spends the majority of her time. Or where she sleeps. Most of what I've learned about her has come from things she's told me herself.

"Sherri was told by Ortega the other day that Dawn hasn't been at that particular shelter since. It's strange, but she says the kids there are disappointed. I don't think any of them really believed she was God, but her presence meant something and they seemed to have had a surprising fondness for her." He sighed. "Dawn's probably upset that Sherri introduced her to me. I think she enjoys our sparring, but otherwise she's a reluctant research subject. Anyway, did that help any?"

"Not really," I said. "I still don't know what happened to her."

"Well, I doubt I can help you there, as I explained; but tell you what, you sit for an interview, and then I'll answer any other questions you might have, to the best of my knowledge."

"Sure."

"You mind if I record it?"

"Um... no."

"Good." He got up and went across the room to retrieve the camcorder. He brought it back with him, and began setting it up. He opened up the tripod and steadied it, then connected the camcorder to his computer.

As he fiddled with the controls, I said, "You're taking videos of everything."

"Sure," he said absently. "I got this camera for my birthday last year, so I'm trying to put it to good use. Why not? I should record all these interviews anyway, and I might make a documentary out of all this stuff. I've always wanted to make a documentary." He looked over and smiled. "Nothing serious, you know, but I might get the Fine Art Department to put it together, give it a professional glean, and maybe it'll get a place in the school library, if nothing else. I don't expect anything more out of it. Though you never know," he shrugged. "I am a well-respected academic. It might get a broadcast airing. You know Howard runs its own Public Broadcasting station? WHUT, Channel 32?"

Wonderful, another egotist. "Yeah. But you have videos of Dawn?"

"Oh, sure. I'll show you a few afterwards, if you want. It's pretty fascinating. Say," he stopped momentarily, "Mind if I see that photo again?"

I handed it to him, and he went over to a scanner and let it capture the image. He handed it back while he saved it, then returned to the camcorder. My image popped up on the monitor, showing the camera was working. I stiffened, feeling uncomfortable being thrust into the spot of having to create a formal record, but I was willing to do what it took to get some answers. He turned the monitor away, so that I couldn't see my image and let it distract me. "You ready?" he said, leaning back in his chair.

"Yeah," I said without enthusiasm.

"You said you ran into her at the National Cathedral yesterday. Is this the first time you've seen her since high school?"

"Basically, yeah." I looked from his face over to the camera. "Which way should I be looking?"

"At me is fine."

"Okay." I focused on his face, and tried to forget the camera. "We broke up that summer because we were going off to different colleges, and that was the last I heard from her. Although I've googled her before, so I did know about the deejaying, but that's it."

"Tell me about your encounter with her yesterday." He seemed very professional in the way he was directing this, like he did it all the time.

I told him what I had seen, how she had been blessing people, and then her conversation with Tyrone, and finally her conversation with me. I repeated most of what we'd discussed, only leaving out the comments about Molly—and Ahmed—but I hadn't understood some of what she had told me, particularly her sermon, or whatever it had been, so I couldn't really explain it. He listened carefully, nodding his head, raising his eyebrows occasionally but remaining silent.

When I was finished, he commented, "Typical cult rhetoric."

"What?"

"You were at a church, but she was holding her services outside. Get the message? You have to leave the church to find the true God. Typical." He thought for a moment, then said, "Just curious, she said your brother knew the meaning of life?"

I repeated what Paul had told me on that subject.

"So I don't get it. Dawn never talks about Christianity unless you specifically ask her. Did she know he was a fundamentalist?"

"Well, she remembered him well enough, so I assume so. He was like that in high school."

"But she'd seen him during her work as a DJ?"

I saw his concern and shook my head. "He turned 21 in April, so he's been playing a little, but it's pretty mild stuff; he doesn't get drunk or anything."

"Still, how did she know he hadn't changed in the intervening years?" That was a good question, to which I didn't have an answer.

Instead I asked, "Did you ever ask her what the meaning of life was?"

He shook his head. "It's a pointless question; purely subjective. Getting back to your conversation—she lied about where she was going to be?"

"Yeah…" I couldn't explain it to him, since my encounter with Molly was too embarrassing to divulge on a potentially permanent video. "I don't understand why I couldn't find her on the web, though. Isn't she running a business? Doesn't she need a website so people can hire her for their parties? I thought everybody had a website these days."

Braxton shook his head. "She doesn't need a website to advertise, she's got notoriety. The best word-of-mouth buzz money can't buy; one of the perks of being God, or insane, however you want to see it. Everybody already knows who she is. You should hear it when she plays 'Personal Jesus' at the clubs. She has this mix of Marilyn Manson's cover of 'Personal Jesus' that she plays at every show, and everybody goes crazy because they know exactly what she's referring to. Yes, and plus, making potential customers hunt her down adds to her aura of mystery. *Why* anyone hires her, though, that I don't know. She has a lot of fans, but it still seems like it would be pretty risky; she must attract plenty of other wackos." He shifted in his chair. "Let's move on. You said you dated her in high school? How did that come about? How'd you meet her, originally?"

"Well," I said with a sigh. I had been anticipating this revelation, in fact it was the whole reason I was here, but I had some trepidations about it being recorded for posterity. I wasn't sure I wanted to share my personal issues with the whole world, or whatever small audience his video would eventually find. "Of course I'd seen her before, in the halls and stuff, but I only got involved with her because we were in a group therapy together."

He nodded seriously. "What kind of therapy?"

"You know, psychiatric therapy. For bad teens."

That, at least, got a grin out of him. "Bad in what way? Drugs?"

"No, depression. Suicidal."

His eyes widened in surprise. "Dawn was suicidal? Did she ever make an attempt?"

"Sure; we all did, that's how we wound up there. She slashed her wrists."

He was stupefied for a moment, so I supposed I had done my job. Finally he shook his head.

"What?" I asked. "That doesn't make her crazy. I was there too; we were just depressed about life. We were all on Prozac and Paxil and Zoloft and a few other things, sitting around talking about appropriate ways to solve our problems and crap like that."

I remembered the whole thing too well; there were nine of us, plus our psychiatrist, Mrs. Dodd, whom we were referred to by the hospital after our suicide attempts. But Dawn was the only one I noticed, the thick bandages around her wrists, white puffy handcuffs that bobbed in and out from beneath the long sleeves of her shirt, the look on her face, sometimes vacant, sometimes tragic, but always beautiful. Me, I had no physical scars; I had overdosed on some pills. I had expected to die, but in retrospect it wasn't a very serious attempt. Paul came home from school and found me passed out and called 911. And my shocked parents made sure I went to this psychiatrist afterwards. So he thinks he saved my life, and lorded it over me for the longest time, as if he wasn't superior enough already.

"Was Dawn depressed over anything in particular?"

"Well, other than serious high school teen moodiness and exaggerated melodrama, I'm not really sure."

"What happened to her mother?" he asked suddenly.

Mr. Gardner has apparently been offended by this question, so I hesitated in answering it, but I didn't think it mattered, not at this point. "I don't really know. Dawn's mother died when she was a kid. I never really asked her anything more about it. Well, I did ask how she died, and Dawn said she had cancer, but that was all. It didn't seem like a useful subject to bring up again." I paused. "Well no, there was one time. In addition to our group therapy, we had individual therapy sessions, and Dawn and I would sometimes discuss what our shrink had said. We saw the same person, Mrs. Dodd. Dawn told me she kept harping on her mother, because she was convinced that was at the root of Dawn's depression. Dawn disagreed. She told me her mother had died when she was three years old, so she had no memories of her, and she had spent her whole life growing up without her. It had never bothered her before, and she didn't think it made any sense that she would suddenly become suicidally depressed over it at 17. But I always thought she would have liked her mother's advice and guidance as she was becoming an adult, graduating high school and going away to college. Maybe the prospect of leaving home was sub-conscientiously more frightening to her than she wanted to admit."

"I see. Mrs. Dodd, you say?" said the Professor.

"I don't remember what her first name was." I had always liked Mrs. Dodd, because while I had some low self-esteem issues of my own to address, she didn't see any reason for a more serious depression, and decided that my major problems were entirely bio-chemical and could be fixed with a higher dose of Prozac. That suited me fine.

"Okay. So did Dawn's mood improve?"

"Sure," I said.

Dawn had been, at the beginning, a bit morose and morbid, and she stayed that way for the first few weeks that I knew her, though her mood brightened when I asked her out. We were encouraged in this, because being with other people, having an active social life, talking about things intimately, and so on, all that was supposed to help us recover. Still, I had a much easier time of it than she did, though I'm not sure why. For me, at least, having gone as far as I did in actually attempting to kill myself, and experiencing a "death" of sorts, had been freeing. I had had a turning point, the moment when I woke up in the hospital and had been relieved, if only slightly, that I was still here. That moment alone was therapy enough. It made me realize I didn't want to die after all. Plus people treated me differently afterwards. They became concerned about me, and paid a lot of attention to me, which I kind of liked. Not everybody, of course; I don't think any of my teachers ever even knew what I'd done. I only missed several days of school, and then I had to go back, as though nothing had happened. That had been weird; I sat in class taking notes, all the while thinking to myself *I could be dead right now.* They only make a big deal about it, with the assemblies and the grief counselors, if you're successful. Nobody ever hears about it if you fail, as Dawn and I had. So it was only the few people who knew that lavished me with attention. All except Paul. He paid attention, all right, but his opinion of me had darkened considerably. For a while he was suspicious and critical of anything I did. This was the main reason he disliked Dawn so strongly. It was never so much about how she behaved, but about how it might affect me. I knew Paul worried that instead of me helping her, she would bring me down again, and that we would end up in some sort of Romeo and Juliet double suicide, as far-fetched as that sounded. Still, Dawn wasn't the same as I was. She had gone through the moment without experiencing the realization. She just continued to float about in her dreams, and it took a long time for her to rise to the surface.

I reminisced in broad strokes about my time with Dawn as I sat there before the Professor and his camera. It was nothing special, just your typical teenage romance. We went to movies, hung out at the mall, made out when no one else was around. Neither of us had been stellar students, and Dawn had no particular interests that I could recall. She didn't write poetry or anything. Occasionally we read together, taking turns reading out loud from a book for a few pages before handing it over. She said, halfheartedly, that she thought she would become a lawyer, but that was because it was what her father wanted. Though what she wanted for herself I don't know. She didn't know either; she was still thinking about it—we both were.

We spent a lot of time together the summer after we graduated, because we were going away to different colleges and had agreed to break up. Neither one of us wanted to, but we'd both decided it would be too difficult to try to maintain a long-distance relationship—and this would have been very long distance, since I was staying here in

Virginia and she'd gotten accepted by UCLA, of all places. It was best not to try to hang on but to make a clean break.

What the Professor wanted to know was whether we'd ever had sex.

"I don't want to be intrusive, but it really is very important," he said by way of an apology. "Sex and how it's viewed is a very important element of religion. But I'm sure you already knew that. All religions seem to go one of two ways. Either they play it down, relegating it to a necessity, or even demonizing it in all its aspects as sin and filth, or else they embrace it and emphasize it, giving it great importance and infusing its practice with spiritual properties. Remember the furor surrounding *The Da Vinci Code*? The idea of Jesus, for instance, having sex is outright blasphemous. He and his mother are virgins, and sex is prohibited for Catholic clergy and considered mostly a mortal sin anywhere outside marriage. Plenty of cult leaders follow this to an extreme, and use it to prohibit most relationships as a means of tightening their control on their followers. On the other hand, some cult leaders go to the opposite end and use their power to demand sex from their followers under the guise of freeing them. I don't think Dawn is either one, but her views are very progressive."

"It seemed to me she was encouraging it," I said, feeling a bit contemptuous. "But yeah, sure, of course we had sex. We were both virgins before we met, if you want to know. I think we did it half a dozen a dozen times over the course of that year."

"All right," he said with a smile. "The point being she had no strong feelings for or against it."

"No," I said. I remembered the first time we had been together. It had been a few weeks before Christmas, sort of an early present to each other. It had been snowing, and the forest of glistening trees completely surrounded her house, from top to bottom, in a burrow of pure white. We stood in her bedroom, naked, and I remember thinking how perfect her body was, how soft and smooth. I felt ashamed because I was skinny and didn't think I was attractive. We played a little, touching each other, before getting into bed. It was wonderfully intense and earthy, but afterwards she said it hurt, and bled a little, and we were both briefly afraid. Later, though, we both felt newly mature and pleased with each other. I wanted those feelings to last forever.

"Is there anything else?" I asked.

"Did she ever go to church? Was she religious or philosophically inclined?"

"Not really. She and her father weren't religious. And she inclined to it in the sense you'd expect. I mean, sure, we had the occasional discussion on the meaning of life or what death was like. Obviously we talked about death, and she was a little obsessed with it at first, which was, after all, why we were in counseling. But she got better and that went away." Well, not entirely; there was her attraction to SADD and their creepy "Day of Silence." That was the most obvious instance, but there were some others. Still, as far as it went, it was a mild curiosity; she never became a goth or drew tombstones or anything.

"What did she think death would be like?"

"She thought it would be nice and peaceful. So did I, which is why we were suicidal. We wanted to escape the stress of life and go to heaven and be happy. I mean, there were some kids in our group who were worried about hell, but that was only after the fact, after they'd lived to regret it." I remember how sternly Paul had lectured both me and Dawn on how we had risked eternal damnation for wanting to end the precious life God had bestowed upon us. We didn't believe it, but by that time I at least had become uneasy and glad I hadn't had to find out. Before the pills, though, I only thought of the peace death would bring. It wasn't so much about heaven—I'd been fairly religious when I was younger but that interest had mostly dissipated by then—because, while I was sure I would go to heaven, it was an abstraction; what I really anticipated was simply being released from the life I was in. I felt so... weighed down. I was so tired all the time I felt like I was already dead. Even then I couldn't get to sleep at night; I was usually up until two AM watching TV before I was finally able to fall asleep, then getting up at six to go to school. I still went to school every day, sleepwalking through my classes without paying any attention, simply because it required less energy than skipping. Skipping involved coming up with excuses, which required thinking. In any case, nobody noticed, nobody cared. I felt so pressured, both mentally and physically. I know now how silly that was; it was only high school, after all, but at the time I was just so miserable and so hopeless all I could think about was escape. Escape from school, family, life, everything. Heaven had to be waiting because anything was better than this. Even the small voice in the back of my mind that warned me I might wind up in a worse state didn't frighten me; how could anything be worse? Hell might even be better, because then at least everyone else I knew (from our group) would be in hell too, and I wouldn't be alone in a world of obliviously cheerful fools. I know Dawn felt the same. For months she had been cutting herself with a razor, working her way up to finally slashing her wrists. No one ever noticed these little shallow cuts up and down her arms, and she'd all but flaunted them; she wore short sleeve shirts most days, even as the weather cooled. She confided in me that she had been troubled enough by the suggestion of hell that she had read things, reports of near death experiences, even fiction like Dante's *Inferno*, where suicides for some reason get turned into trees. She didn't see what was so bad about that, being a tree. It sounded kind of peaceful, actually.

Suddenly I had a weird thought as I remembered from our discussion all those years ago the suicides were on Dante's Circle Seven, the same circle of hell that blasphemers and sodomites wound up in. Hmm.

He then asked: "But she didn't have any particular beliefs? Like reincarnation or anything?"

"We thought we would go to heaven, but we left it vague and undefined. If she thought anything beyond that she never shared it with me."

"Interesting," he said "Did she have any thoughts about the Millennium? You met her before it changed over to 2000, right? What were her thoughts on the end of the world?"

"None," I smirked. "We didn't buy into all that Y2K nonsense." Dawn had asked me, as New Year's approached, if the two of us, at least, should be disappointed the world wasn't ending. I had been pretty sure at the time it was a joke. She'd been doing better by then, so I'd dismissed it with a chuckle.

"How about drugs?" Braxton asked. "Non-prescription, I mean. Marijuana, cocaine, anything like that?"

"No," I said, feeling offended on her behalf. "We both smoked for a while; cigarettes I mean. Everybody in our group did. But it didn't last. Neither of us got addicted. That was all."

"I had to ask," he shrugged. "She is a DJ. One makes certain assumptions."

I was getting pretty tired with the interview, and was relieved when he announced it was over. He turned back to his desk, turned the screen around, and stopped the camera from recording.

"Does the Millennium have anything to do with this?" I asked as he typed. "I mean, she's not claiming to be the Second Coming, right?"

"She's not."

"So whatever happened to her to make her think she's God happened in college, right?" I asked as he typed.

"You're still thinking about a definitive event," he said, without turning around. "It's a Hollywood-esque concept, that something must have suddenly caused her mind to snap, but it's unlikely. Probably she just deteriorated over time. Maybe the Millennium played a part, maybe it didn't. Maybe 9/11 did, maybe not. Maybe it's a little of everything. It's impossible to say. A lot may have happened to her intellectually that we'll never discover unless she tells us. She may not even be able to piece it together herself. Ideas come from reading and thinking, and develop on their own, mixing with other ideas to become something new and personal. And let's not forget the biological aspect. An abnormal brain chemistry could make her prone to delusions, magical thinking, and paranoid fantasies, all symptoms of schizophrenia. Not that she has the usual paranoia, a fear that people are conspiring against her, but that's just a type of defense mechanism to allow someone who thinks they have little value to inflate their sense of importance. Because if the government is putting its enormous resources into spying on you, then you must be pretty damn important indeed. What Dawn has is really just an alternative form of that. She, an insignificant nobody to the rest of the world, thinks the whole universe revolves around her. A literal god-complex."

"Okay, but what about the other people? Why the hell would anyone take her seriously? Especially educated people?"

He finished what he was doing and turned back to me, smiling. "Well, that's a question you could ask of any religion. Believing, in a general sense, that there are larger forces in the universe that we can't understand is one thing, because after all, the universe is pretty huge. But a lot of the nitty-gritty details of most faiths are damned strange, to say the least. Or at least, as things to consider seriously.

Religions all have some grand ideas that are intelligent, and beneficial, but those come wrapped up with a lot of bizarre nonsense, and sometimes it can be hard to separate one from the other, even for an educated person."

"This is different. Dawn's just some girl, an insignificant nobody, like you said. How could she be God?"

"You could ask the same thing about Jesus, or Buddha, or Krishna, or any of a score of others. If you're willing to concede that God could become incarnate and walk among us in human form, then there's no reason to believe that it couldn't happen today. Dawn has made this exact argument to me herself."

This was a repeat of the debate between Paul and Ahmed from yesterday. I found it odd that I was in Paul's shoes now, defending orthodoxy, but I pressed ahead. "But Jesus did miracles to prove himself."

"Did he?" Braxton asked, arching his eyebrow. "That's arguable. The way I see it, if we grant that the biblical account of Jesus is accurate in at least a broad sense, then it seems Jesus was very clearly what today we'd call a faith-healer. You know, where they play on people's own belief and hyped-up expectations of receiving miracles, and toss in the occasional exaggerated or even made-up anecdote, to convince them that miracles are really happening. There are a lot of the elements in the gospel accounts that read very similar to what we find in faith healers throughout history and throughout the world, including my favorite: tell the guy who doesn't get a miracle it's his own fault because he doesn't have enough faith. Even today these people draw huge crowds. Even today, when people should know better, when scientific studies have demonstrated time and again it doesn't work, people still fall for it. How much more easily could people have been duped two millennia ago? And these are just one step up from most cults, where miracles are fraudulent or mere rumors, or even entirely absent, yet they attract followers. On a different level, consider that Buddha and Muhammad never did any miracles at all, yet they accumulated thousands of followers within their own lifetimes who went on to build religions that now have hundreds of millions of believers. Miracles aren't necessary. People are drawn to a particular faith out of a sense of wanting to be part of a group, to belong to something greater than themselves. Humans are social creatures. There's a fundamental human need for belonging, which is a need for the security of the pack. And there's a need for the security of knowledge, to tame the harshness and unpredictability of the world. And the fear of death. Religion answers all of that, and that's all it is."

After taking in everything I was afraid to ask anything else, but he still hadn't answered my question. "But what about Dawn? What draws people into believing that she's God?"

Braxton leaned back in his chair and steepled his fingers. "Well, Dawn knows what people want. She's putting her psychology training to good use."

"What training?"

"She didn't tell you? She got her bachelor's degree in psychology."

"Psychology?" I said, astonished. "How did that happen?"

"You'd have to ask her. After she told me she'd gone to UCLA, I had them send me her transcript. 3.0 GPA, no honors, no minors. She had a single course in religion, a survey course on Eastern Religions, in which, I'm pleased to note, she got an 'A.'"

"But she did graduate."

"Sure. Her mental acuity is fine. She's able to construct very well-reasoned, rational-sounding arguments."

"But what is it she's telling people?"

The Professor then continued: "Well, it's not so much what she says as what she does. And what she does is quite astonishing. Simply put, she goes around telling people that she's sorry. That is, she, God, is sorry for making their lives so screwed up. She's sorry for all the pain and suffering in the world that she created. And people take her seriously! I mean, the implications of it, theologically! Can you imaging God apologizing? Expressing remorse? Plus there's the old debate about free will, and she basically rejects its assumptions. She's God, she made everything the way it is, she doesn't blame anyone but herself for way things have turned out. And all these people! I mean, I sure as hell wouldn't want to be told I had no free will. But to a lot of these people, she's basically telling them they're not responsible for their actions, it's not their fault if their lives are miserable. People like not having any responsibility. They like playing the victim. And that's what she's telling them, be innocent victims, I'm the one who's done wrong, I'm the one behind everything here. But to believe that, you have to accept that she really is the one with all the power. And they do. It's just incredible."

"She apologizes to people?"

"Don't you see how brilliant that is? This is why I've been so fascinated with her. Everybody always says, 'God loves you, Jesus loves you.' It can be a great thing to hear, very uplifting. That's what Dawn's saying to these people. But unlike some deities, she doesn't just love believers, but everybody. And better yet, she's here to tell them in person, instead of letting some minister do it for her. Can you imagine God coming to embrace you personally? And she has total empathy. She doesn't say, you need to get right with God, you need to stop sinning and have more faith. She says, you don't need to do a single blessed thing, because I made you the way you are, which of course jives with what people are taught in school since kindergarten, that you're special and just be yourself. Now, it's a fact that the religions that demand more from the faithful have more devout followers. The more you invest in it, the more dependent on it you are. Religions that make no demands usually don't get very far, because if you don't have to do anything to get into heaven, then what's the point? Why bother believing? Even Buddhism needs its Karma. I think the only reason Dawn gets it to work is that it's not about starting a movement, it's about her personally being God. If she dropped out of the picture tomorrow, I don't think her friends would band together to form a new church in her name. There's not much substance to it, ultimately. Though, she might end up in the New Age's list of luminaries, as one of the 'ascended masters' they all revere. That's what's there, of course. The subtle hint that you, too, can attain a level of higher consciousness and become God if you follow her teachings. You know, be good and meditate and all that. And there's the implication that it's a quick and easy enlightenment, too, given her age. She certainly hasn't spent decades meditating in a cave like you're supposed to. Almost all major religious figures were in their thirties, at least, before they became divine incarnations or prophets or whatever.

"Anyway," he said abruptly, turning back to the computer. He proceeded to disconnect the camcorder and fold up the tripod.

As he carried it across the room to where it had stood before, I said, "So, um, out of curiosity, what is it you believe?" I'd become puzzled about this while listening to him talk; he taught religion yet seemed to have a pretty critical view of it.

"Me?" He set the tripod against the bookcase and looked over at me. "Well, normally I never tell my students about my own beliefs, nor do I ever ask them about theirs, because I don't want to be accused of bias, which has been happening at a lot of universities in the past few years. Plus, I do teach at a divinity school. I don't have tenure yet, so if my fellow faculty members ever found out what I really believed, I could possibly lose my job. But you were honest with me about your personal life, so I don't mind telling you; just don't spread it around. I'm actually an atheist."

"An atheist?" I was aghast. "You mean you don't believe in anything?"

"I believe in what's real. I believe in science and logic. But I don't believe in the made-up fantasies of any religion, or any god." He walked over and sat back down in his chair. "Does that bother you?" he asked, smiling.

"Well, no, I guess not." Despite the vagaries of my own beliefs, I still accepted the basics, and I'd never really questioned them. Often I felt that God didn't care about me, but I never questioned his existence. It was too ingrained in me. "It just seems kind of strange, that you'd teach it but not believe in it. That you'd devote your whole life to it if you don't think any of it's real."

He laughed and leaned forward. He seemed pleased that I'd asked; I was probably the first person other than his wife he could freely discuss it with. "I like religion. I've always been interested in it. I used to be very devout when I was a teenager. I wanted to be a minister. But the thing is, see, that I'm an intellectual. So I approached my faith not with the emotional sentiment that other people have, the desire to feel God's love, God's presence, but with a philosophical attitude that sought to understand God, to make religion make sense, if you will. In college I majored in philosophy, and became very interested in theodicies, the attempts to justify God, to explain how there can be evil if God is both omnipotent and omnibenevolent. Along with that went the study of the various proofs of God's existence. I studied all the proofs that had been developed through the centuries, with the awareness that none of them are perfect, as I studied their criticism, and eventually tried to develop my own. This is all part and parcel of the study of philosophy. Most freshmen go through the same sort of thing, a mental investigation of the divine. It's a major topic of study, in fact, since so much philosophy revolves around God and the nature of reality and morals and all those things. I'm not claiming anything unusual here. It's just that most people accept the arguments that justify belief, allowing it to reinforce what they already believe, even though they implicitly understand those arguments are imperfect. And I didn't. The more I learned, the harder it was for me to continue to accept it. Not just philosophically, but scientifically. All those scientific truths—like evolution, cosmology, and neurobiology—that were impossible to sublimate to orthodoxy. And yes, there was my interest in black theology, with its concerns of justice and oppression and its germane distrust of traditional divine authoritarianism. In short, I came to doubt what I'd believed all my life. Then I finally just gave up on it. I realized I could never be a minister, because I could never give people the easy answers they're looking for, because they don't exist.

"The thing is, I couldn't get away from it. I liked learning about religion, about the many varied religions of the world. It was absolutely fascinating. It was what I loved, and I didn't have any other interest, so I decided to stick with it. And here I am, teaching it at one of the nation's premier universities. I love my job, and if you have that, life is good."

"Even though you think it isn't true. That it's meaningless."

"Lots of things are meaningless, in a way. Do you berate English professors, since the literature they devote themselves to isn't 'true' either? Or the writers, who write that literature? Or musicians, who just manipulate sound? Or actors, or artists, or sports stars, or any number of professionals who work with things that aren't 'real'? Besides, it's not meaningless. It's incredibly relevant to the world at large. Religion is one of the most inclusive subjects there is. Everything relates to it. There's philosophy, of course, then there's history, the history of the faiths themselves and the impact they've had on world historical events, shaping nations, wars, laws. And politics. Religion has a tremendous impact on politics, always has and always will. Many of the issues today are founded on religious principles. So much of what's going on in the world today is directly attributable to the influence of religion, especially in the Middle East. Their beliefs are a driving force, and it's imperative we understand that. And culture. Society. Language. A lot of common sayings we have come from the Bible, you know. Arabic is a unifying language of the otherwise diverse Muslim world because it's the language of the Qur'an. And art. So much art had been focused on religious imagery, religious symbolism. Literature, too, has used religious themes forever. Science. The interplay between science and religion has had a tremendous impact on the world, because both, in a sense, speak to the same thing. They both strive to understand the secret workings of the universe, and sometimes they add to each other, other times they conflict. Religion, in one way or another, influences our lives in every way. The fact is, humans are religious animals. The search for meaning is written into our DNA. The fact that we believe, or at least search for God is, I'll submit, the very thing that makes us human, that makes us different from the animals. All those other things people thought separated us from the lower creatures have been found among them. Language, use of tools, teaching, planning, all those things have been observed in animals. Maybe not to the same extent as we posses them, but they are present nonetheless. The only true limit left, the only defining, unique characteristic of humans is their religion. Since the beginning we have believed. Neanderthal bones have been found laid out in shallow graves. You won't find that anywhere else. No other animals bury their dead. No other animals build temples, or pray, or worship sacred objects. It's a fundamental aspect of higher conscious that only we posses.

I will never accept artificial intelligence as being sentient until a computer tells me it believes in God."

I was struggling to keep everything straight. I probably should have been taking notes. "Even though that would be wrong, as you see it?"

"Hell yes. Disbelief is logical and unemotional. Belief is intuitive and emotional. It is the essence of love and art, of all things human. Even though I'm more certain than ever there is no God, through studying the many facets of faith I've come to respect it greatly, even more than when I actually believed it. Like most, I once thought, 'This is right, everything else is wrong, so why do all those fools not see the truth?' But now I realize they're all wrong in an absolute sense, that they all bubble up from within, from the human experience, I can look at them all equally, as the vivid tapestry of human expressions they are. They all have their elegance, along with their absurdity. If I had a perfect proof for the non-existence of God, something unarguable, that would instantly convert anyone who heard it, I don't know that I would share it. I'm not one of those aggressive people who think the world would be better off without religion. What the world needs is a better religion, something not so divisive, something that can inspire people."

"And you think Dawn can help create a better religion?"

He was surprised. "No. I didn't say that. I'm just speaking in generalities. Though I do think her religion has its value, and I appreciate her efforts. I do think she has the potential, at least in a small way, to do some good in the world." I squirmed in my seat, remembering telling her those very same words as a challenge, to get her to perform a miracle. I doubted she would end up doing much good; I doubted she was truly aware of the larger needs of others, whatever Braxton said.

"So," he said clapping his hands together, "would you like to see some of my videos of her?"

CHAPTER 16

I don't know how many videos Braxton had, but he showed me quite a few of them. Most were very short, a minute or two, or less; if he was going to keep up this documentarian business, he was going to have to buy a bigger memory card for his camcorder. They were outside, in parks and on streets, and inside, in clubs and in a house which I assumed was the youth shelter he'd mentioned.

The first stretch was not of Dawn but of some of the youths who were her presumed followers. They looked invariably like ordinary teens, of all races; their clothes were old and worn and out of fashion, but otherwise they seemed fine. Some of them gave their first names, others didn't. There were little bits of video, practically commercials, of these kids talking about how awesome Dawn was, or how nice she was to them, or how she'd made them feel better. Those last claims were vague but strangely heartfelt, and they led into miracle stories. Braxton must have arranged them, because they got progressively more serious. Dawn had read some girl's mind. She had predicted the future. She pulled money out of thin air. She cured depression and anxiety. She healed twisted ankles and sprained wrists. A fat kid claimed he'd worn glasses all his life until she'd touched him and given him perfect vision. A perfectly healthy looking girl claimed Dawn had cured her of a meth addiction. And then came the final coup de grâce. It featured a Hispanic male who I realized was the youth who had been talking with Molly at the Cathedral yesterday, sitting on a bench somewhere in the city, wearing the exact same outfit I had seen him in yesterday. I guess it was the only one he had. He said his name was Diego, and in awestruck excitement he reported how he had been dying of AIDS and Dawn had healed him with her touch.

After the video parade was over, before Braxton moved on to his next segment, he told me that naturally he was sure Diego was mistaken. "I doubt he had ever had AIDS. He's too old to have been born with it, and he's too young to have been infected, or at least, for the progress of the disease to have developed to an extent where he would have been dying from it. It takes years for AIDS to kill you. I suspect he just had pneumonia or something and recovered from it naturally."

"He did look pretty healthy."

"Sure they're healthy. Why not? These kids are runaways, not drug addicts. Drug addicts wouldn't bother with her. They only care about their next hit; they're not likely to sit still long enough for her sermons."

"That one girl mentioned being healed of a drug addiction."

He smiled over at me. "It's not entirely impossible. The literal presence of God in their lives might spur an addict to get clean; acknowledging God is, after all, part of most twelve-step programs."

He moved on to the videos of Dawn. These were a little longer then the recordings of her followers, but still pretty short—just fragments of what I assumed to be her sermons.

Sitting at an outdoor picnic table:

She was watching someone out of the camera, who said, "Girl, there's nothing spiritual about being poor. People just say that so no one has to do anything about it."

"Oh, no, you're absolutely right," Dawn answered, sitting very still. "That's my point. There is no connection. Just because Jesus and Buddha had nothing, doesn't mean that's the only way to go about it. In fact, they're actually the exception; most of the great religious figures of history were very wealthy, if not outright monarchs. You're absolutely correct, 'poverty is a blessing' is just an axiom meant to keep people in their place." She chuckled, her face lighting up. "I'm starting to sound like Marx! I just wanted to make a point about myself here. Giving away money won't get you to heaven any faster. Indigence isn't a cause of becoming holy, it's a result, because when you've experienced divine unity, you no longer need such mundane things like money. So you give it away to those who do. It's what happened to me. When I was a seeker, I kept hold of most of my money. Only after I found enlightenment did I give it all away, because only then was I free from material longings."

Indoors, in a dark room, sitting underneath a light fixture, leaning against a wall; probably in the back of some club, because there was a faint thumping of bass and she had headphones, the bulky kind that fit tightly over the ears, around her neck:

She was looking directly at the camera, listening to the person holding it. "Tell me, Dawn," said Braxton, his voice booming on the recording. "How did you become God?"

"One doesn't become God. God is eternal, you know that," she said.

"Let me rephrase. How did you become enlightened? How did you discover you were God?"

"Who says I did?" she regarded him blankly, clearly not in the mood.

"Come now, Dawn, don't be argumentative. You know what I want. Even Jesus spent 40 days in the wilderness being tempted by Satan. Tell me about your spiritual awakening."

She hesitated, weighing in her mind what the best answer was, then flashed him that cute, broad smile that scrunched up her eyes. "Sure, Scott, I'll tell you. In college I studied the Bible thoroughly, and some of the other great spiritual books, like the Qur'an and the Tao te Ching. Then I set about trying to put it into practice. I spent all of my free time meditating in a nearby Buddhist temple in Los Angeles. After I graduated from college I joined a convent, the Carmel of St. Teresa, and spent seven months scrubbing floors and praying the rosary. After that, I took a trip to the Vatican, and toured the great cathedrals of Europe. I met a Polish miner who introduced me to the *Bhagavad Gita*, and I decided to head to India, where I spent a year in an ashram in Langhore, studying with a wizened guru named Ramakrishna. One day while meditating I saw all my past lives, and the entire universe unfolded before me. I knew that I was, and had always been, the one who had created it, sustained it, and would one day destroy it."

She was grinning as she spoke, but as soon as she stopped speaking, Braxton sighed loudly.

"Dawn," he said, annoyance in his voice, "I've read the *The Razor's Edge*, too, you know. And I know who Ramakrishna is. Be serious."

"I am serious. You be serious and stop asking such silly questions. I am God, come to walk among you, and that's all there is to it."

Indoors again, seated in the booth of another nightclub, with flashing lights and a booming bass in the background, a ruddy blond-haired boy in a blazer, with a crest on the pocket—a student from a private school who was patently too young to be in a nightclub—and someone off to the side, standing next to the table, bobbing in and out of the frame, watching:

"Okay Dawn," Braxton was saying, "Explain how it is that God is both perfectly good and all-powerful, yet there is evil in the world?"

She laughed. "Oh, an easy one this time!" The boy and what sounded like several other people laughed as well.

Braxton paused the recording momentarily to say to me, "This is the ultimate unanswerable question in theology, one that people have been pondering for millennia. Most people who convert to agnosticism or atheism do so over this one question, usually when it's brought home through some painful experience. I love how smooth she is in answering it. She's probably had this idea all worked out it her head, just waiting for me to ask her."

He let the show proceed, and Dawn said, "Well, it's like this. You're right in saying that I'm all-powerful and perfectly good. I'm also, as I'm sure you've heard, all-knowing. I know everything. The thing is, though, it seems impossible for me to know evil, because, being perfectly good, there is no evil in me. But if I don't know it, then I'm not all-knowing, hence not infinite, and all existence would collapse into nothingness as a result. It's true. So I created something apart from myself, the world. Here evil could exist among the free-willed independent beings I made, so I could know evil through them, vicariously, and thus be truly all-knowing. That is the reason there is evil in the world. It is the very purpose of its creation."

Braxton clapped softly beside me. "Is that incredible, or what?" My mind was being weighed down with confusion. Did her answer actually make sense? Could it, in fact, be the real answer to the ultimate question?

The Braxton on the other side of the camera seemed equally impressed. "Oh, wow," he said. "You've got to be kidding."

Dawn's friends all laughed together. She said, "You know, I think I'd like to dance. Want to dance?" she asked the blond boy.

"Sure!" he replied, springing up. Dawn slid over and left the booth without another word to the Professor, who tracked her with his camera as she melted into the crowd. He also caught the other people standing around the table; there were at least five. I was startled to recognize Molly as one of them, hanging off to the side, wearing a jean jacket over a black shirt. She stood, grinning along with the others, her arms folded across her chest. Braxton turned off the recording at that point.

"So," I said, my voice wavering, "is that the answer?"

"Slick, huh?" he chuckled. "Two questions in one, the question of evil and the purpose of life. Of course it's not the answer. There is no answer; there can't be. I think it's a false question because there is no God, but the question is useful as a demonstration of the difficulty of the concept. But even if you accepted the premise, no, it's still not right. I can't think of any logical fallacies inherent in it, but I haven't done an exhaustive analysis of it either. And there are some mystical traditions, such as Kabbalah, that teach that God created the world to somehow know himself. But it's absurd. No one would take her seriously. We exist to suffer? How depressing is that? Even the standard free will answer, that we cause our own suffering, is better than that, however screwed up it is. Think about it. If your best friend just died, and she comes up to you at the funeral and tells you that, would it make you feel any better? Hell, no. I can guarantee you that if Dawn actually told the guy in the wheelchair her idea of the meaning of life, whatever it was, it wasn't this. This was just a joke, and all her friends seemed to know it. It was an egghead answer she made up to amuse the egghead Professor."

"On the other hand," Braxton continued, leaning back, "if you think about it the right way, it is rather profound. It's a mystical answer, you see. Mysticism is a form of religion which takes a more expansive view of God. Traditional Western religions teach that God is separate from us, the big man in the sky who created the world and watches over it, telling what to do and not do, judging us, and so on. A mystical view sees God as pantheistic, a part of the world, often to the extent that God *is* the world. You know, 'all is one.' I've always thought that to be the only way you can truly understand how God works. See, if you imagine God to be a rational being, like yourself, only far more powerful, then, that there's where the whole problem of evil comes from. You say to yourself, 'I'd change things if I were God, so why doesn't he?' and you try to come up with a logical answer, which leads to frustration and anger because there is no logical answer. The usual one is about free will, the idea that God lets people choose how to behave, then punishes them when the things they choose are wrong. It's an answer that has the comfort of control, of allowing you to say, 'If only I behave nothing bad will happen to me,' but of course it never works out like that, and people are left with a lot of guilt and misery, blaming themselves for things they couldn't possibly have caused. And in times of national distress, whether personal or national, such as in the Middle East of today, it causes people to become more extremist in their religious views, as a means of trying to manipulate God into making things better."

He continued: "The mystical approach suggests that God causes all things, therefore he *causes* the evil we experience. It's not just that it happens and his hands are tied because of some legalistic framework, but that he created a world with good and evil in it intentionally. Now, you might ask why, but that would be a stab at rationality, and no rationality is possible. You're just supposed to be overwhelmed into awe. It's like modern art. Its meaning is derived from its apparent meaninglessness. Does that make any sense? Though of course some try to make it cohere anyway, and the usual answer is 'balance.' Like the Tao. I'm sure you've seen the Tao symbol, the circle divided into two opposing haves that swirl together. It is the way of life, the balance and harmony of opposites. Summer and winter, male and female, life and death, good and evil, so on and so forth."

"The thing about mysticism, though, is what you end up with," Braxton said, " if you take it to its logical conclusion. Because God is not rational, because he's not like us, doesn't think like us, they tell us that God is beyond understanding. Of course, traditionalists say the same thing; it says as much in the Bible. Divine inscrutability. But the mystic viewpoint takes it to the extreme. If God cannot be understood, if his actions to all intents and purposes seem no better than random chaos, then the best way to think about him, and the only useful way, is not to think about him at all. It's almost better to assume that God doesn't exist."

I smiled. I got it—the aim of Professor Braxton's talk was to convert me.

"No, I'm serious," he said. "You know some sects of Buddhism are non-theistic? In certain orthodox forms, at least. Buddhists don't need to believe in a supreme being. They often believe in supernatural beings, to be sure, but not necessarily *a God*. They believe in life after death, and a strict set of morals, but no God. Buddha himself, according to some interpretations, technically doesn't exist anymore. He escaped existence upon his death. That's the aim of enlightenment, you know. Non-existence. They reincarnate through life after life just to get what's there right from the start. As I said, they don't all believe it, and even for those who do, of course that's an oversimplification; the non-existence they believe in is somewhat different from the non-existence I believe in, if that makes any sense. I studied Buddhism, but personally it has no appeal for me. I was raised in the church, that's where I feel comfortable, and it's such an elemental part of Black America it's impossible to abandon. Meditation can be relaxing enough, but I couldn't take it too seriously. You know meditation is simply teaching yourself not to think? Quieting your mind, blanking out all thoughts. As an intellectual who happens to enjoy thinking, I had a problem with that. But it seems to the ultimate point of most religions, to get you to stop thinking and do what you're told. In the West it's called faith, where you shut off your brain by accepting as true things that patently aren't and don't even make any sense."

I had my doubts, but I wasn't going to argue. "So what about Dawn?"

"Dawn's interesting." Braxton continued. "She's trying to create a blend of Eastern and Western thought. Of course, that's the aim of the New Age movement, to unite the two into something better, though usually it ends up nothing but a mess. But here's what Dawn thinks about God: She believes in the very rational, Western tradition of one, single, indivisible God, which is what she is. In another recording I tried to pin her down again and asked how I could become enlightened, that is, become God, and she said it was impossible; all I could do was follow her. She is the only God, and there is no other God beside her. Everything in the world is not a part of her, but merely her creation. On the other hand, she has a very mystical outlook. She creates both good and evil, she causes everything to happen, she doesn't fault anybody and isn't trying to bring people to repentance. She has much more in common with the Eastern avatars like Krishna than she does with Jesus. She's a playful god. Even her deejaying fits; there are lots of traditions of sacred dancing and ecstatic frenzies—like the Sufis. You know, the whirling dervishes? She doesn't see her herself as a messiah. I don't know if you can imagine she has a god-complex but not a messiah-complex, but it's true. She's not here to save humanity or be martyred. She's here simply to observe. That's how she puts it, observe. Observe the world she made, have a little fun living in it, and maybe help out a few lucky individuals while she's here."

He continued: "It's refreshing after considering the heavy-handedness of most religions. But I imagine it makes it harder to understand her personal psychology, which is what you're looking for."

"What do you mean?" I interjected.

"Well… My wife is a social worker. I've heard lots of stories about people who burn out doing that kind of work, or similar work. The endless struggle to help the less fortunate, but for every one you can save there are ten more you can't. Or a hundred more. Burnout is very common for idealists. Or cynicism. You can't help everybody. No one can save the world. So I can imagine how easy it would be to slip into that delusion, to assume a divine appointment to become what no human is, to do what no human can do. To be the one, to be the savior, it presents a special attraction. Even everyday people dream of it; think of how many movies and stories involve one person saving the world."

"But not Dawn," I guessed.

"No. For one thing, she isn't old enough. She doesn't seem to have ever been effected by burnout, to have ever faced a life-altering crisis, to have been confronted with her insignificance. Ultimately I don't really think anything ever 'happened to her,' as you put it. I could be wrong, but I really think she suffers from some garden-variety psychosis. She's God, but she doesn't do anything with it. She does a few things here and there to help out a few people, and she inspires a few people with her presence. But she has no mission. She has no message."

"I thought you were impressed by her apologizing act." I said.

"I am. I think it's awesome, both as theology and as psychology. It's certainly unique, but I also think it's something she does, not something that drives her. I don't think it's her *raison d'être*. Personally, I think she only does it because she can't do the miracles you'd expect from God. I mean, if you're a traveling revivalist, and you go from town to town, with fresh crowds at every stop, you can get faith healing to work for a long time. But Dawn stays here and hangs out with the mostly the same people day after day. People hear about her, and a few follow her around for a while, but in this city she'll never be able to generate the kind of credence you need to pull this off for very long.

"Still, she has a lot going for her. It's pretty well-thought out for a lunatic. Of course, she's not always entirely consistent in what she says, but then again I don't think any religion is. It's more sensible than most of the rubbish that's bandied about these days. Certainly I believe she could inspire people. So, do you want to see some more?" He motioned to his computer.

I shook my head; I think I had learned all I was going to learn. "Do you know how to find her?"

"Sometimes," he said with a shrug. "One of her clique members is a Howard student. Nice guy, chemistry major. Never been in any of my classes and probably never will be, but I had him sit down for an interview, too. He offered to e-mail me with her whereabouts when he learns of them. As I mentioned, she doesn't advertise; all of their communication is word-of-mouth. And of course, sometimes he doesn't hear about her plans—he rarely speaks to her directly. Then there are times she changes her mind at the last minute, presumably not for bookings, but other ventures, like the Cathedral yesterday. I'm guessing she went there to talk to a divinity student—not from Howard—who's also one of her friends. And don't get the wrong impression; I'm not stalking her or anything. Every one of my meetings has been documented, and in all I've only spoken to her eleven times."

"And this chemistry major guy believes in her, too?"

Braxton chuckled and shook his head. "Oh, no, certainly not. Don't be mistaken about her followers. Most of these people don't actually believe she's God. Some take her for a guru or a saint or some such, but most of them know perfectly well she's schizophrenic, or at least delusional."

This was very surprising news, and possibly the most difficult to comprehend. I held up my hand and asked him, bewildered, "Let me get this straight. They know she's insane and follow her anyway? Why would anyone do that?"

"Yes, well, that's the million-dollar question, isn't it?" said Braxton. " It's what I'm writing about in my paper. The insight Dawn's group gives us into embryonic religions. You have to understand, most groups out there are pretty well formed by the time they reach the level of public awareness. They have recruiting methods, indoctrination methods, and means of keeping people in the organization. A very large, established religion is fairly decentralized, even in structured organizations like the Catholic Church. People may be talked into converting, and once they begin questioning beliefs, they may be told that to leave is to endanger their souls. These are mostly come-and-go organizations, because the coming and going of individual followers doesn't threaten the stability of the organization as a whole. Smaller, newer sects are tighter knit and more controlling. They have to be, because members may be pressured by outside acquaintances to return to their previous faith, and there are so few members to begin with even a seemingly small loss could collapse the sect. Some groups go to extremes, keeping members isolated and forcing them to cut off all contact with outsiders. They can become very abusive. Of course I'm talking about cults here, like the Moonies. You're probably too young to remember them, aren't you? Cults were a big issue in the Sixties and Seventies. Lots of cults, with stories of brainwashing, and people being kidnapped and deprogrammed. But all religions start out in a cult phase on their way to becoming a mainstream religion, Mormonism, for instance.

Well, I'm sure you know about that, but did you know Christianity itself started out as a cult? It's detailed in the Book of Acts. The first church had all the elements of a coercive cult. Members initially lived together in a community, and they were expected to give their wealth to the apostles. There's a passage in Acts about one couple who was smited because they tried to keep some of their own money for themselves instead of giving it to Saint Peter. Ever heard that one in Sunday school?"

He continued: "Anyway, these cults don't spring up fully formed, of course. They grow from something even smaller, a simple gathering of people under a charismatic leader. Dawn's group provides an almost textbook example of a nascent religious group. She's one person, and she attracts a large number of people and has fans, of course, people who enjoy listening to her play, which I think is partly due to the novelty, and then she has a smaller but still loose group of admirers around her. As I said, most of these people don't even take her seriously. They just hang out with her for amusement. She's harmless enough; she helps sneak them into cool nightclubs they're too young to be in legitimately. They don't believe her but they're intrigued by what she says. There's something there that pulls them in. I think what she says does have some appeal. Certainly it's flattering for Dawn the Goddess to take an interest in them, especially in that her interest comes without criticism. And they like belonging to something. They have this ready-made set of friends they can just hang out with."

"And then there's the core group, an even smaller number of people who actually do take her seriously. As far as I can tell, this group is—not exclusively, but mostly—composed of these street kids who've latched on to her. This is the center of her cult. These are the people who will become the leaders of new recruits. As time goes on, and her group becomes more organized and her illness progresses, she'll become more assertive and controlling, demanding allegiance, demanding 'sacrifices.' Her carelessness about whether or not people believe her will disappear and most of her current admirers will drop away. The group will become more focused and develop a harder sell. Dawn will write a short book codifying her theology, which will become their bible everyone will be required to read. They'll stop flittering around from bar to bar and move to a single location, their own little 'temple,' where they'll live together under her command and no one will be allowed to leave freely. They may go out to recruit on an individual basis, or Dawn may rent auditoriums and take out advertising, giving talks on how she alone knows the perfect method to enlightenment to entice people into joining."

"You can't be serious," I said, somewhat horrified.

"It's a standard pattern. In ten years, you won't recognize her. She'll be a completely different person. That assumes she retains enough mental stability to control a group, but at some point, if she's successful, it won't matter. She'll be able to isolate herself, occasionally appearing to make a ranting speech, while her apostles control everything in her name. If the group grows large enough and survives her death it could very well become mainstream in a hundred years. Who knows, a thousand years from now there very well may be Churches of Dawn throughout the land, although it's extremely unlikely."

I shook my head slowly; I finally realized he was embellishing. "I can't believe that."

"Well, no, there are thousands of little cults like this. They pop up all the time and usually disappear just as fast. So, no, I don't expect it to get to that point, either; but nevertheless, it is a possibility, however extraordinarily remote. That's why my work is so important. I'm documenting the birth of a religion. Its entire lifespan may only a few short years, or it may be generations. Some day it may actually become significant, and if it does, my documentary will stand testament to the 'real' Dawn."

I shrugged, not wanting to hear anymore lectures on it. I wondered briefly what Paul would say if he were here, if he could stand his ground with this guy. I considered telling him about Paul being a gay fundamentalist, just to hear his reaction, or maybe garner some sympathy.

I decided instead I'd had enough, and stood up and stretched. I felt tired. Braxton got the message, and stood up too. "Look, do you know where she'll be tonight?"

"Haven't a clue. If you want, I can send you an e-mail if I find out."

"Thanks," I said, as he led me back down stairs. As he unlocked the front door for me, I casually said, "One other thing. Are any of these followers of hers dangerous? Violent?"

Braxton looked at me carefully. "I've never seen anything specific. But she is dealing with a lot of youths who live rough lives, who are of necessity both aggressive and desperate. And, as I said, someone like her naturally attracts some real wackos."

"Thanks," I said again, now more worried about dealing with Dawn and her followers.

CHAPTER 17

Paul was sleeping with Kim. Literally; they were snuggled together like kittens, holding each other under the top sheet of Paul's bed. I was too astonished to move; petrified, I watched them breathing deeply, looking disturbingly content. Their clothes were randomly strewn about the floor.

I had known Kim was here because she had parked her powder blue Civic, which she wasn't supposed to drive, in my space in the apartment's lot, right next to Paul's Corvette. I had to park in the visitor's section. I felt lighthearted anyway, thinking, however unreasonably, she had changed her mind. Most likely she was here to pick up her extra clothes and other belongings. And I was right; there were several outfits of hers lying on my bed. But at some point after pulling them from the closet she wound up in bed herself.

It was fairly easy to guess what had happened. Paul had told her about his encounter with Dawn the night before, knowing how much it would amuse Kim, and told her about the wish he had made to be straight. One of them must have suggested they find out if her magic had worked. I would bet it had been Kim who introduced the idea, because she's always been interested in Paul and a chance to sleep with him would obviously be too much to pass up. I wasn't too sure why he had agreed, though.

Or maybe I did. It was the same impulse that had prompted him to make the wish in the first place, the belief that there was something wrong with the way he lived now, that God wanted him to be normal. Having already verbalized his belief, acting on it was a natural next step, given the chance. He must have been much more shaken than he had let on.

I wondered about the open door. Normally Paul was conscientious about keeping his door closed, and I was equally conscientious about keeping his privacy. I don't think I had been in his room at all since he moved in and I helped him unpack. And I hadn't told him what I was doing with my afternoon or when I would return. It could have been at any time. The only conclusion to draw was that he expected me to discover the two of them. He wanted to be caught. He felt guilty, or ambivalent, or uncertain about what he felt he was certain of not too long ago. And he wanted me to know. He wanted me to know... what? How much trouble Dawn had caused? Or I had caused? His commitment to God? How miserable he felt?

I thought he did feel miserable. In his peaceful, dozing face I imagined deeper emotions than I'd ever known him to possess.

I slipped back to the living room and thought for a moment. If I just left now, we could all pretend I had never seen them and had no idea what was going on. If Paul really wanted to tell me something, we could discuss it tomorrow, or any other time. Anything he thought I really needed to know, I would hear about eventually.

But I didn't think I wanted to hear anything from Kim. Surely she wasn't expecting me to find them like this, but I knew she wouldn't be embarrassed by it. Most likely she'd deliver a comparison between us, and that was an analysis I didn't need to listen to. I mean, what if she said Paul was better?

If I left, what was I going to do with the rest of my day? I still wanted to talk to Dawn, and after talking with Braxton, it was more important than ever. I believed I had finally had a glimpse into her mind. I knew, or at least I strongly suspected, what she was up to, and it wasn't about starting a cult. The simplest explanation was that Dawn was suicidal again. I knew how fragile she was. She was claiming to be God because, as Braxton had said, doing so would attract wackos. It was inevitable some wacko she encountered would be fanatic enough, deranged enough, to want to kill her. In other words, she was acting in the way that would be most likely to rile up someone else into murdering her. She could die without having to do it herself. It made terrible, twisted sense.

In a way, this understanding caused me considerable relief. Now her actions made sense. And depression was a mental illness that could be treated fairly easily. If I could reach her, I could actually help her. I'd felt lost before, but now I knew I could do something about it. But first I had to find her, and how was I going to accomplish that? As much as I dreaded going into DC again, I would have to find her at a club; the only problem was that it was Sunday, so there were fewer nightclubs open, which might make it easier to find her, if she was playing any of them, or impossible, if she wasn't. I was sure there must be an easier way than just random searching. If she was self-employed, she did have a business, so she must be in some general business database I could access that would at least list a phone number. Absent that I could always go back to her father. He hadn't been too forthcoming yesterday, but then again I hadn't specifically asked where she lived or how to get in touch with her. But my news might have annoyed him and made him less likely to cooperate again. Still, the understanding I had now about what Dawn was doing would spark his concern. Certainly I would need him to get an involuntary commitment order for Dawn, if that's where this ended up.

I realized I had another option. I could ask Molly instead, at the hospital in Alexandria, where she'd been taken. She would probably be even less likely to help me, but I thought I could change her mind, and she was more likely to know where Dawn was that night. I got excited by the possibility Dawn herself might be there visiting, and that made up my mind.

Then I spied Paul's keys on the kitchen counter. On impulse, I placed mine down next to them, and picked up his. Before I could think about it, I quietly snuck out of the apartment.

CHAPTER 18

I sat in the Corvette and saw my hands shaking as I considered my foolishness. After I'd already decided I wanted to pretend I hadn't seen what I'd just seen, I did something that proved I had been there. And worse, he was going to be furious with me. Absolutely furious. Taking his car was probably the worst thing I could do to him. So why was I doing it? I wasn't angry with him. Not at all. In fact, I was kind of pleased to see his vulnerable side for a change.

He was slipping out of control and I was going to take it up, at least for a little while. I wanted to drive his car; it was that simple. And this was probably the only time I was going to get away with it. I wasn't mad, but he would assume I was and forgive me.

And it's not like I was stealing it. I'd bring it right back.

And I was on a mission to find God. Surely Paul would have to agree that that allowed for special considerations.

Besides, it was a Corvette. It was red. With leather interior.

I stuck in the key, and it *purred.*

I knew Molly had been taken to Inova Alexandria Hospital, because Ahmed had asked the EMTs where they were going last night, but I didn't know how to get there. There was no GPS in the car. I should have looked up the directions online, but I hadn't and now didn't dare go back up to the apartment. So I did the only thing I could think of: I drove to a nearby 7-Eleven and bought a map. It's been years since I actually used one of those, and it took a while to figure out, but eventually I deciphered the directions and was on my way.

The hospital had a bright, spacious lobby with plush chairs and quiet piano music playing over the speakers. I went to the reception desk and tried to explain who I was here for. I didn't know Molly's last name, and I didn't know what was wrong with her. All I could say was that she had been brought in by ambulance the night before; I wasn't sure about the time but I guessed between eleven and midnight. The lady at the desk fiddled around with her computer for a minute before telling me she had a record of a Molly Doe, and that I should go up to the second floor, to the Heart and Vascular Institute, and ask for her there. It made sense she'd be there, since she had needed CPR resuscitation, but at least it was a positive sign Molly wasn't in Intensive Care.

I followed the signs down several corridors before finally arriving at the right place, and told the nurse at the nurses' station who I was looking for. The nurse, a young Indian woman, seemed exasperated at the name.

"I don't suppose you know what her last name is?" she asked. I shook my head. "The previous shift said she was screaming when they brought her in last night, and they had to sedate her. And today, there's been this whole troupe coming in and out of her room, all day. She has a lot of friends, but not one of them knows her last name, and she refuses to tell us. I would say they were all classmates, but there's something funny about all of them, and this is no normal kid. At the least she'd have a last name."

I wondered if her concern had to do with billing issues, but that was irrelevant to me. I thanked her, and went down to Molly's room. She had a room all to herself, charity case notwithstanding, which was nice. It was small, with a TV and a plastic chair by the bed and a window looking out onto the hospital grounds. Molly, an IV sticking out of her arm, was sitting in the bed, and she already had three visitors. They all looked at me when I stepped in, and my first reaction was shock that one of them was Ahmed.

"What are you doing here?" I asked him immediately.

Molly frowned and pouted upon seeing me. "Oh, it's you. What are *you* doing here?" To her friends she said, "This is the guy who tried to kill me," and pulled up her hospital gown to show her belly, where there was still a thin red line that I might have missed, had I not known what I was looking at. She was wearing loose pants, probably also hospital supplied. Ahmed, who was standing behind the plastic chair, didn't move any closer to see, but then he had already seen it, too. The other two didn't move, either. There was a girl leaning against the wall by the window, and a boy sitting in the chair who looked familiar. It took a second before I realized he was Diego, the boy I'd seen at the church yesterday and on Braxton's video, bragging that Dawn had cured him of AIDS. His face was much cleaner than it was yesterday—I guess he'd taken a shower—but he was still wearing exactly the same clothes.

When she raised her gown, I noticed some of the electrodes stuck to her chest. She lowered the gown, still pouting, no doubt annoyed her friends weren't taking her accident seriously by not rushing to her defense. "So Court, what are you doing here?" she asked again. Molly was still wearing her full makeup, just like yesterday, which looked out-of-place in her hospital gown. Without wearing a short skirt or low-cut top, she was dependent on makeup to preserve her feminine identity.

"I just came to see how you were doing," I said, smiling to show my friendly intentions.

"Oh, well, I'm fine, except that you ruined my life!" she said bitterly. She held up her left arm, and then I noticed that not only did she have an IV in that arm, but her right arm was handcuffed to the bed. They were plastic handcuffs, and the IV line was long enough to let her turn over and sleep on her right side, but they were handcuffs all the same. I guess, with her screaming the night before, the hospital staff had realized she was an escape risk and took some precautions. They'd been right to do that; considering what Dawn had told me, Molly was terrified of the social services system and would flee the first chance she had. "They'll send me to some family who'll probably lock me in the basement again. Will that make you happy?"

"You were locked in a basement?"

"Yeah!" she said, suddenly animated. "One time. I was! It was months before I could escape! They were evil! Evil people are everywhere."

I wasn't sure how I was supposed to react to that, or if it was really true. It might be, for all I knew. "Well, I'm sure Dawn won't let anything like that happen to you."

"Humph," Molly said, giving up reluctantly. Apparently she had nothing to say against Dawn, but was in too bad a mood to admit the situation wasn't the hopeless mess she wanted to blame me for.

I turned back to Ahmed again. "So how about you? What are you doing here?"

"Same thing as you are," he said evenly.

"She's not your patient, you know."

He shrugged. "I know, but it was the first time I've actually saved someone's life, and I wanted to follow up and see how everything turned out."

I smiled. "I bet that felt pretty good, right? Saving a life. You won't get that kind of opportunity doing research in some lab. Maybe you want to reconsider your choice of fields?"

He threw me a sharp look. "Don't you start with that, too."

I laughed and turned to Diego, but stopped laughing when I noticed the hard stare the girl behind him was giving me. There was nothing unusual about her; she was a white kid, as young as all the others, a little taller than I was, with lanky brown hair, and like Diego she was wearing stained jeans and a dark long-sleeve jacket despite the weather. She was peering intently at me, like I was about to do something she didn't want to miss. But it was more than the intense gaze; her mouth was a tight line. She looked absolutely furious. I was stunned and took a step back. I quickly shifted my eyes back to Diego. "Hi, I'm Court," I said, to him, feeling a little weak.

"Yeah, I figured that," he said. He, for his part, was restless. His eyes kept darting all around the room and he shifted in his seat. "Dawn said you're an old friend, which I don't understand since you don't look very old to me. I'm Diego, by the way, and this is Gabby," he pointed with his thumb behind him.

I looked back up at her. She was still staring like she was trying to burn a hole in me. "Hi, Gabby," I said to her carefully.

"Be warned, mortal," she growled in a husky voice. "I am the Archangel Gabriel, the Lord's Avenging Angel. I bring destruction and retribution to the earth!"

"Ooookay," I said aloud, taking another step back, preparing to run if necessary. Braxton was right. Dawn was drawing in real wackos. In fact, "wacko" might be too lenient a term; "psycho" was clearly better.

I remembered enough from the Christmas story to know that the Archangel Gabriel had something to do with it, which didn't quite jibe with this girl's thirst for retribution, or the fact that "Gabriel" was a male name, but there was no way I going to ask her for clarification.

"Don't worry about her; she's just kidding," Diego said breezily. She continued to stare at me with a murderous look that wasn't any part of the same universe as "kidding."

I would have left right then and there except I still needed to learn Dawn's whereabouts. I gingerly approached the bed again, and asked, "Molly, do you know where I can find Dawn?"

"Why would I tell *you* that?" she said, angrily.

"Please, Molly," I said gently. "It's very important I talk with her."

"Oh, yeah, I'm sure. You must be real stupid to think you can come here and ask me for help."

"I don't know where else to go." On my way over here I had planned on convincing her by telling her everything, but now I was very reluctant to say anything negative about Dawn after I had used her name to assure Molly she would be all right. Not to mention I might upset the psycho standing there listening.

"Screw you," she said.

I sighed. I had known it was a long shot, but at least, with Ahmed here, I had a backup plan. I could give him a ride home, and he'd probably let me use his computer to search for her.

I was just about to ask him when Diego said, "We'll take you."

"You will?" I asked, astonished.

"No!" cried Molly. "Don't help him!"

"Shut up, Mol." To me he said, "We'll take you to her, but you have to buy us dinner first."

"Dinner?" I asked, confused.

"Yeah, and a real dinner, not just fast food. At a restaurant. I got to have something to eat, dude. I haven't eaten anything for three days. Three days! It's only fair."

"Um, sure…"

"That's not true," said Molly. "What about yesterday?"

"Mol, nobody asked you." He turned to Gabby. "Hey, what do you want? Steak or seafood?"

"All the same dead flesh," she mumbled.

"Steak it is," Diego said cheerfully, turning back to me. "You got to take us to a steak restaurant."

"Okay. You know where Dawn lives?"

"Dude, nobody knows where she lives—"

"She lives in heaven," said Molly.

"Yeah, that's right, Mol," he said dismissively. "We'll take you to the club she's playing tonight."

"What's the name?"

He grinned. "Dude! I'm not giving it away for nothing. You gotta pay the price first. That's how capitalism works."

"I guess." I waited a moment for him to get up, and when he didn't move I said, "Okay, so let's go."

He was already leaning back in the chair; now he crossed his legs and folded his arms. "Dude, we just got here. We're not moving now. We've got plenty of time."

Of course he didn't want leave now; he was enjoying watching me squirm. And I was squirming, with Gabby still staring at me. I was trying not to stare back and risk angering her anymore than she already was, but I couldn't help it and so far I hadn't even seen her blink. I considered offering to buy everyone snacks from the machine I'd seen down the hall just to have an excuse to get out of there, but I didn't want to give this guy any more than I absolutely had to.

Still, I tried anyway. "Well, I don't want to interrupt your visit, so maybe I'll just come back later." I didn't move, though, because I felt I needed his permission.

"Oh, I wouldn't do that. We could leave at any time, and if you miss us we ain't hunting you down." He grinned. "Besides, don't you like our company?"

He had me caught. If I wanted to see Dawn, I had to let him control me, and he knew it. He had the power here. The girl was still looking at me like she wanted to tear my throat out. I didn't understand how Ahmed had been able to stand this, but maybe they had let him alone because he was Molly's hero.

Well, if he was going to rattle me, I could do the same to him. "So, um, Diego, how'd you get involved with Dawn's cult?"

"Dude, it's not a cult. We just hang and stuff."

"But she's God, right?"

"Sure. That doesn't make it a cult. We don't bow down to her or anything. She doesn't run our lives."

"You just listen to her preach about the meaning of life."

He shook his head. "You wouldn't get it."

"Tell me."

"Most of that shit she just says for the jackass with the camera. Most of the time she don't say nothing. She just listens, lets the rest of us talk."

"You mean Professor Braxton?"

"Whoever he is."

"Yeah, I saw some of Braxton's videos, including some which you were in."

Diego grinned. "You did? He is going to use it in his movie, right? Awesome!"

"So what, are you gay too?"

He dropped both feet to the floor and sat strait up, suddenly serious. "What did you call me?"

"Well, in the video you said you had AIDS. And you look too old to have been born with it."

Diego was staring at me. "I am not freaking gay! I would never do any crap that disgusting!"

"It's not true," said Molly. "You do it all the time."

He grimaced at her. "Okay, yeah, a few times, when I was really desperate, when I was starving, and needed the money. Okay? You happy now? I was *starving*. I would never do that crap for any other reason."

"That's not true," she insisted. I think she was enjoying this. "You did it with me."

"What the hell!" He jumped up. "What are you, my damn conscience?" He sat back down, steamed. "Anyway Mol, you don't count. You keep whining about how you're a girl. All the time, 'I'm a girl, I'm a girl.'"

I frowned. At least I'd pushed his buttons. "You better be careful, or you'll wind up with AIDS again."

"I didn't have any AIDS!" he shouted.

"Okay, sorry. I apologize. I was just assuming. You're not gay, you didn't have AIDS. Professor Braxton said as much. He thought you were mistaken, that you'd had pneumonia or something minor and recovered naturally."

"I didn't have nothing! I made the whole story up!"

"You did?" I said, genuinely shocked.

"Yeah!"

"Why?"

"Cause he was making a movie! Damn!"

I stared at him for a minute. "So, Dawn never did any miracles?"

"Hell no! We're just having fun."

I couldn't think of anything else to say. The speakers outside the room paged some doctor to the OR. I watched for a minute as Diego tried to relax in the chair, still fuming. Gabby wasn't watching me anymore. She was now leaning against the window with her eyes closed. I decided to change the subject.

"So Ahmed, did you ever find out what was wrong with Molly?"

"Yes," he said, relieved that I had asked. "She suffers from atrial fibrillation. It's an irregular heartbeat, and sometimes it causes the heart to beat so fast that it no longer contracts fully, which means it's no longer pumping blood, and your brain can quickly die from lack of oxygen. Her episode last night was intermittent, not sustained. It caused her to collapse, but her heart still made enough full contractions to keep her alive until I was able to get to her and start compressions to manually pump her heart."

"So… will she be okay?"

"They've given her a cardioversion—her heart's been shocked back into its correct rhythm—and that should be enough. But if the irregular rhythm returns, it can be controlled on a more regular basis with antiarrhythmic medication. Plenty of people are able to live with this condition with medication. She should be fine. The main concern is with potential repercussions. I don't think any doctor would allow her to undergo any medical surgery that wasn't completely necessary."

He meant the sex change operation Molly wanted. I glanced at her. She was listening attentively, but surprisingly didn't seem too concerned.

"But that means no, ah, you know," I said.

"Right. See, I'm not entirely clear on that. Gender reassignment surgery is really quite complicated, involving many different steps and many possible complications. I don't know if her cardiologist would permit it, but since this won't happen for several more years and her heart condition might stabilize by then, I can't say."

"Of course they'll allow it," said Molly. "I'll just go somewhere and not tell them about all this." She waved a hand in the air to indicate her indifference.

"As I said, Molly, it's not a good idea," said Ahmed, gently. "It's not safe."

She gave him a look almost as incredulous as the look she had given me a few moments before. "I have to have my surgery. I can't live my whole life like this; I'll die."

"But Molly, it's killing you already," he said. Diego snickered.

"What do you mean?" she said, looking worried for the first time.

"Atrial fibrillation mostly affects elderly people. I believe you've developed this condition because of the drugs you're taking."

"I'm not doing any drugs!" she said, sitting up straight.

"It's true," Diego said. "She doesn't spend her money on nothing but food and rent. Everything else she saves for this disgusting surgery she keeps whining about."

"Rent?" I asked.

"Yeah. What, you think we're all bums sleeping on heating grates?"

I took a deep breath. "I guess I sort of did." He shook his head and gave me the finger. I quickly glanced at Gabby; she was once again staring implacably.

"Molly, I meant the hormones you're taking. You're self-medicating, aren't you?"

"Yeah," she said, definitely. "So what? It's just estrogen."

"Well, I'm sure you're not getting them through a legitimate pharmacy." He paused for a moment. "Look, obviously I have no idea what happened to you, what caused you to develop this problem. It could have been any number of things. It might even be entirely natural. Your doctor may be able to make a determination, or perhaps that's impossible. But if you haven't been taking any other drugs, then my best guess is the black market hormones you've been taking have been tainted." Molly's eyes grew wide, and Diego laughed again.

"I told you it was your own fault, you idiot," he said.

"Does that mean . . . ," she trailed off, horrified.

"It means from now on you have to do it right, with legitimate drugs and professional medical supervision."

"But… but if I get stuck in a foster family, they'll never let me do that. All they do is beat me, and I have to run away. Every time!"

"I know you've had some bad experiences, but all foster families aren't like that." Ahmed was speaking with real care and kindness in his voice, and I was amazed. He wanted to instill some hope in Molly, and he was doing such an excellent job, far better than I could have done, that I felt I should thank him for it later. "I'm sure Dawn will look after you," he continued. "And that social worker who was here earlier seemed very concerned with your well-being. I'm sure you'll be in good hands."

"You think?" she asked with a hopeful uplift in her voice, her worry at least slightly alleviated.

"What social worker?" I asked absently. I was thinking I might find someone to help her out in some way too, except that Alexandria was a different jurisdiction from Fairfax, and I didn't know anything about their system.

"There was a social worker here earlier; she was leaving just as I came in, and we talked briefly. She seemed nice. Her name was Sherri Braxton."

My mouth fell open and I stared almost as hard as Gabby. "Do you know her?" he asked, looking worried.

"Jesus," I said mostly to myself. "Dawn actually knows what she's doing."

CHAPTER 19

Even though the Archangel wasn't staring at him, Ahmed decided he couldn't take it and told us he was leaving, but first he wanted to talk to me in private. We stepped outside the room into the hallway, where he leaned against the wall. He didn't want his back to the door.

"I know," I said, holding up my hand before he even started. "I heard. Don't ask for a miracle, don't talk about religion, don't do anything that gives the impression I'm taking her seriously."

"That's right," he said, nodding curtly. "I would recommend you not talk to Dawn at all, but since you knew her in an earlier part of her life, you at least might be able to maintain a conversation on wholly neutral topics. You have to keep her grounded." He thought for a moment before adding, "I don't think you should go with those two. They don't seem very trustworthy."

"You're just saying that because he sounds like a homophobe."

He shook his head. "That's just part of it."

"Yeah. And the girl, too, she has it in for me," I said with a nervous chuckle. "Oh well, if I turn up dead at least you'll know who did it."

He drew his lips tight. "Don't joke about that. I mean it. I'm worried for you."

"That's nice," I said with sarcasm.

"Look, these people didn't trek all the way here from DC simply to visit. I'm certain they're here to steal drugs from the hospital. They might check themselves into the Emergency Room complaining about pain and get a prescription for Percocet or Vicodin or some other painkiller. It's a common scam. They're not giving that up just for a free dinner," said Ahmed.

"You're probably right, but I'm sorry, I have to do this."

He nodded. "I suppose I can understand why you think you need to do this. Paul told me about Dawn—what she did—so you have my full sympathy. Just be careful."

I smiled. "Thanks, Ahmed. You have money for a cab?" I wasn't about to tell him I'd borrowed Paul's car.

"No, but it's still light out; I'll walk."

"Walk? You don't live anywhere nearby."

"You Americans, afraid of a little exercise! That's why you're all so fat, because you drive everywhere."

"Hey," I said, patting my slender stomach.

"I didn't mean you personally, just society in general. Anyway, I'll see you around." He started to go, but I put a hand on his arm.

"Wait a minute. Before you go, I have to know something."

"What?"

"How long have you and Paul really been dating? And please, just tell me the truth."

"Not long. Since the end of June."

That was what Paul had said. "Oh, come on. The way you two talk looks pretty long-term to me."

"Well, we've know each other for a while, the whole year actually. We met at a New Year's Eve party. We've had plenty of conversations, but it was only in June we decided to get serious. Now we're monogamous," he said proudly.

I stared, rapidly approaching the bail-out point. "And you weren't before?"

"We were in other relationships."

"Okay!" I said, "I was just curious."

"Splendid. Now can I leave?"

I took out my wallet and removed a twenty-dollar bill and held it out to Ahmed. "I'm not sure how I feel about this at the moment, but I want you to do me a favor. Get a cab, and go over to my place. Paul was really upset earlier, and I think you should talk to him."

He peered closely into my eyes. "You actually want me to go over there?"

"Yes. To talk," I added quickly. "I really think he needs to talk to you."

"I'm sure he'll be fine. It's his own fault, anyway; let him stew for a while. I'll see him next week."

"Please, Ahmed." I held out the bill again. "I don't want him to do anything he's going to regret."

"Okay," he said carefully, and took the money. "What do you think Paul might do that he'd regret?"

"I don't know. I swear. I'm just saying."

He gave me another careful, searching look. Finally, he said, "All right."

"Thanks."

"Don't you like it, though? That Paul secretly wishes to be straight? Isn't that what you want?"

I smiled wanly. "I am glad he take things seriously. But Ahmed, you were wrong yourself. He's not as happy-go-lucky as you thought."

"I believe I said well-adjusted. And he is. If he's having any crisis of doubt, it won't last long. He knows who he is. What I thought was more aggravating, was that he took her seriously and then asked for something so self-centered and insignificant. Having come from a poverty-stricken nation controlled by a despot, I could think of a few more pressing issues to address with God than my sex life. But beyond that, it was disappointing he didn't listen to me at all, that he gave Dawn what she wanted so easily. Don't play any of her games, Court. You can't win."

"We'll see." We nodded to each other. As I watched him walk away, I thought about what he said and thought it might actually be a good game to play with Dawn. What if I did take her seriously, or at least pretend to? Very seriously, the way Ahmed was talking about?

This thought preoccupied me enough that it wasn't until much later in the evening, long after it was too late to matter, that I realized if Paul was stupid enough to still be in bed with Kim when Ahmed arrived, he would discover exactly what had happened. How angry Ahmed would be I couldn't guess. The consequences for Paul were karma as far as I was concerned. And because of my part in sending Ahmed over there, he would probably never forgive me.

Back in the room, Diego had decided he'd had enough. We said goodbye to Molly, who wanted them—not me—to help her escape, or at the very least stay longer, and Gabby momentarily became human when she bent down and gave her a hug. I led them out to the car in the parking garage. Diego's eyes popped when he saw my car. "Sweet! It's a Corvette!" he said excitedly to Gabby. The two of them had to share the passenger seat, which looked uncomfortable. At least the seatbelt still fit.

"So, do you have any place in mind, or do you just want me to drive around until we find something?"

He opted for just driving around, so that's what we did for ten minutes, stopping at the first building that looked like a restaurant of the non-fast food variety. It wasn't as crowded as it would have been on a Saturday, but we still had to wait in the lobby ten minutes for a table. As soon as the waitress came around to ask what we wanted to drink, Diego went right ahead and ordered the 12 ounce steak dinner for all three of us, with the baked potato side. I hadn't wanted steak but wasn't going to argue. Gabby stared down at the table.

For the twenty minutes we waited for dinner to arrive, Diego spent the whole time chatting aimlessly. It wasn't a conversation; it was a monologue. He told me about how they and their friends spent their days on the street, pulling minor thefts and burglaries, and then consuming and dealing various types of drugs. However lackadaisical his conversation seemed, Diego was careful to avoid providing incriminating details for these and other small-time crimes. Occasionally he and his friends turned tricks as well, surprisingly mostly the boys; the girls would be risking their lives in reprisals from the people who organized prostitution rings in the city, if they started taking away their business. I couldn't believe it. There are plenty of stories about politicians and their high-priced call girls, of course, but when I think about crime in DC, I just think about the murder rate and drug trade and gang violence associated with it. I hadn't thought of prostitution as a major business here, with pimps and everything. Diego insisted the tricks were very rare for them; even Molly, he claimed, wasn't the whore I assumed her to be, though she did it more often than the rest of them because she commanded a higher price, thanks to her unique attributes, which were apparently a selling point to the kinds of people they dealt with. I didn't ask for clarification.

Diego and his friends were not the ones who stayed in youth shelters, they were a more independent sort. They slept in abandoned buildings—the rent payments he'd mentioned earlier were just for very occasional motel stays in the winter—they smoked and drank all the time, and they wandered freely about the city. He had a prescient view of his situation, seeming to hate his indigent life while at the same time contented by its complete freedom. I said something about panhandling, and he snickered; they weren't bums, or at least didn't think of themselves that way, and they apparently did nothing I had associated with homelessness. They didn't take food from garbage cans, they didn't sleep on heating grates or under bridges in parks, and they didn't beg anything from anyone. They grifted for money, or more commonly, simply stole it, at knife-point when necessary, but they didn't beg. From listening to him, I didn't think it was a matter of pride, but they'd been rejected by everyone around them and forced into self-reliance. And they were simply younger, and with youth comes a certain energy, a viciousness.

He didn't say much about Dawn, other than that she gave them money sometimes and invited them to the clubs she played, occasionally naming them her guests so they could skip the cover charges. I didn't ask if he was old enough to be in any clubs, but he certainly didn't look it. He also said she wasn't one of them; he didn't know where she slept but it wasn't in any abandoned building or heating grate. I hadn't thought so, since she had a real job, of sorts, but her behavior was too unpredictable to make comfortable assumptions.

He stopped talking only when the food arrived, and spent the next twenty minutes absorbed completely in the process of eating. He savored his food and chewed slowly. So did Gabby. I'd half expected them to tear their steaks apart like wild dogs. When he was finished, he noticed I still had some of mine left, so I slid it on to his plate. He kind of scowled, like he didn't want my handouts, but he ate it all the same. Then, when the waitress came back, he ordered deserts. I was too stuffed to eat anything else, but they both scarfed down thick slices of chocolate cake.

I paid with my credit card. I had no cash left. "Does this club have a cover charge?" I asked. "Because I'm going to have to stop off at an ATM if it does."

"Yeah, it does," he said. I noticed him eyeing my wallet, and at the ATM card. I took my cards out and put them by themselves in a different pocket. I also only took out $40, enough for a cover charge and maybe a drink or two, but not enough to worry over if it got stolen, which I was pretty sure it would be.

CHAPTER 20

I drove up the Shirley Highway across the George Washington Parkway and across the 14th Street Bridge into DC, then up past the Mall. Diego gave me directions as we headed somewhere well north of DuPont Circle. He still wouldn't tell me where we were going, though I don't think it would have helped. I don't know the city well enough and a club name or even a full address wouldn't have been enough to get me there; I needed his directions. The Archangel stared silently out the window the entire time.

I followed Diego's words down one street and across another long past the point where there were still buildings I recognized. From the restaurant it was easily forty minutes before he finally pointed out an unattended parking lot and told me to pull in. As I did, I looked but couldn't see any brightly lit building nearby which might suggest a club.

I pulled into the only available space, the last one over, next to a brick wall. I got out and locked the door. He pushed Gabby out and practically stepped over her.

"Lock the door," I said, after he'd slammed it shut.

"Sorry." He opened it, locked it, then slammed it again.

"So? Where is it?" I asked, looking around. All the buildings were dark and quiet. I checked my watch. It was approaching nine o'clock. Not bad. Not even nine yet! With any luck I could speak to

Dawn before she started her performance, which meant I might not have to stay here until two in the morning as I'd thought.

He shrugged. "Couple of blocks away."

"A couple of blocks?" I asked, angry.

"What, you were expecting valet?" he sneered.

"Fine, let's go. Which way?"

He stepped over to the wall, but didn't go any further.

"Well?" I asked impatiently.

He looked at me with eyes that were blank. "Give me your keys," he said dryly.

"What?" I shuddered.

"Dude, I'm sorry, but your car is just too nice. Give me your damn keys, and we won't have to beat you. And your wallet."

"You're robbing me?" I said quietly, astonished, afraid. After everything, after I bought them dinner, he was going to do this to me?

And the worst thing was that it was Paul's car. If I had driven here in my old Tercel, I would have just handed the keys over, not a problem. Hell, I'd have been glad for a chance to get a new car. But I couldn't let something happen to Paul's baby.

He saw my reluctance and punched me in the stomach. It happened so quickly I couldn't respond, except to cry out. He hit me again and again, until I doubled over. Then he started kicking me in the shins. He kicked me several times until I fell to my knees in pain, howling.

He kicked me in the ribs and I collapsed completely to the ground. He stood over me a moment, then gave me another swift, hard kick in the ribs. I could hear something crack.

"That's for calling me gay!" he shouted. He bent down and reached into my pockets, removing my keys, cell phone, and wallet. He put the phone and the wallet into his own pocket, then turned back to the car and unlocked it.

I pushed myself up on my hands. My body was in a lot of pain. I could taste blood in my mouth and I felt like I was going to pass out. I glanced up. Gabby was towering over me, staring down impassionedly.

"Well, come on, let's go!" Diego shouted at her, and came over and grabbed her arm.

"What about Dawn?" I said weakly.

"Dawn?" he said, and looked down and laughed. "What about her? You think she's gonna do anything? You think I'm afraid of her? She ain't gonna do crap! I mean, if you die she'll probably tell the cops, but otherwise she don't say jack. I'm not responsible, I'm just some poor helpless kid."

"She's God," I gasped. "Doesn't that mean anything to you?"

He shook his head at me and swung the keys around his finger. "Dude, she's not God. She's just some crazy bitch."

The Archangel Gabriel put her hand on the side of his head, and smashed him into the wall. His skull impacted with a sickening thud. He collapsed without another sound.

She bent down and picked up the keys. Then she held out her hand to me. As shocked as I was, I took it, and she helped me stand up. That was all the help she gave me, though. She opened the driver's side door of the car and got in, and started up the car while I shuffled around to the passenger side. She leaned over to unlock the door, and I sat down carefully. Then she backed out and took off.

"What if he's dead?" I asked, looking back.

"Do you care?" she replied.

I swallowed. "Where are we going?"

"The club."

"Can you take me to a hospital instead?"

"I thought you wanted to go to the club."

"Please," I moaned. "I'm in a lot of pain."

"*Fine*," she said, irritated, and took the next left.

CHAPTER 21

Gabby took me to Washington Hospital Center, which is a little north of the city's center. I didn't know where we'd started out from so I didn't know if this was the closest or just the one she was most familiar with, or if she'd just picked it at random. It didn't take all that long to get to, but that didn't matter much since the traffic was very light. She was going to drop me off in front of the Emergency Room entrance, but I insisted she park in the garage and then give the keys back to me, despite the risk of setting her off again by admitting I didn't trust her not to simply drive off with the car. She certainly did nothing to help me as I limped along to the Emergency Room on my sore legs. I was having trouble breathing and my whole side was aching painfully. I was very glad I had pulled my cards out of my wallet when I did, because I still had everything important: driver's license, credit card, and most importantly, insurance card. I prayed the wait wouldn't be too long, and I didn't think it would be. The lobby of the Emergency Room was only about half-full. It was Sunday, after all, and the night had barely started.

"Say whatever you want," Gabby said to me suddenly as we sat waiting. "But you don't want to file a complaint with the cops."

"Sure I do."

She turned to bore me with her eyes. "Don't."

Having seen what she was capable of, I didn't want to do anything to cross her, but this was important. "Can I ask why not?"

"When you leave here, you'll go home to your safe house and your nice family and you'll never see us again. I'll go back to him tomorrow. I don't want things to be worse for him than they already are." She spoke in a clipped, impersonal tone. I was still impressed, since this was the longest statement I'd heard from her all evening.

"You might have killed him and you're worried about him getting arrested?"

"He's my family; I have nowhere else to go." She turned away.

"That's not true. You don't need him. You could find a place at the shelter I keep hearing about."

Still looking away, she said, "Just don't talk to the cops."

I sighed. "But Gabby—" Her head snapped around to stare with her flaming eyes. "Gabriel," I corrected. "He took my wallet. I kept some stuff but there are personal things still in there, like my car registration."

"So?" she snapped.

"If he's dead, the police are going to come looking for me. It'll look very suspicious if I haven't filled an assault complaint like people normally would."

She glared, disbelieving. "Are you saying you'd lie for me?"

I suddenly felt caught. That was what I'd said, wasn't it? Or implied, at least. She was asking to make sure I wasn't going to turn her in. Was I going to turn her in? I felt absolutely petrified. I seriously doubted I was capable of lying to the police about something as serious as murder, or manslaughter, or whatever it was. So what was I supposed to say to her? My only hope seemed to lie in the fact that she couldn't kill me here, not with all these people watching.

Her eyes smoldered as she waited for my answer. After a long moment of silence passed, she must have decided she'd gotten her answer, and reached into her coat pocket. I was horrified and started to get up, thinking she was about to pull a knife, when instead she withdrew my wallet and held it up for me.

"And when were you going to give the wallet back to me?" I asked, astonished, carefully taking it from her. I hadn't noticed that she'd taken it along with the keys.

"You said you had everything. I was going to keep the cash."

"I see." I opened it and withdrew the $40 that was still inside. I put the wallet in my pocket and gave the bills back to her. "You can have the money."

She took it and stuffed it in her pocket without looking. "No cops."

"Okay. But aren't you concerned he might be dead?"

"I'll call someone to check it out."

I was about to ask whom when I suddenly realized I was also missing my cell phone. I quickly checked my pockets to be sure.

"I don't suppose you also have my phone?"

"Do you want me to call someone or not?" she asked with barely concealed rage. My God, didn't this woman have an off switch?

"So that's a yes." I held up my hand. "Fine. Call whomever you need to."

"Richards!" a nurse called out. Thank God! I got up slowly and followed her through a door into the ER.

It turned out I had three fractured ribs. I also had a number of bruises, both external and internal. I had given up the fight too easily for his punches and kicks to my legs to lead to any significant damage. It was the kicking he delivered when I was already down that really did the worst. But after getting poked and prodded, sent to some basement lab to be given multiple X-rays—which only took five minutes, though getting there and back took over an hour—I was told by the ER staff I was very lucky to have not sustained more serious injuries. The bones had only been cracked, not broken. There were no punctures or tears in any blood vessels or organs, and there was bruising but only mild internal bleeding which had already stopped. The ribs would heal in a month or two, and I should move cautiously and not do anything too strenuous in the meantime. Breathing, particularly deep breathing, would be painful for a while, but I should take some painkillers and continue breathing as normally as possible. That was it. I was discharged with no medication stronger than Tylenol. And when I said I'd been attacked by someone trying to rob me, and asked if I wanted to file a police report, I dutifully said no, that my injuries were only from falling down some cement stairs.

Gabby was still sitting in the lobby, exactly where I'd left her. I sat next to her, easing myself into the chair. It was now after two in the morning. Five hours had passed since I'd parked in the lot, excited that I might get to see Dawn early, and now it was too late. I guess I would have to try again next week. I wasn't sure how wise it would be to wait, now that I'd seen the kinds of people who followed her. I guess I didn't really have to personally speak to her before I tried to convince her father to get her committed, or at least evaluated, because it was possible that if I simply confronted her outright she would deny any problem. But I had wanted to talk to her anyway, if, for no other reason, to hear how she wound up as a DJ.

"So, did you find out about Diego?" I asked Gabby.

"Yeah," she said, sounding less on edge than she had earlier, maybe because she was tired, too. "He's fine. Dawn sent Eddie to get him, and he showed up complaining about both of us. But she knows he's full of shit."

"You talked to Dawn?" I said with a touch of awe. If she had called Dawn on my cell phone, then I now had Dawn's number. I had her number! Now I could just talk to her anytime, without hunting her down, without trawling the web or begging shady acquaintances. This assumed I was getting my phone back.

"You still want to talk to her?"

"What?"

"Dawn. She said you could stop by and talk. Unless you were tired."

"No, I'm not tired at all." And suddenly I wasn't.

Gabby pulled out my phone, and pressed the redial number. "Hi, Miss Dawn," she said, instantly sweet and girlish. She was actually smiling! "Yeah, he's out. He said yes. Okay, we'll be by. Right out front. See ya." She snapped the phone shut and handed it back to me. It felt as light as my wallet but was worth as much as gold. Before I stood up, I quickly checked my calls. In addition to a number I didn't recognize, which I joyfully assumed to be hers, I saw that Paul had called me once around eleven and then texted me twice. The calls hadn't been answered and he left no message, and the texts were just a string of question marks. I had realized while lying in the MRI it was a mistake to send Ahmed over there this afternoon. The fact that Paul left no messages was ominous, but I chose to assume he was merely worried about his car.

CHAPTER 22

I never did find out what club Dawn had been playing that night. Whatever it was it was already dark by the time we pulled up. She was standing outside talking to some burly guy in a black tee shirt who I hoped was a bouncer. When we pulled up, she came over to my door and opened it.

"Hi, Court. I heard you went through a lot of trouble to talk to me." She was wearing what seemed to be the uniform she'd worn in all Braxton's videos, a white tee shirt and headphones around her neck.

"Yeah," I grinned stupidly. I unsnapped my seat belt, thinking, and praying she was going to slide in right next to me, but she held up a black satchel.

"Hey Gabby, pop the trunk for me."

Gabby turned off the ignition and pulled out the keys. She got out, and met Dawn at the trunk of the car. It opened, then shut. Gabby came around and slid in next to me, and Dawn took the driver's seat. I felt miserable, because I really wasn't the least bit comfortable pressed up against Gabby. At least she wasn't staring at me any longer.

She turned the key and listened to the purr of the engine for a moment. She grinned, relishing it. "Nice car you got here, Court. I was thinking we should blast some ZZ Top or something, but I didn't bring my '80s stuff with me." Then she noticed the tape deck.

"But I see it wouldn't matter anyway. So! What do you do that you can afford such a nice car?"

"It's not mine; it's Paul's."

"Oh!" she said, sounding delighted by this information. "So what does he do that he can afford such a nice car?"

"He doesn't do anything. He's still a student."

"And in debt up to his ears, I see!" she laughed musically.

"It's the American way," I shrugged.

She put the car in first and tried to pull out, and the car stalled. She giggled as she started up the engine again. "Sorry, I don't drive much these days." This time she got it right, and as we drove away, she asked, "And how's Paul doing, by the way?"

Instead of answering her, since telling her what happened would clearly be a violation of Ahmed's rules, I asked her where we were going.

"A little pizza place I know that's open till five. I go there pretty often after my shows. You like pizza, right?" As if she had to ask. As if we hadn't fought over who got the last slice more than a few times back in the day. As if—well, yeah, it was usually me.

"Could we go to your house, Miss Dawn?" Gabby asked.

Dawn frowned as she stared ahead. "Gabby, you know I can't do that. I don't let anyone see where I live. People follow me wherever I go; I need to hold on to at least a little bit of my privacy. I know you guys make money on your own, but some of you expect me to give you whatever I have. If anyone found out where I lived, they'd hang around twenty-four-seven and expect me to put them up, like a hotel." She paused. "Yes, I know, I'm God, I'm able to provide. But it can't just be that easy." Another pause, and when she spoke again I could hear the very real sorrow in her voice. "I'm sorry, Gabby."

"Please? Just this once? I won't tell Diego, or any of the others. Not even Molly. Molly says you live in heaven. I want to go, please?"

Jesus Christ. I shook my head, keeping it imperceptible. What was Dawn doing to these kids?

"I can't, Gabby."

"But I saved your friend and everything! Please?"

I turned to look at her, and she had somehow assumed an adorable sad-puppy expression. It was freaky. "Gabriel, if you want someplace to stay, you can stay with me. I'm the one who owes you." I didn't at all want her staying in my apartment; even though she'd given me a great deal of help, I still considered her dangerous. But for that very reason I was willing to do whatever it took to keep her out of Dawn's place.

Her adorableness vanished instantly as she shifted her eyes to me. "I don't want to stay with you." Then, aware of how she looked, she managed a halting parody of a smile, and said, "But thanks anyway."

She looked back to Dawn and her features softened again, even though Dawn remained focused on the road. "Please, Dawn? Just once?"

For a long moment Dawn kept silent. Then finally she sighed and said, "All right."

"Thank you," said Gabby promptly.

Dawn kept on driving as she had been. She made no u-turns or other noticeable departures, which suggested the pizza parlor was in her neighborhood anyway.

Dawn lived in a studio apartment. It was tiny and cluttered. She had a bed—at least it was a real bed and not a mattress on the floor—pressed into a corner, a small table with a single chair on the opposite side of the room, a desk with a computer and a second chair next to it, a small television on a stand roughly in the middle of the room and sitting on a dirty beige carpet, and a bookcase that held stacks of CDs and not a single book. There was also a small kitchenette and a bathroom, and a single window. That was the entire place. The carpet was worn thin, the walls were dirty, and while there weren't any holes or leaks or any other obvious signs of squalor or decrepitude, it had a despairing aura. I felt I was seeing confirmation of my worst fears about Dawn.

She giggled, embarrassed by the tiny space. "Well, here we are." She took off her headphones and dropped them on the computer keyboard, and set the satchel next to it.

"This is heaven?" asked Gabby, looking around, troubled. I was truly afraid about how she was going to react to discovering the real Dawn. She could flip out at any moment, and I doubted I could protect Dawn in the state I was in. But at least I *was* here, and maybe this was exactly what I needed to demonstrate to her the danger she was in. That was why I had gone to so much trouble to find her, after all.

"Of course not," said Dawn. She looked Gabby directly in the eyes. She had to look up; Gabby was an inch taller. "Did you think I lived in a mansion? Would that be heaven?"

"Well...," she said slowly, and took a minute to mull the question over. "No, I guess not," she finally said.

"Heaven isn't any one place on earth. Some people find Heaven on a beautiful beach, or a nice clean house, and some people can find it in a little jail cell. Heaven is where you find your peace. Heaven is right here." She touched Gabby on the forehead with one finger.

"Okay, Miss Dawn," Gabby said without enthusiasm.

Dawn watched her carefully a moment longer, trying to read her eyes, then moved off into the kitchenette. "Besides," she said lightly as she went, "this place is huge compared to the room I had at St. Teresa's when I was a nun. Hey, you guys want anything? Sorry we didn't get the pizza after all, since I don't have much around here, but there's some cereal. And some juice. Or I could make coffee.

"You weren't a nun," I said in spite of my caution. "Professor Braxton said you just made it all up."

She came over to the counter separating the kitchen area from the rest of the room and smiled at me. "And you met Scott, too! You've been busy! I don't know if I should be flattered or worried. I bump into you and you investigate my whole life. Or have you been stalking me for a while?"

"I'm not stalking you. I was just trying to find you, since you don't have a website. Besides, how can I be stalking you if you're God? When you stalk God, isn't that being devout?"

Giggling again, her eyes twinkled. "Touché." I pulled out the chair at the table and sat down. I was feeling very tired and the pain in my side ached every time I inhaled. Gabby wandered over to the bed and sat there.

"And I really was a nun," Dawn continued. "Well, a postulate. You're a postulate for a year, then a novitiate for two years, then you presumably know you want to be there for life and you take your vows and they throw away the key. And I was there a whole seven and a half months. That's two and a half months at a time over each of the three summer breaks I was at school. So that part was true. I really did spend my summers there scrubbing the floors and saying the rosary and doing my darnedest to peer deep into my soul. It's pretty interesting peering into your soul. You should try it."

"Is that why you studied psychology?"

She laughed. "Boy, you just know everything about me, huh?"

"Not everything. I still don't know the most important thing." She raised her eyebrows expectantly, and I continued, "How you became a DJ."

Now her smile turned quizzical, wondering if I was kidding or if I thought there was a connection. But after a moment she laughed again. "Oh, I see. Ahmed gave you a little lecture, didn't he? Don't talk to the crazy woman about her silly delusion. I guess that's why you don't want to tell me about Paul." She looked around. "I was in here for a reason. Oh, right, did you want anything, Court?" I shook my head. "Gabby?" I looked over and Gabby was lying down on the bed. She was still wearing her jacket and sneakers.

Dawn went over and sat down beside her. "You tired? You're not still disappointed I don't live in a mansion, are you?"

"It's just... that even Molly has a bigger apartment than your's; it's got two bedrooms," said Gabby, quietly struggling in a crisis of faith.

"That's because Molly shares that place with five other girls," countered Dawn. " And they need the second bedroom for their business."

"Are you going to have sex with him?"

"With Court?" Dawn asked, surprised. Then she chuckled. "Of course not. Court's just an old friend of mine. And after what happened tonight, I'm sure he's not going to be having sex with anyone for a while." Gabby giggled a bit at that last comment. Boy did I feel insulted, even if it was true.

Dawn grabbed the headphones from the keyboard and brought them over to Gabby. "I'm going to have a quick talk with Court before he leaves. You ignore us and get some sleep." She put the headphones over Gabby's ears.

Gabby stared up in awe, trying to see the headphones, as though they were a crown of light. She was like that for a minute; I was starting to worry she was going to hurt her eyes, when she finally rolled onto her side. Dawn came back over and dragged the desk chair to the table and sat down across from me. "Just the music?" she asked. "Don't want to lecture me, tell me how I need to teach these kids some morals?"

"Just the music. Just a friendly chat, like you wanted yesterday."

"Oh, so now you want to chat."

"Yeah. I'm sorry about yesterday. I was shocked, is all."

"Well, that's all right." She thought for a moment, leaning forward and putting her arms on the table, then said, "You missed my show tonight. All metal. You like metal?"

"I hate it."

"Yeah, it's not my favorite, either. I get hired by those clubs more often than others because they get a kick out of having God play their devil music. But it lets me play my favorite remix. It's a mix I did with Marilyn Manson's cover of 'Personal Jesus.' You've heard that song?" She smiled mischievously, and then sang the first line in case I hadn't. "'Reach out and touch faith.'"

"Yeah, I've heard it. And I heard how you bring down the house with it. Is that your theme song?"

"No, but I try to play it at most of my shows. You already know that? People love it when I put it on. It's too bad you didn't get to hear it, you know. It's not just the obvious that people cheer for; it's actually a really good remix in and of itself. My best ever. It's such a repetitive song that breaking it up with some random stuff improves it quite a lot. In my opinion, at least. You want to listen?"

I shook my head. To be honest, I was glad to have escaped a night of deafening noise and unintelligible screeching. Of course, if I had my choice, I would have taken the music over the trip to the hospital, but now that it was all over I could pass on it easily.

"All right then. Let's see, how I became a DJ. Not really much of a story, to tell you the truth. When I was in college, I went to a lot of raves. My original intent wasn't in music or dancing, but trying to score some hallucinogens." She smiled, embarrassed again.

I was taken aback. I'd, um, dabbled a little in college myself, an occasional joint, like everyone did, but somehow I'd never imagined Dawn doing the same. "Praying wasn't working?" I managed to quip.

"Yeah. Well, it's a different thing. They say these things, these drugs, and meditation, are all mind-altering, but they're mind altering in different ways. When I sat in silence in the convent, everything was clearer, more real. When I was taking Ecstasy, everything was hyped up, different, less real, somehow. I still felt alive, but being centered and being blasted are two different experiences of aliveness. Although there was some melding. The meditation really helped ease the landing when I was coming down off my highs. And I think it's why I never got addicted. I enjoyed it, I got to dance like crazy, but it never gripped me like it did some people.

"Like my boyfriend. In my senior year I started dating this guy, Iggy. Well, his name was Ignacio, but everyone called him Iggy. He was one of the guys who helped put on a lot of these raves I attended. In fact, he was usually the DJ. So that's the short answer; I got into it because I dated a DJ.

"Iggy sort of took me up as his protégé and showed me all his equipment and taught me all this stuff about how to deejay, which I thought was weird at first, since I didn't know a thing about it and wasn't interested in music. But then I found out he was doing it to keep our relationship secret from his other girlfriend."

I coughed politely. She shrugged.

"Anyway, I could be at his house all day and supposedly her suspicion wasn't aroused because I was only there to learn the trade. Although I'm sure she wasn't an idiot. But yes, I went along with it, because it was cool. He let me do a few of the parties, and I enjoyed rocking out as an active participant. Being the DJ, you're the center of everything, running the show, and at the same time nobody pays attention to you, unless they have a request. I kind of like that."

"Sort of like being God?"

"Very apt," she nodded. "Eventually I did more and more of Iggy's shows. He, unfortunately, had developed all kinds of addictions: to marijuana, to Ecstasy, to cocaine, to liquor. A lot of times he would be so stoned, or high, or just plain drunk that he couldn't perform. See, that was the real point of teaching me how to do it. It wasn't just a cover for his girlfriend, it was so he'd have someone to take over when he couldn't perform. Someone soft and manipulatable, like a former nun. I told him about my stint in the convent. That really turns some guys on, you know? It's creepy. But he wanted me covering his jobs and not be some potential competitor; in that way, he could shirk it and still get the money, and not worry about losing his business.

"It lasted a while, but eventually I did end up a competitor. I got tired of it and broke up with him and struck out on my own. I'd met a lot of the people responsible for these things, so I had some contacts. I played raves and other private parties, and then got some bookings for real clubs. I made a lot of money—well, it seemed like a lot when I was a recent graduate, now I realize it's barely enough to pay the rent. At least I get to write all my music purchases off my income taxes."

"No radio?"

She shook her head. "No. I interviewed, sent in some tapes and that sort of thing, but I've never gotten a spot. They all tell me I don't have a good 'radio presence.'"

"What does that mean?"

"It means my voice is too quiet for them. And I don't have a 'dynamic' enough personality. So no radio. And I've never been offered a permanent position as a house DJ for any club either, and I've applied to a lot of clubs."

"And are you surprised? Why would anyone hire someone who's crazy? I can't believe you find any work at all."

She pursed her lips. "No, I mean even before that. I didn't tell anyone I was God out in LA. It was only when I came back here that I decided meditating wasn't enough, and that God should be active in the world. There are so many people out there I can touch." She stopped and smiled. "But I guess that's not the story you're interested in?"

"I guess not. But I am interested in knowing why you came back. Was it to influence the nation's capitol with your divine presence?"

"No, no," she laughed. "I came back here for work. I'll tell you a secret, Court. I'm actually a lousy DJ. I mean, LA is the entertainment capitol; out there, everybody's a showman. Every DJ I know in LA is a wannabe rap star, a would-be Dr. Dre or Daft Punk. It's not just turntables anymore, you know. Mixes are just the start. They do their own tracks, riffs, whole albums of electronicia, whatever. It's a very serious profession. I can't do any of that. I don't know enough, I don't have the equipment, I don't have the right style or the right attitude. I'm not a musician. Don't get me wrong; I like my job, but I'll never be as enthusiastic about this stuff as they are. I can't compete. That's why I could never get a permanent job. So I came back here, because, frankly, there's less competition. There's still a scene here too, but I can keep afloat."

I shifted uncomfortably in my seat. "Dawn, that sounds kind of suspicious. Please don't tell me this whole thing is just a publicity stunt." A little notoriety was far too trivial for something as smite-worthy as what she was doing.

"Of course not!" She raised her eyebrows and frowned, trying to look hurt. Then she smiled again. "It's not doing me any good; you said so yourself. But you're not the first person who's asked me, and it bothers me. I sometimes wish I could find a new job so I won't have to deal with it."

"Wait a minute." I held up my hand, feeling especially disturbed. "You want to get out of the business not because you're lousy at it, but because it casts suspicion on your divine status?"

"More or less. The tricky part is trying to find something better. What kind of job should God have? At least now I have an outreach. And I can meet people, go places, keep on top of the *zeitgeist*, all that stuff. Where else am I going to get that? Most people imagine God doing some kind of quiet, dignified, manual labor, mostly because of Jesus being a carpenter, but also because of the idea of God's empathy with the poor, His humility. A God with money doesn't make much sense unless you're the emperor or something. I don't know. Buddha was a prince but he gave it up to become a wandering mendicant. I thought about it, but there really isn't much of a place in our society for alms begging. People don't seek the spiritual there anymore. Most people don't give because there are government programs, and I couldn't take money that might have gone to someone who actually needed it. And to be honest I don't really want to live out in the open. I've gotten used to my roof and my radiator and my late-night pizzas."

I wondered if she'd forgotten the headphones and this confession was more intended for Gabby than for me, and I glanced over at her and saw she was still curled up.

"Maybe you could teach yoga," I said, tongue-in-cheek.

"I don't know any yoga."

"Well, meditation, then."

"Yeah, then I could be like one of those Indian gurus, and wear flowers in my hair and talk about Karma. Meditation's easy, Court. It'd feel like stealing to take money for teaching it."

I watched the vivacity that shown through her eyes. She really was a different person, and it really was because she'd gained something during the years we'd been apart. Maybe she'd uncovered something with all her mind-altering adventures. She wasn't daydreaming any longer. I though maybe she'd found what she had missed out on when we were both recovering.

"Were you really a nun?" I asked, smiling at her.

"I really was. For seven months. Don't worry, I didn't lie to them. I didn't pretend I wanted to sign up. They knew I was getting my psych degree and had other goals and I was only there to learn from them about peace and the love of God."

"Did you have to convert?"

"To Catholicism? Yeah. They kind of expect it before they let you in. So yeah, I'm Catholic now. Ridiculous, huh? I still haven't told my dad. I don't think he'll care, but it's kind of tricky to bring that sort of thing up."

"You had to confess to convert, right? Must have been some confession."

"Not really. I've never sinned, of course, but I have done a few things they frown upon—like sleep with you!—so I told the priest about those things."

"But you left out the part about being God. Seems odd you wanted to learn about the love of God without mentioning it's self-love. Or were you not God back then?"

She pursed her lips again and leaned back in the chair. "Come on, Court. You didn't want to talk about it but you try to sneak it in anyway. It's okay, just go ahead and ask. Ahmed will never know."

"Okay." I took a deep breath. I'd been waiting for this all evening; it was the whole reason I'd gone searching for her. I knew what was truly going on, and I knew I had to confront her to stop it. I thought I had time, maybe weeks, but after what I'd seen tonight I feared nothing could wait.

"I want to start off by saying I know you're not insane," I said.

"Of course I'm not insane; I told you that yesterday," she said, amused.

"I know this because you lied to your father. You told him you didn't know what the Professor was talking about, that it was all a misunderstanding. You couldn't do that if you were genuinely insane. You wouldn't be able to turn it on and off."

She sat silently, trying to read my face. "You think that was wrong, to tell him that?" she asked finally. "Daddy wouldn't understand; he'd just get upset. I don't want to hurt him."

"Well, it's a little late for that." I regretted having to tell her this. "Tomorrow I'm going over there and telling him everything. I'm going to ask him to help me get you committed. And if he doesn't I'll do whatever it takes to see to it myself."

She shifted in her seat, sitting up straighter and folding her hands in her lap, but her expression returned to amusement. "Why's that? I don't understand; you just said I wasn't insane."

"You're not insane in the way Ahmed and the Professor think you are. You're not schizophrenic. But you're dangerous, Dawn, and that's why I have to get you help."

She tilted her head to indicate curiosity. "Is this because of Diego? Court, it's not a cult, please understand that. They're just a bunch of kids. They were their own little group long before I came along. I hang out with them sometimes, but I'm only trying to help them, to get them past their fear so they can find some stability, some security."

"Dawn, Diego said you were just some nut, and as soon as he did, that girl," I pointed to the sleeping Gabby, "bashed his head into a wall."

"She didn't bash his head into a wall, she just knocked him out. I told you, he was fine."

"He was lucky. What's she going to do to the next person who mocks you?" I leaned across the table and spoke softly, afraid she might hear me anyway. "What's she going to do to *you* when she finds out the truth?"

"Court, Gabby's not a monster. She's harmless. She just acts tough. It's all an act, to protect herself on the streets."

"It didn't look like an act to me."

Dawn was beginning to show a flush of anger. "That's because Diego was really hurting you; he was really trying to steal your car. Court, she drove you to the hospital and sat in a waiting room for what, four, five hours? Holding your cell phone, and your money, and she sat there waiting for you. For you. Not for me; for you."

"Yeah. I'm your old friend, remember? Gabby only helped me to please you. She made that clear when she was begging to see your apartment. And she obviously hates me."

"She doesn't hate you. I told you, it's just an act. Why don't we wake her up and ask?"

I shook my head, certain she was bluffing. "Absolutely not."

She slumped in her chair, but seemed to have gone back to merely being entertained. "So I don't get it, Court. If she's the dangerous one, why do you want to have *me* committed?"

"It's not about her. She's just an example. I know what your true intentions are, Dawn."

"What?" she asked, honestly baffled.

"You asked me what kind of job a messiah should have, but a messiah has only one job."

"Court, I'm not a messiah."

I shook my head. "You are. You're Jesus, and you're just waiting for your Judas." Finally she must have put it together, because her eyes widened in shock.

"Court!" she said harshly, sitting up. "You think," she said, in an acid whisper, "that I'm suicidal again? That's why you're stalking me?" She relaxed again. "Why on earth would you think that?"

"Dawn, I know what you're doing," I answered. "This whole thing is nothing more than an elaborate way to commit suicide. It's so simple. All you do is call yourself God, and the crazies come out of nowhere. Eventually you find someone crazy enough to kill you, and you finally get out without having to spill your own blood, still an innocent. Hell, you're Catholic now; maybe they'll make you a saint."

She stared at me like I was the crazy one. "Really? Seriously, that's what you think?" She shook her head slowly. "That's absurd, Court. First of all, it was a long time ago. I'm no more suicidal now than you are."

"No, no. We were never the same. You never got over it."

"And second it doesn't even make any sense. I've been doing this for months and no one's even threatened me."

"Well, sure it's not very efficient. But it trades efficiency for subtlety."

She leaned over the table as far as she could and pleaded with her eyes, trying to convince me with sincerity. "Court, death is the furthest thing from my mind. I'm not that girl anymore. I found what I was looking for. I found my mission. I found the answer."

"You found the answer? Is that like the meaning of life? What's the meaning of life, Dawn?"

"To live!" she exclaimed, frustrated. "Everyone knows that."

"That's your answer? It's pathetic. Why all the games yesterday?"

"I was just being mysterious." She slipped down in her chair and laughed a strangled laugh. "I do that a lot."

"So telling me to ask Paul was just a distraction?"

She shrugged. "Basically. Why, did he say anything interesting?"

"No! He said exactly what I thought he was going to say. He hasn't changed, Dawn. He hasn't gained any special insight from being gay."

"I gathered that after last night." She focused on me again. "Look, you know perfectly well you won't get me committed. I know what they'll ask, and I already know the answers."

It was my turn to lean across to her. "Dawn, I have to try. You're not going to convince me I'm wrong, because there's no other explanation for what you're doing."

A wan smile spread over her face. "Court, I really am God. That's the explanation. It's true. I really am God."

I put my head in my hands. I was getting too tired, but thought of one more thing to try. "How about this, Dawn: What was it you told the guy in the wheelchair? Because I don't think it was 'to live.'"

"I told Tyrone that being God changes how people relate to me. Whether they believe me or not, it colors everything I do with them. It becomes holy, or if they don't believe me, adventurous. It's not every day you talk to a crazy woman. Even the actual schizophrenics see me as otherworldly. People open up to me in ways they never would otherwise. I'm God, and I've come here for them. My mere presence makes life special. These kids I've been following, they confide in me, they trust me with their secret dreams and fears and things they wouldn't tell anyone else. All of them, even those who doubt me, like Diego. They open up and sometimes find truths about themselves they weren't even aware of."

Or like Paul, I thought. He'd been mocking her and it still affected him. I sighed. "So is that it? Is that what you're out here doing? Some weird social work project? Some experimental form of therapy?" She thought for a moment, and I pressed, angrily, "It's not, is it? Please don't tell me that's what this is about."

She shrugged. "Not intentionally. It's sort of become that, I guess, since I've gotten involved with these kids, but it didn't start out that way. That was never the point. I was God, and I thought I should act in the world, at least a little on the margins, not just watch it all passively, the way I was doing."

I was buoyed by her reference to there being a "point" to this, but I still couldn't fathom what it entailed. "Well, I should hope not," I said. "Because you wouldn't let the Professor pin you under his magnifying glass for that. And you wouldn't have lied about it to me. Dawn, you've done things, said things, that are going to follow you around for the rest of your life. And even if none of these 'kids' of yours snaps and kills you, they'll be pretty heartbroken if they ever find out."

She looked away from me, down at the table. "Listen—"

"No, forget it. I think I've had enough for tonight. I would like it if you'd make me that cup of coffee now, because right this moment I'm way too tired to drive. I'll get pulled over if I even attempt it, if I don't crash first."

"Okay," she said, still not looking at me. She got up and started fiddling around in the kitchenette. I didn't know what to think anymore. I had been so sure earlier she was suicidal, which explained everything neatly and simply, but now I wasn't so certain. I wasn't entirely dissuaded yet, but there was no longer any evidence I could point to. Maybe I'd been wrong about Gabby, and maybe Dawn... I was beginning to think she really was insane, after all. Hell, maybe she really did have schizophrenia. She didn't seem to, but I was no psychiatrist. What did I know? There just wasn't any explanation.

I was afraid for her. I'd felt reassured earlier after deducing that she was acting out some complex suicide plot, because it was something that could be fixed. But even other mental illnesses could be helped with medication. Now I realized that there was no therapy that was capable of curing her; there was something inside of her that was too subtle for any pill to reach. That frightened me in a way that was new to me, an unfocused terror of being completely beyond my depths, of drowning in a forgone hope.

While the coffee brewed, I called my supervisor and left a message on her voicemail that I had been in a minor accident and had just been released from the hospital, and wouldn't be in today or tomorrow. After I hung up, Dawn came back around to the table and kept me awake by asking me questions about my own life. I told her all about my pathetic college career and the only job I'd ever been able to hold on to and for that reason would probably be stuck doing for the rest of my life. She displayed no sympathy, and like everyone else, she was amused to hear where I worked.

CHAPTER 23

I drained my coffee cup. The heat of it, the rich smell, these alone pricked my senses. I could relax now. The caffeine would take effect in a few minutes, and hopefully be enough to get me home. It still wasn't safe, but there was no other way. I doubt I would trust anyone else to be driving at this hour, either, not even Dawn, who wouldn't take me anyway because she couldn't leave her guest here alone. The hardest part, of course, would be getting out of the city, where I was unfamiliar with the roads. For several minutes, Dawn explained to me how to get back to 14th Street, which was the quickest way home.

I sighed. "Well. I guess that's everything then."

She smiled softly. "You're not still going to tell my Daddy, are you?"

"No, there's no point. I guess the whole thing was too convoluted. And even if it's true, you're right, you know how to get out easily enough. Hell, even I could get out of it. I remember the questions on those risk assessments. 'Have you been feeling depressed for more than two weeks?' 'Have you had thoughts about suicide?' Pretty stupid."

"Yet they still work because most people answer honestly. Depressed people don't want to die. They really do just want help."

"I remember." But I didn't. I recalled genuinely wanting to die, but maybe the years of living with it had clouded my recollection. But I did know she was right. Part of my expectation in coming here was betting she'd admit what she was up to when I confronted her and break down and ask for help. The fact she hadn't asked abetted her insistence that I was wrong.

"Pretty silly, huh?" I grinned at her. "Us still talking about it all these years later."

"Well, you brought it up."

"Yeah, well. How about I call you tomorrow, just to check up?"

"And after that? Will I see you again soon? Are you going to become one of my followers?"

"No." I was surprised she'd asked.

"Why not? Look at all the effort you've put in to follow me tonight."

I shook my head. I would follow her to the ends of the earth, but not like this. "Dawn, there is no way I could ever believe you were actually God."

"Well, you don't have to believe. A lot of my friends don't."

"No, Dawn. I know you too well to go along with it."

She smirked. "Because you've had sex with me?"

"Well, yeah. It's kind of hard to take you seriously as God when I know how much you liked it. Besides, it's not just that. We were best friends for almost a year. We talked about everything, but I never had any idea that you were divine. If two people can be friends yet not know the most important things about each other, what kind of friendship is that? Either you weren't God then, or you were deceiving me, and how could anyone ever trust a god who did that?"

She appeared concerned for a moment, and I hoped I had scored a point. But then she said, "Okay. When did you learn Paul was gay?"

I shook my head. "What does that have to do with anything?"

"Well, you knew Paul a lot longer than you knew me, but you didn't know the most important thing about him until… whenever."

"I can't believe you said that!" I said, screwing up my face. I thought of objecting that they were completely different situations, and that it wasn't the most important thing about him. But I didn't, because she was right. Was she truly insane, that she kept lying to me like this?

"Court, I only ask that you keep an open mind," she said impassively.

"Give me a miracle," I blurted. I had intended on this earlier, but my reaction had been instant and unconscious.

She smiled, sadly. "Ah. At last, there it is. I knew you couldn't resist. But are you forgetting I already gave you a miracle yesterday? To fix Molly?"

"It hasn't happened yet," I answered quickly, piqued. "She's still in the hospital. Besides, you said it was inevitable. And I hope you realize she could have died. If Ahmed hadn't been there…"

"Then what? You think he was the only person in that club who knew CPR?"

"It was still risky. You knew something was wrong with her, but you let her carry on as usual."

"I've noticed something was wrong with Molly over a week ago. And since then, the entire time, I've had someone follow her around. Someone has always at least been in earshot every moment of the day."

I had to give her credit; that was probably true. There had been that woman with her yesterday. And Diego had trailed her earlier Saturday, though the fact that people like Diego were involved meant it wasn't as secure an operation as she was implying. Still, I guess she had done what she could.

I drummed my fingers on the table. "Fine, point taken. I still want a miracle."

"Sure, Court," she said lazily. "Whatever you want. Just ask."

She was expecting a challenge, I thought. I felt pain with every breath I took, so it would be obvious what I would ask for. I almost did, just to see how she would handle it, but that wasn't the plan I had thought of. No, I was going to take her seriously.

I took a deep breath and mustered all the solemnity I could. "Dawn," I said, "I want you to fix it. Everything. All the suffering in the world, all the sadness and neglect, I want you to fix it all, put things the way they're supposed to be. Make the whole world right."

For a moment she looked stunned, then amazed, before she finally started laughing, laughter which quickly became little hiccups of mirth. "Nobody's ever asked me that!" she said, when she'd regained her composure, still amused. "I think you've got it, Court. You've got it."

"Do it, Dawn. Make the world right."

She shook her head. "Court, the world *is* right." She opened her arms wide to encompass the room, the building, the whole of creation. "Everything is beautifully and wonderfully made. I created all things, I cause all things to come to pass. I am perfect, and my world is perfect. I know it's hard to see, but the Hand of God is in everything, and everything is as it should be." She lowered her arms and looked at me, a self-advertising look of beatific calm on her face.

I didn't believe it. It was the exact same ludicrous thing she'd told the guy in the wheelchair yesterday. I'd sat here talking to her for the whole evening, and she hadn't moved an inch. I was right earlier; her mind was in an unreachable fortress, or perhaps a dungeon. Either way, I was wasting my time here.

"Okay, Dawn. That's bullshit. I know it, you know it, everyone knows it."

"Not at all. It's the heart of every religious faith on earth."

"Bullshit."

"I know it's difficult to make sense of, but it's true. That's what I've learned by being God. I've experienced it directly, from the inside. I've been able to feel its truth, its ecstatic, rapturous truth."

"Show me," I said desperately.

She leaned back and looked at me with sweet sadness. "You can't let it go, can you? You're stuck, buried in the turgid clay without noticing the wonders right above you. You resist the touch of awe. You can't even just sit back and enjoy the magic like everyone else."

"There's no magic. There's no magic, no miracles, and no mystery. I *know* you Dawn. I know you to your core."

"You don't know me."

"Yes, I do. I know you because—I love you, Dawn. I *love* you."

For a moment, she was very still. Then she carefully spoke. "Court, that was six years ago."

"And not a day of it has gone by without regretting that I let you go."

She closed her eyes for several seconds. When she opened them, she said quietly, "See, this is exactly why I didn't want to talk to you yesterday."

"What do you mean?"

"Why I lied about where I was playing."

"I thought that was because you wanted me to hear Molly's sob story direct from the source."

"I did. But that wasn't the reason. You caught me off guard, and after the short talk we had, I didn't think I could simply have a normal conversation with you. I wouldn't have agreed to talk tonight, either, except you went through so much to find me, I couldn't turn you away."

I smiled, hesitantly. "You do still care, don't you?"

"I… I…" She became serious again. "I care for everyone, for all of my children, for the whole creation."

"But you and I, Dawn…"

She shook her head. "Look, if I tell you what it's all about, will you be satisfied?"

"Never. There's only one thing you can say that will satisfy me, and it has nothing to do with religion."

"We're not soul mates, Court. We can't be. I'm divine, and you're just a man."

I felt a sudden flash of anger and smacked the table. "Damn it, Dawn. Stop lying to me." I managed to contain myself after that, because I'd wanted to avoid accusations at all costs, but I was immensely frustrated. I realized my hands were trembling slightly.

"I'm not lying, Court. I'm really not. To be honest, I don't know why it's such a big secret. I was going to tell everybody; that was the whole point. To share what I've learned, to open their eyes. I never wanted to run a cult, or have people worship me. I never wanted to be God. I just wanted to understand. I've spent my whole life trying to understand, like I missed something vital that everyone else knew. For the longest time I was searching."

"Every freshman does that," I added weakly. The tremors had stopped. "I mean, I know there was 9/11 and all that."

"No, no. It wasn't a phase for me. I kept looking until… until…"

"Until what?"

She sighed. "At the end of my senior year, I had a professor who, for his last class, gave this silly little lecture for 'inspiration.' It was one of those motivational speeches, you know, with trite epigrams like 'think big' and 'do what you love.' You know the kind I mean?"

"Yeah," I said, already on edge. I knew the kind only too well.

"Well, in the midst of all this fluff, he said something that really affected me, that finally showed me what I needed to do."

"What?" I silently begged her not to tell me she found enlightenment in a cheap motivation speech. Dear God, she was going to say "Believe in yourself, and you can do anything." Or you can be anything. Something like that. The moral of a thousand children's stories. Kim would say things like that. She believed in thinking yourself into good fortune and positive coincidences and a lifetime of happiness. But thinking yourself into divinity? How could she be serious?

"Now, when I tell you what he said, you'll laugh, because you've probably heard it a million times. It's nothing original; I'd heard it a million times myself, but for some reason this one time it really struck me as truly profound. He said, 'You can't know someone until you've walked a mile in their shoes.'"

Well, she was right; I had heard it a million times before. I didn't laugh, though, because at this point I was incapable. I was still waiting for her to say something about believing in yourself... "So?" I asked sharply.

"And here I was, trying to know God. I put two and two together."

I understood. I understood so much I wished I hadn't come. She wasn't trying to think herself into divinity. She was doing something even worse. I stood up suddenly, my mouth agape. "Shit, Dawn. You're just *pretending*? This whole thing is nothing more than a game?"

"Court," she said, calm and reasonable. "It's not a game. It's a form of meditation. That's all. That's all *all* religion is. Religion's all about trying to know God, whether through prayer or scripture or experiences or actions. It's to make you think about God. I'm thinking about God, all the time. And more than that, I'm learning to think the way God thinks. I see the world the way God sees it."

"Real blasphemy is what you're doing!"

"It's not blasphemy. I do it out of love. I love God, and I want to learn from Him. That's all. I imitate Him to learn from Him. To learn how He thinks, how He acts."

"But Dawn, you're pretending—so, what about all those people you have following you—"

"—Most of whom don't really believe I'm divine. You found that out pretty well for yourself."

"But some do."

"I know. That's why it's so hard to stop." She gave me a quick smile. "Do you want to hear what I've learned? How God sees the world?"

"Dawn, I don't care!"

She stood up then, slowly, her eyes on me always, and spoke carefully as she motioned expansively. "I look out at the world, Court, and I'm responsible for everything I see. Everything that exists, every person, every animal or plant or building, every star in the sky, I created them, every last one of them. Everything that happens, I caused. Or at least, I allowed to happen, which is really the same thing, because I'm all powerful. I know everything. The world is my domain. It's sort of like the exact opposite of traditional religion. Instead of being selfless and having nothing, I'm completely selfish. I claim it all, and I have it all. No matter where I am or what I'm doing, I want for nothing. The whole universe belongs to me. Everything is under my control. I can feel it, Court, the limitless power."

"You don't seem to have much power to me."

"That's just it." She swept her hand in the direction of the room's window, towards the city, a city filled with men and women lusting after power. "This is the world that God has made. It's exactly the way God wants it, right now. It's not about getting power to change things; He doesn't change things. It's about understanding God. If this is God's world, I learn from Him by looking out and imagining that this is my world, and that I orchestrate it just as He does. I take the responsibility upon myself. I say to myself, 'Why would I create the world like this? Why would I let things happen the way that they do?' Court, in the end you have to see that everything is perfect, with the good and the bad, just the way it is. It's not a view that you can justify with logic. It doesn't make any sense; it's just something you know. It truly opens your eyes, gives you a sense of peace."

"That's why I feel love for everyone, and could never judge them for anything. I created them, just as they are. They only do as I intended them to do. How could I fault them for that? I created them, they're part of me."

"Not even when they beat the crap out of somebody?"

"I don't judge; I acknowledge people the way they are. That doesn't mean he's going to get away with it. There are always consequences." She stepped a few paces closer to me. We could touch each other, if either of us just reached out.

"That's not very comforting, Dawn."

"But it is! If only you could see it the way I do. The way God does! Everyone should try it. It's the ultimate meditation. People are often unhappy because they're confused by the dissonance between the ideal represented in religion and the reality of the world. They struggle to make sense of it all, but all the theology in the world can't clarify things any better than the experience of living it. If people saw the world as God does, all this division, all this hatred and fear would vanish."

I chuckled barrenly, without feeling. At least her comments were getting me to focus on her again. But all the same, it was absurd. She thought she was going to bring world peace? She thought anyone would convert to her nonsensical religion? Such utopian dreams are and have always been nothing but pure fantasy, and she would be sorely disappointed if she thought hers were any different. She was drowning in her own lies, her own myths. "You can't be serious," I said.

She was still watching me, calmly. "It's the answer," she said.

"Dawn, you only think about love and peace because that's what you already believed. Your God is a creature of your imagination, and so He confirms what you already thought about Him. It's a Rorschach. If some more critical, or say, more callous people tried what you're proposing, all they'd do is see exactly the world they already believe in. They'd look around, pretending to be God, and they'd say, 'I gave these people life, and see how they're sinning against me night and day. I hate them all, and the bad things happening to them are my well-deserved judgments, and if they don't repent I'm going to send them to hell.'"

She shook her head. "No they wouldn't, because that's not consistent. If you didn't like things, you'd want to change them. But God doesn't change anything, even though He could. This is because He made the world, just the way it is, because this is the way He wants it. This is perfect."

"I don't know, maybe God likes being angry."

She smiled at me. "Doubt it. Nice try, though. Maybe you should test it. Do you know anyone who thinks like that?"

I shook my head. "There's so much misery in this world. Are you going to tell me that's what God wants? What kind of kind of God is that, that wants this? How does it make sense? What could possibly be the reason for that?"

"Court, it can't be learned with words, but through experience."

I shook my head and gave up. All she had were *feelings*. That was her great revelation. "Dawn, I think you just like being God. You're leading the Professor on, and these friends you keep talking about, not just so you don't upset the handful of nuts who actually believe you, but because if you told them, then they'd all be their own gods and you'd just be some random girl again. You like being the center of attention, having people cheer you on, crowd around you, hang on your every word. Those people are in awe of you, and you don't want it to end. You can claim otherwise, but you do want a cult and a movie and your name in the books. This isn't about world peace, or knowing God, it's about you being superior to the rest of us."

"No—it's not like that, Court. I really am trying to help those kids. They don't have a place of their own, or families, or hope for the future, but they listen to me. I can guide them in the right direction."

"Not from what I've seen. And what, are you going to send them all to the hospital?"

She looked away, down at the ground, just for a moment. "Well, a few of them do need psychiatric treatment."

I gave her another half-hearted chuckle, but this time it arose more naturally. "All right, Dawn. I guess I should be going. It's really, really late." We had probably gone as far as possible, but at least I had gotten a confession out of her. It was something, and maybe tomorrow, or next week, I could try to reintroduce her to the real world.

"Did you really mean that, what you said?"

"I really and truly meant it," I answered gently. "You were never a random girl to me."

"Oh." She glanced away again, uneasy. "Okay, Court. Goodnight."

"Goodnight, Dawn," I said, and opened my arms in the hopes I might at least get a hug out of this. Instead, she placed her hand on my forehead.

"Bless you," she said.

CHAPTER 24

I walked back to the car, despondent, kicking myself for being so stupid. I couldn't believe I told her that I loved her. Well, it had pushed her into opening up, but her cold indifference was piercing. What kind of a response was that? "Oh." That was all she could say. It hurt. Was the pain worth it? I guess. The worst of it was, because I was feeling this pain, I knew what I had said was true. It wasn't just some trick to affect her emotions, but an honest, desperate plea. Yes, I had exaggerated; I hadn't spent every day of the last six years pining for her. I had counted her gone and had moved on, but seeing her again yesterday made it impossible to think there could ever be anyone else, and now I felt bereft.

When I got outside, it was very dark, nothing but street lights, and it was completely silent. At this hour, there was absolutely no one around, and nothing going on. The loudest sound was the breeze passing by. If I strained my ears I could hear some cars a couple of blocks over, but that was all. I stood for a moment, absorbing this tranquility.

I could imagine being spiritual in such tranquility.

Well…damn it, there was only one way I was going to understand Dawn.

Feeling like a complete idiot, I opened my arms to embrace the world and thought to myself, I am God, this is the way I want things to be.

I wanted to be standing here, my side aching, rejected by the woman I was in love with. I wanted to have a low-level job, with no chance of advancement. I wanted my brother to be gay. I wanted to live in a world of misery and hate, of terrorism and disasters and disease. Sure I did. I wanted all of it. The whole world is the way I want it to be. I created it. I created these cars, and those buildings, and the moon in the sky, and the clouds surrounding it. And the people, the ones sleeping inside those buildings, they were a part of me, and I had given them their happiness, and their pain. Their lives would have ups and downs, all arranged by me. The waves would crash, and the birds would sing, all for me. I was aware of the wind; I felt it against my skin, because I had caused it to blow.

The minutiae of the scene around me filled my senses. Every movement, every smell, every sound. I heard a car horn blaring in the distance, I heard the scraping of a piece of trash as it blew across the parking lot. The world, as empty and dark as it was, swirled around me, vibrant and alive, and I stood in the oasis of calm at its center, absolutely still. I could feel my own heartbeat, hear my own breathing.

My skin tingled. I came back to myself, and realized, strangely, that I did want it.

I really did.

And I got it. I understood what Dawn meant, and I also understood she had left a line open to me when she said we couldn't be soul mates because she was divine and I wasn't. She was still offering an invitation to share her life with me.

I laughed and went back inside to Dawn, because that, too, was what I wanted.

THE END

ABOUT THE AUTHOR

W. JASON PETRUZZI

Jason Petruzzi was born in New Rochelle, New York in 1977, and within days was diagnosed with complex congenital heart disease. In spite of these severe life-long physical limitations, he maintained a cheerful disposition and intellectual curiosity.

After a family move to Northern Virginia, Jason graduated HS in 1995 and worked as a Fairfax County administrative assistant, beginning in 1996. He later earned a B.A. degree in English from George Mason University in

2006, and an M.A. degree in Library & Information Studies from Florida State University in 2011.

Jason had just begun his 19th year of service with Fairfax County when he was seriously injured in a car accident (due to a critical malfunction of his vehicle). After a week in intensive Cardiac Care, he died in 2014 at the age of 37.

Capitalizing on his intellectual strengths, Jason spent much of his free-time creating and writing several novels, poems and short-stories. Knowing full well how fragile his health was, he left a note to his parents asking for help getting his works published, should he not be able to do it himself.

This novel, "Dawn of All Things", was Jason's favorite. His own life-long struggles gave him insight into the courage, kindness and compassion for others, which define "Dawn's " journey; the need to be accepted for all that you are. Publishing this story gives the reader an opportunity to experience the world through their eyes.